# POPULAR GOVERNMENT IN AMERICA

# THE AUTHORS

CHARLES S. HYNEMAN, a former president of the American Political Science Association, has been involved in political science in both its theoretical and practical applications since 1928. He has taught at Syracuse University, the University of Illinois, Louisiana State University, and Northwestern University, and is now Distinguished Professor of Government at Indiana University. He gained practical experience in administration and politics at various levels of government. He was Executive Secretary of the Louisiana Municipal Association, adviser to the Governor of Louisiana, and a member of the Civil Service Board of a Chicago metropolitan district. He served the federal government in the development and management of training for military government, as Director of the Foreign Broadcast Intelligence Service, and as Executive Officer of the Federal Communications Commission. He currently advises the Committee for Economic Development on governmental problems.

Since his first book, *The First American Neutrality*, appeared in 1934, Professor Hyneman has shown continuing imaginative insight into American political problems in *Bureaucracy in a Democracy*, *The Study of Politics*, *The Supreme Court on Trial*, and *A Second Federalist*, and in numerous articles in the leading political science and legal journals.

CHARLES E. GILBERT was educated at Haverford College, the London School of Economics, and Northwestern University where he was awarded his Ph.D. Co-author of *Planning Municipal Investment* and author of *Governing the Suburbs*, Professor Gilbert is also a frequent contributor to professional journals in the areas of local government, public administration, and political theory. He has been a consultant to the Cleveland Metropolitan Service Commission, the Pennsylvania State Department of Public Welfare, and the Committee for Economic Development. He is professor of political science at Swarthmore College.

*Atherton Press · New York · 1968*

# POPULAR GOVERNMENT IN AMERICA

## Foundations & Principles

**CHARLES S. HYNEMAN**
*Indiana University*

**with the collaboration of**

**CHARLES E. GILBERT**
*Swarthmore College*

TO: WILLMOORE KENDALL
EVRON M. KIRKPATRICK
HAROLD W. STOKE

*They set me to this task and prepared me for it.*

# PREFACE

In his Introduction, Charles Gilbert tells how this book was prepared. If I disputed any point in his statement, I would say that a greater proportion of the volume was written after Gilbert assembled the earlier materials. The issue is unimportant, however. Even though some of the content was in its present form as much as twenty years ago, I am able to say that the entire book represents my present thinking. If I had written all of it anew, some matters would have been approached differently but judgments and conclusions would not have been changed.

The circumstances of its construction—piecing together, revising, and supplementing manuscript written over a period of two decades—accounts for three features of the book that readers may find puzzling. One, my examination of the democratic idea and the democratic way of governing is more topical, less systematic, than I like; much that deserves treatment is passed over and emphasis is unevenly distributed among things that are treated. Two, there are sharp and perhaps distracting changes of purpose and method. At one point my aim is analysis of a complicated problem, at another point description of arrangements and practices, at still another point expression of my personal apprehensions and preferences. Three, the vocabulary and the level of discourse are not consistent. In discussing some matters the vocabulary and tone are appropriate for young people starting their serious study of government and politics; at other points the presentation is suited to an audience of mature political scientists. These difficulties will be rendered less disturbing if one brings to the reading the tolerance he must display in perusing a collection of related but separate essays.

The assertion that the book represents my own thought must not obscure the fact that Charles Gilbert contributed enormously to my thinking. Recognizing that I do not know how much I owe him, I venture to cite three principal gifts. He made me see that I had not settled my mind on many questions that were vital to the analysis I had partially developed. He confronted me with inconsistencies and other inadequacies in analysis that I thought had been completed. And he convinced me that what I had written suppressed many implications which ought to be firmed up and elaborated and brought to the front. Without doubt his greatest impact on my thought is revealed in the discussion of requisites of democratic government. In none of my earlier writings had I attempted to identify social conditions that must be present in order for democratic government to persist, and I did not plan to discuss that subject as I set about revising and supplementing the earlier pieces. Gilbert insisted, however, that a belief in social requisites was implied in what I had written, urged me to make my beliefs explicit, and gave me the three terms—autonomy, equality, and commonalty—which I subsequently lifted to prominence throughout the book.

My keen awareness of obligation to Gilbert does not drive from mind the great debt I owe to many others. I made a deliberate decision not to refer, in the text, to the stimulating and informative literature upon which I have drawn in my many years of study. I find a partial justification of this decision in the fact that it would not be practicable, if possible, to credit colleagues and friends with the instruction they gave me in conversation. I cannot say that the thought I encountered in books was more imaginative, more discriminating, or more compelling than the thought impressed upon me in several decades of intermittent conversation. I talked to too many to allow a listing of all I remember to have introduced an idea, moved me from a position, or confirmed a judgment. I see them as generations. Working on me before and during World War II (and in later years as well) are the three men to whom this book is dedicated. I could get along with each of them better than they could get along with one another, so far as beliefs about democracy and self-government are concerned. Each of them prepared me to put hard questions to the others; collectively they reduced to something like normal the overload of naiveté which I brought to the study of politics. The second generation confronted me during my ten years of teaching at Northwestern University. Most influential on my thinking, among the Northwestern group, were Jean Driscoll, Charles Gilbert, Lawrence Herson, and Roland Young. Charles Hagan and Austin Ranney of the University of Illinois also administered some severe discipline during this period. Finally, those who have joined in debate about democratic theory since I came to Indiana University in 1956. Here, theory of democratic government entered more prominently into my courses than formerly, and I refrain from naming those students who presented me with the stiffest challenges. Of the faculty, I have argued the subject matter of this book most vigorously with Byrum Carter, Charles McCall, and P. J. Vatikiotis. Several persons read this book in manuscript and gave me valuable criticism. These include Charles McCall, Robert McClure, Donald Lutz, Richard Hofstetter, John Miller, and Roy Speckhard (all of Indiana University), and George Carey of Georgetown University. Edward F. Kenehan brought me up to date on federal broadcasting policy. Marlene Mandel and Mary Lacey Kelly of Atherton Press patiently improved my sentences without overtaxing my capacity to defend a nice distinction. Any sin I commit by omitting persons who should be mentioned is matched by understatement of the debt I owe to those who are cited.

Finally I acknowledge with pleasure and gratitude the opportunities afforded me to lecture on the subject matter of this book at several colleges and universities. Some of the pages appearing hereafter were presented to audiences at Florida Presbyterian College, Georgetown University, Iowa State University, Pennsylvania State University, University of Illinois, University of Oklahoma, University of Tennessee, University of Texas at El Paso, and University of Washington.

CHARLES S. HYNEMAN

# CONTENTS

PREFACE ix

INTRODUCTION by CHARLES E. GILBERT xv

## I Democratic Ideals

1 DEMOCRACY: GOALS AND METHODS 3
2 THE DEMOCRATIC SOCIETY 14

## II Popular Government

3 TWO SYSTEMS OF DEMAND AND RESPONSE 37
4 THE CITIZEN'S ROLE 54
5 THE RIGHT TO VOTE 64
6 THE CITIZEN'S EDUCATION 82
7 POLITICAL ACTIVITY AND ELECTORAL BEHAVIOR 102

## III The Structure of Authority

8 THE ELECTIVE PRINCIPLE 127
9 THE LEGISLATURE AND THE EXECUTIVE 139
10 CONTROL OF ADMINISTRATION 152

## IV Limited Government

11 GOVERNMENT BY LAW 175
12 CONSTITUTIONAL GUARANTEES 197
13 FREE SPEECH AND SUBVERSION:
   AN HISTORICAL EPISODE 214

14 FREE SPEECH AND SUBVERSION:
    A CONTEMPORARY SOLUTION  232

V *Democracy on Trial*

15 THE NEGROES' CHALLENGE  245
16 ORGANIZED PROTEST AND RESISTANCE  261
17 CONCLUSION: ON THE PRESERVATION OF
    DEMOCRATIC FOUNDATIONS  277

OTHER WRITINGS OF CHARLES S. HYNEMAN  293
FOR FURTHER READING  297
INDEX  317

# INTRODUCTION

I hope that readers, on finishing this book, will find the introduction both superfluous and presumptuous. Little explication is called for because the author takes little for granted in his argument.

A description of how this book was written may, however, help to explain why the argument takes the form it does and why some topics are dealt with while others are not. A few comments on the book's relations to the literature of political science may be useful to the undergraduate student.

The original plan for this volume was to bring together Charles Hyneman's views on democratic government. When the project was first suggested by the publisher and when I began it, we were thinking of already published views that could be welded into a unity or, at least, a continuity. As selector and welder I asked Hyneman to provide me with all his old articles and published addresses; but I also asked for unpublished lectures and manuscripts, many of which I had read before. When this material was collected several themes in Hyneman's thinking during the last decade became apparent, and it seemed better to develop these than to include earlier articles on a wider variety of subjects.

Accordingly, I blocked out the themes, assembled Hyneman's writings with liberal use of scissors and paste, and wrote transitions based on past conversations with Hyneman. Then Hyneman re-entered the project personally: he rewrote all the transitions, developing a couple of them into separate chapters, and then revised all his own material extensively. The result is a book that is largely based on manuscripts and ephemerally published lectures; but nearly half of it is newly written, and almost nothing written earlier has escaped alteration or interlarding. Some of Hyneman's revisions stemmed from changes in his thinking. Some of them were attempts to make the style consistent and the argument easily accessible to students. Many of the materials on which this book is based were written for teaching or as general lectures; the book is meant for freshmen and laymen as well as for political scientists.

The main themes in Hyneman's recent work have to do with the nature of democratic theory, the ideology of American democracy, the relations between the basic ideas of limited government and popular government, the implications of the popular government idea for public institutions and of the limited government idea for political action, the social requisites of democratic government, the balance of pluralism and populism in American democracy, and the ways of participation open to the citizen. Hyneman has original things to say on each of these themes. One cannot do justice to his argument by abstracting or summarizing it; but identification of the major elements in it may help readers to appreciate its balance and capture its details the first time through.

Political theory, for Hyneman in this book, consists in clarification of language and concepts, in description and analysis of institutions and behavior, and in appraisal and evaluation. Hyneman's theory is not one of the behavioral or functional varieties that rely on special language and concepts drawn from other disciplines than political science. It heavily emphasizes, however, a central concern of both conventional and behavioral theory: the distribution of "power," or what proportion of people have how much influence over what aspects of government; and how power is shared, divided, checked, and balanced. The theory also emphasizes the role of ideology in controlling and distributing power.

Hyneman says he is pessimistic about the prospects for a precise description of the distribution of power in any situation. He does not, therefore, define "power" precisely, though at points in the book he tries to identify mechanisms and processes—models and analogues—in terms of which the mobilization of influence and the application of controls might be studied. For the most part his method is to reason from recorded history and careful observation with the naked eye. Implicitly, then, this book raises the question of whether conventional or behavioral methods are more helpful in understanding democratic government; whether conventional observation and language are adequate for description and analysis, whether behavioral concepts and methods can be linked to appraisal and evaluation without tending to alter the norms by which we "normally" judge the performance of institutions and the behavior of individuals.

Hyneman's theorizing is concerned with values, institutions, and behavior; but it does not distinguish these things sharply. The values dealt with are beliefs and commitments expressed in documents or inferred from action, and they refer to social states instead of intellectual abstractions or constructed traditions. Similarly, institutions and behavior are characteristically discussed as "practices" or "ways" and as direct expressions of belief. For Hyneman, the materials of politics are both more variable and more readily observable than ideological ends, sociological structures, or psychological motives. It follows from this conception that Hyneman is not dealing primarily with democracy in general; instead, his book is about the American democratic political culture as manifest in statements, institutions, and practices.

The first task of theory, Hyneman thinks, is clarification of the values served by and sustaining American democracy. This task gives meaning and direction to analysis of the elements of democracy and to empirical research on the processes of democracy. In this sense political science is not "value-free"; it is most useful in pursuit of the implications of basic beliefs and ideals.

These beliefs and ideals can be found in historical statements as well as inferred from institutions and behavior. Hyneman's approach to the sources of American democracy is the kind of historical explanation favored by the late George Sabine in his famous essay on two democratic traditions: "the sympathetic appreciation of men in terms of their own conscious purposes and problems." Like Sabine, too, Hyneman finds liberty and equality closely combined in American democracy. The basic concepts are those of limited government and popular government. These were vaguely stated in the Declaration of Independence as personal rights and public consent: general principles to which governments should defer. Later, in the early debates on the Constitution (both before and after its adoption), the ideas of legal limitations and popular control of government became more definite as institutions, practices, and understandings became more definite. Of the two ideas Hyneman argues first, that the idea of popular control was probably dominant over that of limited government in the beginning, and second, that the two conceptions are inseparable in American thought and practice.

It has usually been maintained that limited government is a condition, or necessary antecedent, of popular government. Hyneman's position, however, is the reverse—at least in terms of practice, if not of ideology. One reason for this position is the ambiguity Hyneman finds in all legal standards; another is the incompleteness of legal controls over power. The electoral sanction is more effective, and is the main instrument of popular government. Stable and orderly democracy rests, however, on certain social requisites (autonomy, equality, and commonalty, for short). Is democratic government in America, then, at bottom a problem in political sociology? Are constitutional provisions largely derivative from social pluralism, economic opportunity, or ideological agreement? Not entirely so for Hyneman within American society *today*: the social requisites are important, but they are reinforced by governmental arrangements for dispersal of power and for effective representation. Such arrangements rest in large part, however, on the ideology of limited government as well as on that of popular government; on the balance of American concerns with liberty and equality, limitation and participation with respect to government. Ultimately, a spirit of toleration is required to make the social requisites consistent with one another and allow political competition and participation to operate consistently. The result of all this is an analysis in which legal institutions, governmental arrangements, belief systems, and socioeconomic structures figure reciprocally, and in which neither structure nor culture, neither political nor social variables have clear precedence. But, to return to popular government and limited government, the former has priority for Hyneman in his analysis of institutions, if not ideologies, and in his own value system.

Most scholars have emphasized the potential conflicts between the notions of limited and popular government; Hyneman stresses the consistency of these notions in historical context and the ways in which they support one another today. The same emphasis appears in his discussion of the democratic ideals of liberty and equality, of the pluralist and populist aspects of American democracy, and of the social requisites of democracy (individual and group autonomy, equality, and commonalty). In each case it is clear that conflict is possible between two or more ideals, institutional patterns, or social requisites. However, by dealing with values and behavior not in abstract categories but as concrete traditions, institutions, and practices Hyneman discovers the consistencies among them.

To some readers it may appear that he overstates the consistencies and understates the tensions in the ideals, practices, and social requisites of the American system. Hyneman identifies these ideals, practices, and requisites at some length, and readers will find in his discussion parallels that may seem forced to some but that may also be historically sound. The liberty and equality that, as ideals, underlie limited and popular government are close to the autonomy and equality that serve as social

xix    *Introduction*

requisites of democratic government more generally; and the view
that democracy is a way of life as well as a set of institutions is
close to the "commonalty" that is the third social requisite. Commonalty is suspiciously like the "consensus" emphasized by many
conservative theorists, though it refers more to shared ways of
life and less to explicit ideas or material interests; and it is not
simply a residual category of explanation. Ideals and social requisites are not sharply distinguished in this analysis; instead, in traditional language, Hyneman is recognizing the roles of both
political socialization and social organization in democratic government.

Similarly, the leading ideas of the rule of law are so defined as
to consist readily with a system of popular representative government, or, indeed, to support it: the old *ultra vires* notion is expanded to the principle that crucial decisions should be lodged in
elective offices; while the other two elements of the rule of law
are equal protection and the public welfare (public interest, public
purpose) as the legitimate ends of legislation or administration.
Thus: quality of office, equal protection, public welfare; autonomy,
equality, commonalty; liberty, equality, democracy as way of life.
Hyneman's discussion of the ideals of limited government—the
principles of the rule of law—is broader than those to be found in
most law books; but it is highly suggestive, it rests on original
scholarship, and it is not at all clearly inconsistent with the common law and Lockean traditions or with American legal doctrines.

Turning to Hyneman's analysis of the *politics* of American
democracy, three aspects merit special comment. The first of these
is his treatment of two interpretations of the American system that
emphasize different aspects of it. The contrasting emphases may
be identified as pressure versus electoral politics, pluralism versus
populism, group competition versus equality of influence. Hyneman tries to identify the complementary and antithetical relations
between the two patterns and the ways in which they alternate in
importance. He stresses the need to know more about the detailed
processes of influence in each pattern, its distribution of benefits,
and how each pattern relates to the political ideals and social requisites of American democracy. Hyneman rather neglects a prominent approach to modern political science: the conceptualization of
the mechanics of group influence on government, including David
Truman's discussion of interaction and access, the organization
theory of Herbert Simon, and Robert Dahl's notions of direct and
indirect influence. He evidently believes that this line of theorizing
has not greatly helped us to deal with the question how many have

how much influence over what aspects of government, or to explain the stability of American democracy. Specialists may be challenged by his argument to evaluate the theory of group influence, competition, and equilibrium as it now stands. Hyneman's own analysis emphasizes the majority-forming process that is also stressed by such scholars as E. E. Schattschneider, which is not surprising in light of his preference for what he calls the equalization-of-influence thesis with its emphasis on electoral politics, and his view that in clarifying value positions the theorist should also work out their implications for research.

A second noteworthy contribution is the analysis of ways of popular participation in government. Hyneman identifies six, of which three—elections, appeals and pressures by individuals and groups, and mass protest and resistance—are most important in this book. Here again he stresses the ultimate importance of elections, partly because they, far more than the other processes, are subject to regulation in accordance with democratic ends. He also notes, however, the inevitability of the other processes, the insufficiency of all regulations, the significance of voters' differing intensities of concern, and the consequent lack of realism of majority rule doctrines of democracy. As he deals with elections and appeals-and-pressures, Hyneman's search for a proper balance between the equalization-of-influence and the group-competition processes is again evident. In looking beyond the decorum of both these processes to the important role of mass protest and resistance in politics he also challenges the emphasis of many contemporary theorists on political equilibrium and stability. This leads to important normative issues in the concluding section of the book, especially with respect to the importance of "commonalty" and the spirit of toleration that allows commonalty and political competition to coexist.

Third and finally Hyneman deals with the implications of his emphasis on electoral direction and control for the electoral process itself and for governmental structure. Here especially, he points to issues where the clarification of value positions would be likely to reorient research. His analysis may strike some readers as neglectful of the existing literature in its effort to look freshly at subjects like voter rationality, the legislature, the executive, and federalism.

It is fair to ask, then, whether the main links in Hyneman's chain of reasoning about the implications of popular control of limited government have been broken or weakened by recent research findings. I think the answer is no. The discussion of voter rationality is a reasonable, if controversial, interpretation of Survey Research Center findings and is not invalidated by other data. The argument for popular control of elected officials is carefully qualified and supplemented by the group-competition thesis. The position on control of administration by elected officials (for which, perhaps, Hyneman is best known) is qualified in the same way and is thoroughly consistent with the skepticism about the prospects for effective hierarchical control to be found in modern organization theory. Because of his own skepticism on this score and his corresponding doubt that *party* organization can secure popular control of the presidency Hyneman tends to favor federalism and decentralization, together with emphasis on the legislature, as a variety of means of preserving popular control of government. Hyneman's own value position—his preference for electoral, equality-of-influence politics over group competition—is largely shared by writers of the "party government" school. But his skepticism about centralization and executive power and his emphasis on the legislature as a center of representation may well be more consistent with both this value position and the empirical knowledge of political science today than is the party reform, presidential hegemony program.

Hyneman's emphasis on popular control, electoral politics, and equality of influence also tends to challenge both of the antipodal "pluralist" and "ruling elite" schools—though it should be clear that he is not engaged in a scholastic contest. The freedom of his analysis from specific reference to professional controversies is one of its strengths and a probable source of originality. I have, however, tried to connect it explicitly to the literature of political science at a few points.

In these comments I have not followed closely the sequence of the book but have simply tried to call the reader's attention to major themes and contributions. The book's last section is an attempt to work out the implications of all the foregoing concerns for policy toward political action. Three kinds of action are considered: "free" speech as a personal right; speech and political action that may be seditious or subversive; and organized protest or resistance to law. The first question Hyneman asks is an old one (though his analysis is new in several respects): How are personal "rights" and public "welfare" to be adjusted in cases of speech whose effects range from inconvenience and irritation to sedition and subversion? This was the question involved in the post-World War II controversies about policies to deal with domestic Communism, and Hyneman deals with the history of legislation against sedition and subversion in a highly original analysis.

The second question is a little less traditional but it is still more topical: In what circumstances is organized protest-and-resistance justifiable and legitimate? Here the relevant controversy is the civil rights movement. As political action goes beyond electoral campaigning and group importuning toward militant protest and resistance to law, what are its consequences for the social requisites of democratic government, and how does such action square with the concepts of popular and limited government? The categories of analysis that were applied to free speech—the values damaged or advanced by the speech, the probable effectiveness of either speech or its regulation as means to valued ends, and attitudes toward uncertainty where probabilities cannot be calculated—these same categories are applied to protest-and-resistance, where effects on autonomy, equality, and commonalty, or the social requisites of democracy, are in question.

In the concluding chapter Hyneman returns to critical questions for the future of American democracy that are disclosed by his analysis. These questions include: how to preserve the main avenues of participation against attrition from protest and resistance; how far, to this end, to apply legal limitations to political action, using limitations imposed *by* government to preserve the processes for control *of* government; how, within the latter processes, properly to balance pluralism and populism, or the roles of elites and the population at large; how to render the three social requisites of democracy (autonomy, equality, commonalty) compatible? The last issue receives primary attention because it is fundamental to the others. Hyneman's analysis is directed to policy and the emphasis is placed on commonalty. Is this simply the usual conservative fear of disorder and preachment of togetherness, however fictitious? I think not. In light of the entire analysis it seems closer to old-fashioned, Lockean liberalism in its stress on toleration, on the populace as a whole as well as a collection of individuals, on a balance of governmental action and popular control of it, and on limited government and popular participation, on pluralism and populism, liberty (autonomy) and equality. It is, however, unlike modern theories of "participatory democracy" in its emphasis on commonalty. For Hyneman, it is commonalty, with toleration at its core, that enables the foregoing balances to be maintained. Thus, as a result of this analysis, Hyneman's admonitions are directed to what he calls "communicating elites" rather than to government alone. Policy toward political action is a matter for citizens as well as for officials, and Hyneman is asking for more public attention to the whole range of conditions of democratic government insofar as we understand them.

It follows that the first concern of the book is to enhance this understanding by identification of critical elements in democratic government (including values, commitments, and attitudes) and by analysis of the relations among them—that is, by a democratic theory. Such a theory will be concerned not only with tendencies of individual and group behavior, and with results of institutional structure, but also with continuing analysis and interpretation of norms like liberty and equality in their relations to peoples' wants, the working of institutions, and the making of policy decisions. The second concern is to bring the theory's implications to the attention of citizens, especially of intellectuals but not necessarily political scientists. This is one reason why the theory is stated in nontechnical, readily understandable terms and deals with human behavior as most of us experience it.

I have stressed the structure of Hyneman's argument and its implications for policy so as to orient the reader. It is important for students to note, however, that no democratic theory can be final or complete; and that the one they are about to read is not intended to be. A good political theory is a challenge as well as an explanation or evaluation. One test of a theory is its fruitfulness of questions susceptible of answers. Another test is the theory's relevance, or the case it makes for the importance or centrality of its propositions; and this test is nearly as important as the theory's conformity to evidence.

Students are likely to read this book as a supplement to other literature about American government and politics. They should use it, then, to evaluate that literature as well as to sharpen their own direct observations of government and political behavior. To help them begin, and thus to read Hyneman's argument critically, this introduction concludes with a random list of twenty questions that are implicit in the foregoing discussion.

1. Are the social requisites of democracy in America well-enough defined to be useful in policy decisions affecting them; and are the definitions open enough to take account of social change?

2. As among autonomy, equality, and commonalty, as social requisites of democracy, is Hyneman right in his judgment that American democracy is more seriously threatened by defects in commonalty than by failures of autonomy or equality; and is heavy emphasis on commonalty, as Hyneman conceives of it, in itself a threat to autonomy or equality?

3. In terms of the ideals of American democracy as Hyneman has identified them, what kinds of behavior should be legislated against or considered illegitimate for persons attempting to win

the favor of public officials by lobbying or consultations or of the general public in elections?

4. Does careful study of elections encourage a belief in the rationality of the average voter (Hyneman's common man), or does it appear that competition among interested elites is more likely to promote the general welfare; or is the average voter's rationality relevant to this issue?

5. As to the general welfare, has Hyneman correctly identified the legal and political conceptions that give this term meaning in America; or does the term have any consistent meaning at all?

6. Do the ideologies of limited government and popular government sufficiently recognize differences in opportunity to influence government that stem not only from social and economic position but also from disposition; that is, from habits and attitudes that people have probably learned by the time of adolescence and that are linked to social and economic position? As to the social requisites, how are the right attitudes about autonomy, equality, and commonalty learned; and how can such learning be encouraged?

7. How good is the evidence that close electoral competition tends to produce well-organized political parties, and that disciplined competition between them tends in turn to promote inclusiveness of consideration or equality of treatment of the population by government? What are the effects of electoral competition on strategically placed elites on one hand, or on "discrete and insular minorities" on the other?

8. Is there a viable alternative to our primary reliance on electoral competition for popular control of government? As a beginning, how important are enforceable legal and constitutional limits on government in promoting popular control and official responsiveness to popular wants? What are the prospects for radical decentralization of government so that more citizens can reach it directly?

9. What are the institutional conditions of effective direction and control of administration by elected officials? Has Hyneman adequately elaborated these? How well do our institutions now fulfill these conditions?

10. How do different methods of election, and of regulation of elections, determine which interests are most effectively represented in government; and how nearly sufficient is Hyneman's discussion of elections for drawing conclusions on this point?

11. Given Hyneman's premises about the ideals and social requi-

sites of American democracy, is he correct in favoring federalism and decentralization?

12. Similarly, is Hyneman's emphasis on a large congressional role in policy making and control of administration consistent with his premises, with congressional possibilities, with administrative tendencies, or with the social necessities of our time?

13. Should courts not only help control the actions of administration according to Hyneman's standards of limited government but also invalidate congressional legislation when, in their judgment, it conflicts with these standards?

14. Does Hyneman's analysis pay enough attention to the small minority of the population that is actively involved in politics? Is it the beliefs and practices of these people that largely account for a stable democratic order in America?

15. Are the traditions of public education and of the communications industry more important than political institutions in maintaining—or, potentially, undermining—democratic government; and what do you conclude from Hyneman's discussion about the tendencies of those traditions?

16. By what tests, if any, can we properly limit organized protest and resistance in order to preserve the essential procedures of American democracy? Are Hyneman's tests the right ones?

17. If a modicum of social and political "integration," as well as toleration, is implicit in commonalty, how helpful are American political institutions now in accomplishing this? How might they be improved in this respect?

18. Is the rhetoric of politicians, either past or present, proper material for a theory of American democracy, or should such a theory refer only to the performance of institutions and the actions of men in specific situations?

19. Hyneman's argument is expressly confined to American democracy; but, considering experience elsewhere, would you say it is likely that a democratic system can function effectively if the population does not conceive of government primarily in terms of law, and of politics in terms of personal participation?

20. What obligations or responsibilities of citizenship, if any, do you infer from Hyneman's analysis, and do you accept the implications of the analysis?

CHARLES E. GILBERT

# I

*Democratic Ideals*

# 1. DEMOCRACY: GOALS AND METHODS

Democracy, democratic institutions, and democratic practices refer to a popular base; they presume purpose and effort by a substantial part of the population. This point needs no labored justification; all thoughtful writers and propagandists who use the words *democracy* and *democratic* relate them in some way to a general population. But exactly how institutions, practices, and states of mind must relate to the population in order to create a democratic regime is a point of sharp dispute.

In contemporary classifications of political systems, the words *democracy* and *democratic* are given one or another or an admixture of three principal meanings:

a. A regime in which those who compose the government (the officialdom) are under some compulsion to find out what the people want done and to do what they understand the people want done. Ordinarily compliance with public expectations is effected by popular selection and replacement of the officials who make the most important public policies and who have supervisory power over all other officials and employees of the government.

b. A regime in which the officialdom conscientiously seeks to satisfy the expectations and preferences of the people, but without an obligation to do so enforced by disciplinary action by the people. In this view, a regime is labeled democratic if it voluntarily gives the governed what they want or will be content with.

c. A regime in which the officialdom does what it believes is good for the people, regardless of whether the people do or do not like what they get. Benevolent despotism is an old name for this kind of government, and this conception of democratic government holds that benevolent despotisms are democratic.

I formulated these three statements to differentiate clearly three significantly different conceptions of democratic character. Actual governments, or political systems, cannot be classified with certainty according to these tests because of the near-impossibility of establishing cause and effect in human relationships. We cannot prove that an elected official made a particular decision because he wanted to be re-elected and believed that this decision was necessary to win votes. We can only infer that the acts of elected officials were made with a view to winning the approval of the electorate, basing the inference on the behavior we observe and the reasons officials give for their actions.

Definitions of democratic character that cannot be fitted with high confidence to actual situations nevertheless can be of great utility. They specify ideals toward which people can strive and they challenge thoughtful people to develop practical tests for determining how closely their political system approaches the ideal.

My concern throughout this study is with the first type of regime —a political system in which the people have effective means for expressing expectations and preferences and for inducing compliance with their demands. At many points my words may suggest that I count a government democratic if the people approve of its acts. On all such occasions the reader must understand that I refer to governmental action that responds to public wishes because of the presence of instruments that induce such response.

This is a good place at which to introduce some cautions about the meanings of words and phrases that will recur again and again. An essay that is broadly descriptive and provides elementary analysis must use words that are general rather than precise in meaning. I twice referred to "the people" in the preceding paragraph. But who are the people? Certainly infants who are still in mothers' arms are irrelevant to a discussion of popular direction and control of government. The term "the people" will at no point be given a precise meaning in this book; sometimes the reference will be to those persons who make their wishes known, at other times to those persons who participate in political campaigns and elections, at still others to all persons who may be conscious that their interests are affected by government. What words ought one use when he wishes to speak of attitudes and behaviors of the people? On any election day some persons have clear perceptions of interest, have definite preferences, can express firm demands; other persons only vaguely perceive their interests, have expectations that they might abandon under scrutiny, or appear to be totally indifferent to what government does. It would encumber the pages that follow if I were to remind the reader of this variety in states of mind every time I speak of a popular response to acts of government. I must ask the reader to bear in mind that I may speak of popular preferences when I readily acknowledge the presence of expectations that have not been elevated to preference by rejection of alternatives. I shall hereafter say "popular demand," "the public wishes," "will of the people"—using these terms interchangeably and in no case intending to specify an exact state of mind. So also I shall speak of popular control of government when I am uncertain as to how many people exert influence and when the influence I refer to is either more than control or less than control. People suggest courses of action that their officials might pursue, they induce their officials to move one way rather than another, they press restraints on officials, and they deal out rewards and punishments. Perhaps at most points in this book when I speak of popular control of government I have in mind more of direction-setting than of coercing, rewarding, and punishing.

There is good reason for addressing my inquiry to the first conception of democratic character presented above—the view that a political system is democratic if public officials are under some compulsion to satisfy the people. Government in the United States, in its conception and development, is government of the people, by the people, and for the people. A study of its origins makes it clear that this political system rests on two main principles: (1) government is to be controlled by and to answer to the people; and (2) government's power over the people is restricted in scope and restrained in method. The germ, but not a full statement, of these two principles is in the Declaration of Independence. There it is stated that all persons, equally, are made in such a way (so endowed by their Creator) as to require that they shall always enjoy certain conditions of living which the authors of the Declaration called inalienable rights; under any rightful form of government these rights are to be respected. Further, it is the function of government to make these rights or conditions of living secure, and to guarantee that this is the fruit of government, the just powers of any government are derived from the consent of the people. Finally, if any government does not meet these requirements—does not secure the inalienable rights, exercises powers which are not derived from the people and so are not just—it is appropriate and right for the people to terminate it and create a new government thought more likely to conform to the objectives which have been stated.

There is not, in the Declaration of Independence, any direct assertion that a rightful government will be controlled by and readily answerable to the people, or that, in order to enforce a due regard for the inalienable rights, limitations should be imposed upon the authority of government. These assertions, which I have offered as the two foundation principles of our political system, were to be announced shortly thereafter. The state constitutions that were formulated and declared effective during the decade of the Revolutionary War made clear the commitment of the American people to the two principles I have noted. Some of them made formal announcements that government rests upon the will of the people; all of them provided for an elective law-making body; and several of them contained elaborate statements of personal rights or claims to immunity from political control.

Scarcely more than a decade after independence from Great Britain was achieved the federal structure was invented and promulgated. The new Constitution, effective in 1789, placed in the national government important governing powers. With very few exceptions (notably diplomatic relations and treaty making) it declared these powers to be vested in Congress. Congress was to be an instrument of popular government. The House of Representatives was to be chosen directly by the people, and the Senators were to be chosen by state legislatures which were, at least partially, chosen by popular vote. Furthermore, the Constitution required the national government to see to it that every state maintain a republican form of government. That requirement, I think there can be no question, was intended to mean that every state government must answer to the people.

The Constitution also charged the new national government to have a proper regard for personal claims to freedom, but on this one of the two fundamental principles it was less than adequate in the view of many persons who displayed an active interest in constitution making. The Constitution specifically forbade the new Congress to pass any bills of attainder or ex post facto laws, and limited its power to curtail the rights that English citizens had long been able to enforce by the writ of habeas corpus. But the new national Constitution did not contain a statement of immunities from governmental power comparable in scope to those found in some of the state constitutions. The demands of those who thought an elaborate bill of rights to be necessary were largely satisfied by the adoption of the first ten amendments to the Constitution during the first three years of its operation.

The record of the adoption of the constitutional amendments that gave us a Bill of Rights is most instructive. It reveals sharp differences of opinion as to whether any guarantees against excess of power on the part of the national government were needed, and if needed what they ought to be. A study of what was said in the House of Representatives when the amendments were proposed—we have no record of what was said in the Senate—strongly supports a conclusion that most of the congressmen believed that the great battle for security of inalienable rights had been won when the principle of popular control of government was made effective. A view strongly pushed forward in Congress, and I think probably the view of most members of the House, was this: When a government is truly answerable to the people, declarations of personal immunity from acts of government are definitely of marginal value. If James Madison, who managed the campaign for adoption of the amendments, thought they were of more than marginal value, he did a poor job of saying so.*

The natural result of my historical report, up to this point, must be a conclusion that the American political system is dominated by a single principle: popular control of government; that if this principle is effectively secured, all the benefits envisaged by constitutional safeguards of personal freedom are also secured. If I based my judgment only on what was said in Congress during the first decades under the Constitution, I would reach that conclusion. Those men were talking only about the need or lack of need for guarantees against abuse of power by the national government. They did not discuss the need for safeguards against abuse of power by government where it had the greatest opportunity to encroach on the inalienable rights of individuals—the state governments. When one looks to experience in creating state governments he has to conclude, I think, that the idea of limited government, of safeguards of personal freedom, was companion to and not wholly subordinate to the idea of popular control of government.

The two fundamental principles that underlay the creation of this political system have continued to control its character. American political leaders and writers about American politics have consistently maintained that this is a government by the people, and a government committed to the security of individual rights. When crises press upon us, they are discussed in terms of "fundamental principles" such as division of authority (separation of powers, federal arrangement, local self-government) and rule of

* Madison's several statements in support of his proposed amendments are reprinted in Charles S. Hyneman and George W. Carey, eds., *A Second Federalist* (New York: Appleton-Century-Crofts, 1967), chapter 11.

law (e.g., respect for the Constitution and independence of the judiciary). Support for these principles is marshalled in the name of the yet more fundamental principles of government by the people and individual liberty.

In this American experience, I contend, lies sufficient justification for the special view of democratic character that fixes the content and emphasis of this book. A book written by an American principally for an American audience may appropriately assume that government which perforce responds to popular demands and is sensitive to individual rights is democratic government, and that particular policies and practices that significantly contradict the principles of popular control and individual rights are departures from the democratic way in government and politics. No heed will be taken, hereafter, of contentions that the word democracy also applies to despotisms that, because of the generosity or superior wisdom of the rulers, voluntarily give the people what they want or forcibly impose upon the population what the rulers know to be good for them.

A reader who vigorously applauds the position just asserted may, however, have little or no sympathy with another bias pervading the pages that follow. This is the priority that I place on popular sovereignty, or the people's ability to control their government. I find myself firmly attached to the view that I believe to have been persuasive with the architects of our political system. If I read them correctly, those men were predominantly of a mind that their first great task was to create a government that would have to respond to the wishes of the people. They believed that the accomplishment of this task was the first indispensable step toward the achievement of their other primary goal—a government that would heed individual claims to liberty, make an honest effort to resolve conflict among competing demands for exercise or quiescence of governmental power, and pursue a course of action that would enable men to live in dignity as individuals and in fruitful connections as a society.

Because of this conviction about priorities in political architecture, I will treat the ability of the people to control their government as the prime distinguishing characteristic of democratic government throughout this book. Proof that a government is controlled by the people is established by evidence that those who possess the authority of government are obliged to exercise that authority within limits acceptable to the people, or, failing to do so, are obliged to give up their authority. Later in this essay, the general perspective of democratic government as government by the people will be modified by observations about the securing of personal liberties in circumstances where a popularly controlled government may threaten to impair or deny them.

The ideal in democratic government is obligatory response to the wishes of the people. Popular government, popular control of government, government by the people are short terms for instrumentalities and practices designed to achieve this goal. We can estimate the closeness of approach to the ideal by finding answers for these three questions: (a) how much of the population shares, (b) in how much of the critical decision making, (c) with how much impact or influence? If practically everybody in this country were heard and his wishes heeded in the making of every important governmental decision, we would have a government as democratic as anyone could hope for. If, at the opposite extreme, one man made all decisions of importance, paying attention to nobody's wishes but his own, we would have the ultimate in nondemocratic government.

Looking at it this way, it is hardly proper to say that a nation's government is democratic or not democratic. Rather, one ought to say something like this: Country *A* has enough of the democratic quality in its government to suit me; but country *X* has so little of that same quality in its government that I shall not call it democratic. Perhaps this is just what we do in common speech. We conclude that Great Britain and the Scandinavian countries have provided a fair amount of popular control over their governments so we call them democracies. We conclude that Russia, China, and Yugoslavia have too little popular control so we say that those countries do not have democratic governments. There are even times when a thoughtful American citizen can say with good reason: there is too much response to popular demand in this area of public policy and I would be happier if we had a little less democracy in these matters right here in the United States.

The three questions that I proposed for estimating an approach to the democratic ideal direct attention to three main points of inquiry that must be pursued if one wishes to describe a political system in terms of its democratic character or evaluate a nation's effort to manage its public affairs in a democratic manner. Specific tests could be formulated that would enable one to measure popular participation and so make it possible to place political systems on a set of scales showing how much of the population shares in how much of the critical decision making with how much impact on the outcome of decision making. But the formulation of tests and the process of measuring would be heavily beset by difficulties. It may be relatively easy to determine how many people take part in formal actions such as voting. But how is one to estimate the number of people who affect the conduct of government by inducing other persons to vote differently than they otherwise would have done? Can one hope to identify the persons who make their voices heard in appeals and pressures directed to public officials? Or can one hope to find out how much of the population makes an impact on the conduct of public policy by cooperating with public officials, clandestinely violating the law, or boldly marching in protest against a public policy and its enforcement?

The difficulties one would encounter in determining how many people share in control of government are small compared with those that would beset an effort to determine how much influence is exerted by those who seek to intervene in decisions. The number of persons who testify in a congressional hearing can be counted, but one cannot know how much weight the congressmen attach to their recommendations, or even whether the congressmen listen to them at all. One can fix the exact number of persons who march in the streets or lie down in the doorways of public buildings, but he cannot know how profoundly these demonstrations disturb the minds of officials who formulate the public policies.

Finally, we ought to recognize the unlikelihood of easy agreement in scaling the importance of decisions. The choice of a President will be a critical decision for you if you think only one candidate promises vigorous and enlightened leadership, but it may come to the tossing of a coin for me if I can see no significant difference between the candidates. Into which decisions may the common man intrude with reasonable expectation that the advice he offers will advance his personal interest? If widespread public demand is ignored in making tactical decisions in foreign relations, ought one enter this on the minus side of a democratic/non-democratic scale? If farsighted statesmen yield to shortsighted public demands, ought we mark up a victory for the democratic ideal? How one looks at these questions and many others of comparable perplexity will depend in good part on his view of the whole social environment in which government functions. If I believe the society is sufficiently pluralistic, I may think that unwisdom in government is corrected by countervailing forces that collectively advance the objectives of the population at large. In that case I shall attach small consequence to many governmental decisions that will be thought critical indeed by another man who thinks the society is monolithic in structure and that his only hope of protecting his own interests is to mobilize pressure on government immediately.

This brief catalog of obstacles to be encountered in fixing tests for democratic character may prompt the question: Why propose the application of tests if there is so little prospect that meaningful and administrable tests can be devised? To this query, three things must be said in reply: (1) It is most important for the people of a free country to know where they stand in relation to their government. (2) They can know where they stand in relation to their government, and therefore can hope to prevent or reverse a drift toward an authoritarian form, only if scholars and other trusted observers inform them about where governmental authority is placed and whose wishes are attended to when important decisions are made. (3) It is the function of theory to guide those who search for such knowledge; and it is the fate of the theory maker to build his house on the sands of uncertainty, starting with such knowledge as he has and trusting a disciplined imagination to foretell what will be found when the next round of exploration is carried out.

Mankind has come a long way from the rude and practical knowledge of his environment and the consequences of his acts, which we suppose to have characterized his early experience. The route he has traversed from the days of primitive knowledge must, in large part, have been determined by happy and unhappy accident. But also, in large part, that path was plotted in advance by a shrewd foretelling of what was bound to occur and sound judgment as to what could be made to occur. Theory makers must make a mental survey of the route that has been traveled in getting to the present, project that route into the future, and predict the consequences of expected future events. The object of this book is to prepare the ground for theory making, and perhaps to take a few first steps in proposing theory about democratic government.

A democratic people pursue a democratic style of living and maintain a democratic type of government. The importance of the interrelationship of these two emphases can hardly be overestimated. Government is democratic if it comes out well on the tests proposed above; but no people can establish and maintain that kind of government unless they meet certain standards in their day-to-day living. A democratic way of life may thus be said to be a condition necessary for a democratic type of government. But governments that are democratic in character are inclined to pursue policies and carry on public activities that support and strengthen the very standards of behavior and living that make democratic government possible. Democracy in government is therefore both a consequence of and a contributor to the democratic way of life; the connection between the democratic type of government and the democratic way of life is a hen and egg connection. For that reason we must examine the body of ideals and practices that not only gives us a democratic government but also makes us a democratic people.

Democratic ideals and aspirations are based on the conviction that everybody counts. There have been societies, and may be societies today, in which a great part of the population did not count. Certain parts of the population were only tolerated; their interests were not a primary consideration in deciding what would be done. For those who are excluded, such a society is not democratic. And if the number of excluded individuals seems unreasonably large, the person who looks at that society objectively will conclude that, as a whole, it is not a democratic society.

What standards can we set up for the treatment of individuals that will enable us to judge whether a particular society can properly be called democratic? What measures can we apply that will tell us whether, as a matter of fact, everybody does count? This is a subjective matter, and perhaps no two persons will arrive at the same answer. But two things seem to be agreed on: all persons must enjoy a certain amount of liberty, and there must be a certain degree of equality in the treatment accorded everyone. If the necessary measures of liberty and equality are lacking, the individuals who make up the society do not have the status which is essential to democracy.

It is easy to see why liberty and equality are essential to democracy. If the individual is the center of concern, then what the individual prefers is a matter of importance. Since different people want different things, a nation cannot fit all its affairs to one rigid pattern and expect to please everybody. Consequently each person must be allowed a wide choice as to how he will conduct his life. This is the same as saying that he must have a wide range of liberty. The argument for equality is just as simple. The degree to which I share the good things of life determines the extent to which I enjoy equality with others. If all the things that men want were divided among them in equal amounts, man for man, we would have the highest degree of equality attainable. If, on the other hand, some people got everything they wanted and others got only what was left, the nation would be at the opposite extreme from equality. In the latter case, it would be abundantly clear that some people count in the society and that other people do not.

One hundred per cent liberty and one hundred per cent equality are not likely ever to be attained. Each person wants things that are incompatible. I cannot attend the basketball game and see the prize fight too, for they are scheduled at the same time; I cannot buy a new car and also pay off the mortgage on the house, because I haven't enough money to do both. So I choose between alternatives. It is the same for society as a whole. It is not possible for one man to have things entirely as he would like, because his interests conflict with those of other men. As individuals, we are constantly making concessions to other individuals. The organizations and institutions that we set up are largely engaged in working out these concessions and compromises. The result is, of course, that our liberties are constantly being limited, for we are obliged to respect and comply with the compromises that are made.

The process of curtailing my liberty also determines where I shall stand in the matter of equality. When compromises are made they not only limit what I can do; they affect my chances of getting what I want. That ought to be clear on its face, since the main reason for wanting liberty is to increase the likelihood that one can obtain the good things in life. Some of the arrangements and rules of the society will tend to even up the opportunities of individuals to get what they want; others will give an advantage to certain groups or sectors of the population. We view them as democratic in character, according to their tendency to establish and maintain equality of opportunity.

# 2. THE DEMOCRATIC SOCIETY

When we examine a society in order to judge its compliance with democratic ideals we are really trying to find to what extent it provides freedom of action and equality of status to the individuals who compose that society. There is, of course, no end to such a search, for all aspects of life bear some relation to these two things. But some interests seem more vital than others, and some aspects of living bear a greater relation to one's happiness than others. In searching for evidence of the status of individuals in any society, we must look most intently into those areas where the enjoyment of liberty and equality are of most critical importance. We shall conduct that search by examining a series of questions about the distribution of opportunities and advantages in a society. Having the results of this inquiry in mind, we shall next consider whether certain social conditions are necessary for the maintenance of popular control of government.

## Tests of Democratic Character

One should not expect agreement on the relationships that must persist in order for any society to be generally regarded as democratic. My study causes me to believe that the democratic character of a society will be disclosed by a close inspection of the conditions brought to attention by these five questions: (1) Does everybody enjoy a right to be treated with respect? (2) Does everybody have a right to express himself? (3) Does everybody enjoy a right to worship according to his own conscience? (4) How equitably is economic welfare distributed? (5) How nearly equal are men in controlling their government?

Before we take up these five questions for separate discussion, three general observations must be made. First, the word "right," as used here, refers to claims of the individual that are thought to be justifiable and defensible; the discussion is not confined to rights that have been secured by law. Some of the matters involved in each of these five questions may be provided for by law and recognized as legal rights, but they are presented here as ideals to be achieved. They are, for any man who accepts these ideals, defensible claims and they are often referred to as moral rights. Anyone who is deeply concerned that these claims be honored will hope that they will come to be recognized as legal rights.

Second, the ideals that prevail in any one of these five areas are closely related to the ideals encompassed by each of the others. A nation can, in practice, approach the ideal in one area of affairs only if it also moves nearer to the ideal in the others. Furthermore, they overlap; each of these five questions will lead us into matters that are involved in one or more of the other questions.

This makes necessary a third observation. A nation cannot achieve all these ideals in equal measure. At their margins they conflict with one another. One man uses his right to speak to cast aspersions on the character of his neighbor, and freedom of expression is in conflict with the right to be treated with respect.

## DOES EVERYBODY ENJOY A RIGHT TO BE TREATED WITH RESPECT?

It may be that the right to be treated with respect is merely a summation of all the other rights that men aspire to; that when the other rights are well established, it will inevitably follow that individuals from all sectors of the population are being accorded the respect that we set up as an ideal. Whether this is so or not, there are a few things that should be said directly on the subject of respect.

First, who should treat whom with respect? The practical problems we face in trying to relate this matter of respect to the ideals of democracy lie in the relations that exist among substantial sectors of the population, and in the way institutions that are set up and maintained by the dominant part of the population affect other parts of the population. If white people do not treat Negroes with respect (or vice versa); if rich people do not treat poor people with respect (or vice versa); if any sector of the population refuses to accord respect to some other substantial sector of the population—in any of these instances we had better look into the nature of the relationships that exist. For if the withholding of respect is evidenced in things that men count important, and if such behavior is painful to those who suffer from it, we may have a serious shortcoming in our democracy. How serious a shortcoming it is will depend upon the number of people involved, the importance of the matters in which the objectionable attitude or behavior is evidenced, and the sense of injury that people feel as a consequence of the treatment they are accorded. If those persons who persist in the objectionable attitudes or behavior are dominant in the society, they ordinarily will use their organizations and institutions, including government, to maintain their superior position. Then it becomes increasingly difficult for the mistreated groups to win better treatment.

When we have said this much, we have called attention to a second aspect of this problem of treating people with respect. What kinds of attitude or behavior constitute a serious offense against the ideals of democracy? The answer to this depends on what the different elements of the particular society consider important. If all people in the United States consider it important that they be spoken to courteously, that they be allowed to ride from place to place in public conveyances, that they be able to eat in cafes and restaurants—then it is certainly an offence against the standards of democracy for one sector of the population (whites for instance) regularly to speak insolently to another sector of the population (Negroes for instance) or deny them admission to public conveyances and public eating places. We are forced to this conclusion because we have acknowledged that attitudes and actions of this character constitute serious discrimination in matters that all regard as important.

Are we required by force of logic to conclude that the right to respect is breached if white people insist that Negroes must ride in seats at the rear of the bus and eat in special dining rooms apart from white people? This is discrimination, certainly; but some persons have argued that it is discrimination of a trivial character if the seats at the rear of the bus are just as comfortable as those in front, and if the food and service are identical in the two dining rooms. If Negroes, unconditioned by previous discriminatory treatment, found those arrangements satisfactory and voluntarily accepted them, we could surely say that no offense had been done to the democratic ideal insofar as this matter of the right to be treated with respect is concerned. We have not supposed that democratic standards are breached if men and women are required to use different toilets, and there has been no great outcry that a religious sect is a blemish on the nation's democratic record if it requires men and women to sit separately by sex in the church. If only Negroes go to watch the baptism of a Negro and only whites go to cockfights, and this dividing up is strictly due to personal preferences unaffected by social pressures, it would seem farfetched to argue that people in both races should repudiate their personal tastes and mix in order to avoid an appearance of social discrimination.

The truth is, of course, that segregation and other manifestations of unequal treatment that confine and restrict the Negro in the United States are regarded as offensive by the Negro, and are generally now regarded as invidious by whites as well. In the view of Negroes, therefore, the racial discrimination that abounds in this country constitutes a substantial departure from the ideals of democracy. Such discriminating practices are substantial departures from the ideals of democracy in the view of anyone, whatever his place in the society, if he accepts the proposition made above— that democracy is based on the conviction that everybody counts.

## DOES EVERYBODY HAVE A RIGHT TO EXPRESS HIMSELF?

If we accept the proposition that everybody counts, we are forced to conclude that everybody must be allowed to express himself. If a man cannot express himself in some fashion other people can hardly know that he exists. The principle that affirms every man's right to make his existence known is not likely to be contested in any society. The debatable questions, in a free society, relate to the means by which the individual may express himself, the circumstances under which he may do so, and what he may say when he gets ready to make his wishes known.

The right to express oneself involves a great deal more than the right to put thoughts into words. The composer makes his thoughts and feelings known by notations on paper, and the performer interprets and embellishes them in the production of music. The artist expresses himself by creating an art object. And the dandy reveals his conception of God's greatest handiwork by public display of his body and its garb. All means of expression, from those highest in refinement on down to those most raw and ugly in taste, must be contemplated by the architects and critics of a democratic order. We shall tackle enough in this book, however, if we confine ourselves to what men say and write. The discussion must start with recognition of the primary interests at stake in all controversies about free speech and press.

There are two basic reasons for cherishing freedom of speech and press. A man may simply want to get something off his mind without caring what effect it has on anyone else; or he may wish to communicate his ideas to other people and benefit from the ideas that other people have to offer.

Not much need be said about the first of these considerations independently of the second. The right simply to get something off one's chest is like the right to go fishing or the right to play a banjo. The fact that I want to do any of these things establishes the presumption that I ought to be able to do it. But it is only a presumption that can be overcome by proof of injury to somebody else. My idle fishing can destroy another man's food supply, and my banjo playing can disturb his sleep. So also, a blasphemous outburst that is directed only to God may cause pain to sensitive people who overhear it.

We are most concerned about the right of men to express themselves when their interest in saying something coincides with the interest of other people in hearing what they have to say. For it is by men talking and men hearing, and men writing and men reading, that a group of people come to understand one another and have the relations with one another that make them a society. The difference between the amount of freedom of expression in the most democratic society and in the least democratic society is a matter of degree. But the difference of degree is of greatest importance, for it determines the likelihood that people in the two societies can understand what they have and where they are, what they might get and where they might get to, and what courses of action offer some promise of making things over to their liking.

Common sense tells us that there must be some limitation on freedom of speech and press because what some men choose to say or write will conflict with other things that are valued highly by great numbers of people. Who would contend that a man should go unrebuked if he stood up in the midst of a religious service and blasphemed God? Who would argue that no restraints may be imposed upon young men who loose the foulest words in their vocabulary on old ladies they encounter by chance on the county square? Until recent years theory and practice in the United States was dominated by public conviction that freedom of speech and press is frequently abused, that it is proper for communities to adopt regulations designed to prevent such abuse, and that law and government are proper instruments for effectuating restraint. Since World War II these suppositions have been vigorously challenged. It is now argued with great persistence that public taste and public thought profit from talk and writing that formerly were counted reprehensible; that all restraints on communication threaten if they do not actually impede the instrumentalities of democratic government; and that, if it ever be proper to impose restraint on any kind of utterance, it should not be done by law or acts of public officials. Support for all three propositions in this newly developed free speech doctrine is inherent in the contention, recently heard with increased frequency, that the First Amendment to the United States Constitution absolutely prohibits any abridgment of speech or press by the national government and that the due process requirement of the Fourteenth Amendment makes that prohibition applicable to state and local governments also.

A serious effort to appraise the democratic character of any society must examine the conditions under which communication takes place in that society. A full inquiry will take into account the readiness of people to communicate with one another, and their preparation for generation of ideas and persuasive address, as well as the regulations under which communication is carried on. Some aspects of this complicated world of thought and expression will receive considerable attention later in this book. However, it may be helpful to provide at this point some general observations about the clash of values which has made reconsideration of free speech doctrine inevitable in the United States since World War II.

A belief that the people should be untrammeled in the dissemination of information and ideas has repeatedly collided with a stubborn determination that law and government shall be used to thwart any efforts to bring this democratic experiment to an end. Speech and writing intended to criticize and stimulate improvement of government get confused with statements designed to excite overthrow of the government by violence; and men who aspire for renown as the philosophers and architects of a better order withhold their counsel out of fear that they will be viewed as traitors and punished as conspirators.

The argument for allowing individuals to attack the institutions of a democratic nation follow simple lines. In a democracy, everybody counts; everybody has a right to say how he thinks things can be improved and to hear what other people have to suggest, so that anyone who is convinced by the argument can join with others in working for what they believe will constitute improvement. This line of reasoning is persuasive, but it leaves one question unanswered. What shall we do if we are convinced that freedom of expression is being used to destroy the very things that make democratic living possible? Do we have to say concerning freedom of expression: "We value this freedom so much that we will not limit it, even though we are convinced that the way it is being used today will result in our having no such freedom tomorrow"?

At the risk of unpardonable oversimplification, we may say that debate on this great issue is dominated by three principal positions: (1) Some people do not see any likelihood that freedom of expression will contribute to the destruction of our democratic ideals and democratic practice. In defense of their position, they contend that facing a reprehensible proposal prompts people to think seriously about their condition, stimulates the development of counter argument, and results in the triumph of truth and sound judgment over falsehood, deceit, and unwisdom. (2) Other strong defenders of unrestricted communication are less sanguine about the certain triumph of virtue over evil. They readily admit to a state of danger, but they are willing to take a chance that serious injuries can be averted. Adherents of this position acknowledge that evil designs and injurious actions originate in the minds of men, and they freely concede that communication is a necessary instrument for cultivating evil designs and accomplishing injurious acts. They are willing to take a chance that the injurious act can be averted by governmental intervention at the edge of its occurrence, but unwilling to assume the risk that socially useful communication may be seriously curtailed if the government makes a selective effort to cut off communication which develops the hostile design and directs its progress toward final realization. (3) The third position differs from the second in placement and assumption of risk. Adherents to the third view are less confident that the danger can be averted after an evil design has been perfected, and they are more confident that particular statements can be neatly excised from the general body of communication without a serious inhibition of speech and writing. Persons in the second and third groups may also differ in their estimates of the health of public discussion in the United States. Many persons who take the second position identified above appear to think that even a very slight fear of being punished will blot out lawful remarks that lie along the margin of the unlawful. Those who take the third position may or may not agree that this is likely to happen; in any case they are pretty certain to contend that any band of silence will still leave enough thought in the forum to assure full consideration of every proposal that a democratic nation will seriously entertain.

Any person who sets out to build a state of mind on these great issues has a long and stony road to follow. He must scrutinize his value holdings, reach judgments about relations of means to ends, and be prepared to take risks. It will be apparent at once that a free flow of information and ideas is essential for the advancement of some things he values (e.g., the Negro's march to freedom), but he will realize also that speech and press are powerful instruments for accomplishing other things that he contemplates with horror (e.g., the sharpening of racial animosities and the mobilization of a Ku Klux Klan). Before he endorses a law designed to curb the speech or publication he abhors, he must not only be convinced that the law will have its intended effect; he must also identify and weigh the unwanted consequences that are likely to follow. Too often for comfort, the evidence will be inadequate and decisions will be clothed in doubt. The risks assumed when decisions are made in a cloud of uncertainty may be viewed as a price citizens must pay to live in a free society.

### DOES EVERYBODY ENJOY A RIGHT TO WORSHIP ACCORDING TO HIS OWN CONSCIENCE?

Like the right to speak his mind, the right to worship according to his convictions is important to a man simply because he is a man. History shows that there are few things people cling to more stubbornly or fight for more stoutly than the right to have and to pass on to others the religious faith they have embraced. It is difficult to avoid the conclusion that a society has significantly breached the principle that everybody counts if it denies to any part of the population the right to embrace particular doctrines and forms of worship.

The justification for freedom of worship in democratic societies does not rest solely on the point that people like to choose the religion that suits them. Genuine freedom in the choice of religion is pretty certain to result in the appearance of many different sects. Of all the groups into which society may be divided, few if any are more jealous of their integrity than religious groups. Leaders of the strongest sects may favor institutions which would permit them to decree their faith as the only authorized and lawful religion for the country. But the less powerful sects, afraid of being persecuted, hold out for institutions that give them a voice in making decisions and offer them hope that their faiths will be allowed to survive. Freedom of worship thus becomes a support for other elements of a democratic system.

There must be limits to the right of men to worship as they please, just as there must be limits to freedom of expression. We encountered this problem when most Americans found the practice of polygamy by Mormons objectionable and it was forbidden by law. The Supreme Court met the situation by reasoning this way: admitting that religion involves practices as well as faith, the court asserted that a distinction should be made between those practices that are clearly essential to the faith and those that are not essential. The latter could be forbidden, but the former could not. By holding that the practice of polygamy was not essential to the religious faith of Mormons, the judges were able to rule that the act that forbade plural marriages did not violate the constitutional provision that Congress should pass no law prohibiting the free exercise of religion.*

But there are situations for which this reasoning would not be adequate. Certain American Indian tribes once followed the practice of sacrificing young people, believing that the whole population would suffer in an afterlife if the sacrifices were not made. If this was really their belief, then the act of taking human life was surely essential to their faith. Yet we may be sure the American people would not permit a declaration in their Constitution to keep the government from putting an end to such a practice. And surely we can say that no reasonable interpretation of the ideals of democracy as a way of living would permit such practices to be tolerated. In the list of things essential to democracy there are many items more important than an unrestrained indulgence of the beliefs of imaginative men about their relation to the universe and the hereafter.

## HOW EQUITABLY IS ECONOMIC WELFARE DISTRIBUTED?

The opportunity that a man has to make a living deeply affects his ability to enjoy other rights and privileges. The beautiful things of life have little attraction for a man with an empty stomach and no place to sleep. All our professions of respect for a man because he is a man are a mockery if we deny him a chance to obtain a decent income. Freedom to say and write what one pleases is only a limited privilege for the man who cannot avail himself of modern means of communication. Some measure of wealth is essential even to the enjoyment of religion, if the religion calls for pilgrimages or worship in churches.

* *Reynolds* v. *United States,* 98 U.S. 145 (1878).

We must always keep in mind two things about the ideals of democracy—that ideals are a subjective matter, every person being required to establish his own; and that in establishing the ideal on any point we must bear in mind its relation to our other ideals. These cautions are especially important in considering the relation of the economic system to democracy. There is no reason for hoping that we can get general agreement as to how much equality of opportunity there should be in economic affairs. There are two points, however, on which we may all agree, and a third that will be acceptable to most if not all Americans.

First, each one of us, in formulating his concept of what is democratic, must provide for an amount of equality in economic affairs that permits the realization of his other goals. If the standard that I have set for freedom of expression requires that every man be able to read and write, then my standards for the economic system must make it possible for every man to learn how to read and write. If my standards for freedom of expression require that every man be able to address a particular audience, then I am committed to an economic system that enables every man to address his appropriate audience. The same principle must be applied to my standards regarding a right to be treated with respect, to enjoy freedom of worship, and so on.

The second point upon which we may all agree is that there is bound to be great inequality in the wealth of individuals in any society which permits wealth to be accumulated on the basis of competition. Even if we were born equal in talents we could not control our environment sufficiently to bring people to manhood with equal capacities and identical interests. Some people will work harder than others at accumulating wealth; some have skills that others cannot equal; some are more persuasive than others and will have their neighbors working for them. Therefore, we must expect differences in wealth in competitive societies; it has not yet been demonstrated that people can devise an industrial society so free of competitive effort that there will be no substantial differences in the ability of men to control material goods.

There is a third point on which most of us may agree, but probably not all. Must there not be some mitigation of the extremes of wealth and poverty? There are two aspects of this issue. Of the very rich we may ask: can we allow some men to control the amount of wealth that can be acquired in a competitive economic system? In the United States we do not set a maximum to the monetary value of a man's estate. But we do, with our income and inheritance tax laws, hold down the disparities between top and bottom income groups. Much of our other legislation, for instance that forbidding certain kinds of business combinations, limits the power that men can exercise through control of wealth.

The other aspect of income distribution concerns the very poor. Many people feel that in a democracy everyone should be assured a minimum level of comfort. We recognize this, though we may not acknowledge that we are affirming a "right," when we provide unemployment relief and some medical care at public expense. Every society makes some provision for individuals who have temporarily lost their means of livelihood, though many societies are not as liberal as the American people.

As a nation, we have reviewed our standards on this point in recent years. Underlying the New Deal was a conviction that people are not personally responsible for many of the hardships they suffer. During that period we put a new floor under the living standards of low-income people by the enactment of social security legislation. These laws, though subsequently altered, do not apply equally to all persons in similar circumstances. As one would expect, the level of security now guaranteed by national and state legislation is not high enough to satisfy many people who persistently demand more ample guarantees. But, equally to be expected, present policies are much too benevolent in the view of other people who fear that income which is not the fruit of personal effort destroys incentive and willingness to produce.

Governmental programs that provide for a man who cannot take care of himself, or that carry him over hard times, can be adequately justified by the purposes they carry on their face. They are a way of saying, "This much a man is entitled to because he is a human being." But there is a further justification of social security legislation. We want the whole adult population of this nation to share in the running of our government, but we want people to use their best judgment, not their worst, when they participate in political affairs. They will not use their best judgment when they are governed by hysteria. Programs of social security that free people from the prospect of destitution are a first step toward the avoidance of widespread hysteria.

### HOW NEARLY EQUAL ARE MEN IN CONTROLLING THEIR GOVERNMENT?

A man who has no voice in the control of his government is in a poor position to defend himself. If a society denies any important sector of its population an opportunity to share in the direction of political affairs, the scope of governmental action being what it is in modern times, we surely have to conclude that that part of its population does not count for much. Our democratic ideals call for widespread participation in control of government, but they do not require that everybody be allowed to participate —certainly not newborn infants. Furthermore, to say that certain people ought to be given a voice in government leaves unanswered many questions about how much influence they should exert.

An effort to reach conclusions about who ought to have how much influence in deciding policies of what importance must be guided by a sharp appreciation of how ability to control government is related to other democratic ideals. Earlier, we said that the connection between democratic government and the things we call democracy in living is a hen and egg connection. They have to be developed together; you cannot have one of them unless you have the other. If the terms on which people live together are not in sufficient accord with the ideals that we have discussed here, those people will not be able to establish a democratic system of government and run it in a democratic fashion. And if a people living according to these ideals loses control of its government, it will thereafter have no assurance that it can continue to live according to those ideals.

Anybody who has had his eyes open during recent decades must appreciate that when people lose control of their government they lose their power to control the conditions of their living. Autocratic regimes permit some of the people to live a very beautiful life indeed. They may even permit the mass of the people to live according to their own preferences for a time. But when the people as a whole have lost control of their government they have lost assurance that they can use it to support or defend their ways of living and they face a prospect that government will be used to terminate their style of life.

We have been forced by the events of our time to think about the importance of democratic government to the security of a democratic life. But we have not given comparable thought to the importance of democratic ways of living for the achievement and maintenance of a democratic type of government. That the relations of support run both ways is readily seen. Democratic government, as it was defined at the beginning of this essay, imposes a minimum requirement that those persons who have the authority of government exercise their authority within limits that are acceptable to the people as a whole, or failing to do so, give up their authority. Obviously, there can be no conducting of government within limits acceptable to the people unless the people have opinions about what government should do and not do, and unless there are ways of finding out what those opinions are. Since there will not be very many people, if indeed as many as two people, who agree on everything that the government is concerned with, there must be ways for men to find out what others think, so that compromises can be made and a course of action can be planned that will satisfy a great many people and be acceptable to a great many more.

Now this business of bringing a nation to agreement on affairs of government is not accomplished simply by announcing that a question is up, and polling everybody to see what each wants done. The complications of an issue cannot be explained that easily. People need to hear explanations from individuals who see the issue from different points of view. They need to have some impression of how deeply other people feel on a matter before they can decide how much of a concession to make.

The knowledge that must guide people in making their decisions is not handed out to them when the time comes for them to act. It is acquired by their whole experience. If every man lived as a recluse, there would be no possibility of group judgments that satisfied anybody; the more fully men live in association with other men, the greater the chance that something will come about that can be called the common will. It is for this reason that the conditions of a democratic life which were discussed above are so important to democratic government. If people do not treat an important sector of the population with respect, that part of the population will lose its capacity for making its position on public issues known to the rest of the population. If there is not a wide range of freedom for men to express themselves, there will not be the flow of knowledge and conviction that is essential to democratic government. If part of the population is on the edge of destitution, it will not have the time or resources to find out what the government is doing. It will not be able to inject its beliefs and wishes into the general body of public knowledge and opinion, and its notions as to what constitutes sound governmental policies will be warped by the narrow and distorted conditions under which it lives. Finally, if the disparity in the wealth of different sectors of the population is great, there will be a consequent disparity in the political power of sectors of the population. Wealth gives men the ability to influence the minds of other men; an equal voice within the polling booth is not a guarantee of equal influence in the political life of the nation.

The ideals we set up to guide us in our effort to achieve a democratic life are worthy of being striven for, each for its own sake. But each of them is essential to all of the others. To the extent that we yield on one of them, we jeopardize the others. To the extent that we advance on one, we make more certain our ability to advance on the others.

## Social Requisites of Democratic Government

The contemporary efforts of people in many parts of the world to establish self-government in a democratic style have excited considerable debate about the social prerequisites of democratic government. The appropriateness of such an inquiry is further demonstrated by growing awareness that several nations that long ago adopted formal institutions of the Western democratic model have not yet succeeded in establishing government that is reasonably sensitive to the expectations and preferences of the population at large. Concern about prerequisites for democratic government is accompanied by a growing apprehension that the institutions and ways of popular government may not be as firmly implanted as one would like in countries where government by the people has been thought most secure. There is widespread uneasiness about the future of democratic government in our own country. Many thoughtful and informed persons appear to be convinced that further development of certain states of mind and social practices might result in loss of popular control over government in the United States. Persons who believe that their government is securely democratic may be forgiven for an in-difference about *prerequisites* of democratic government. They have pressing cause, however, to be concerned about *requisites*— conditions that must coexist with popular government in order for government to remain sensitive to the wishes of the people.

Although there may be utility in trying to determine whether certain social conditions must be well established before experiments with government by the people can succeed, I do not wish to make the search. The courses pursued by nations that have arrived at democratic government are marked by many and great differences in social experience. For all such nations much of what must have been critical experience is lost in the mists of history. The search for prerequisites of democratic government therefore is one of speculative inquiry as well as empirical research. Speculation on this subject ought to prove interesting and useful, but it will not find a place in this essay.

A consideration of requisites of democratic government—social conditions whose coexistence is essential to the continuance of popular government—is of critical importance to this essay and cannot be avoided. That there are social requisites of democratic government is implied in my assertion above that "the democratic way of life [is] a condition necessary for a democratic government," and that "democracy in government is both a consequence of and a contributor to the democratic way of life; the connection between the democratic type of government and the democratic way of life is a hen and egg connection." This testifies to my conviction that the totality of beliefs and practices that constitute the democratic life of a people include some that are necessary for the maintenance of popular government. I think it unlikely that we shall ever make up a list of clearly defined states of mind and social practices and say for each of them: If this characteristic of the social situation were extirpated, popular control of government would immediately become precarious and soon disappear. I think it may be possible, however, to array a number of carefully defined states of mind and social practices and get agreement from students of politics that a substantial number of them must be operative in the society in order for popular government to have a vigorous career.

Agreement on such a battery of mind-sets and attendant practices can come only after elaborate empirical inquiry guided by appropriate theory. Some of this theory, in the absence of adequate comparative experience, is necessarily speculative. It is hoped that this study will offer helpful suggestions for the construction of such theory.

A body of theory may well presume that popular government can be achieved only where three states of mind and behavior are in clear evidence. They are: (1) commitment to and provision for *individual and group autonomy*; (2) commitment to *equality*; and (3) *commonalty*—a common mind on the objectives and methods of government.

It is undeniable that popular government has been most successful in societies marked by free choice for the individual and a pluralist social structure. *Individual and group autonomy* will serve as a label for such a social condition. It would be an enormous undertaking to catalog the opportunities for personal choice in the United States today. They would include such things as deciding on a career, preparing for a career, and deciding on places and conditions of employment; deciding where to live and purchasing a home; utilizing vacation time and making investments; and so on *ad infinitum*. It may be that a society can achieve a high degree of productiveness in economic affairs with a citizenry that is subjected to enforced roles; witness the records of certain nations that depended heavily on slave labor directed by more favored men who were still in servile status. It seems most unlikely, however, that a citizenry born to fixed status, unused to making choices about employment, place of living, and other matters of like significance, could make the judgments and perform the acts required for popular control of government.

The necessity for a pluralist social structure and group autonomy is equally apparent. As the power of government is enlarged, we incur an increasing risk that the men and women who hold public office will use their power to keep themselves in office and defeat our central purpose that public officials must do what the people want done or give up their places.

We protect ourselves against this risk in large part by the structure of our government. However, the safeguards provided in this way are not enough to guarantee that government will be democratic. We need centers of power outside of government which can stand firm in opposition to those men and women who exercise governmental power. We need focal points of loyalty which enable people to find leaders they can trust whenever there is growing apprehension that governmental power is being used to impair the ability of the people as a whole to control their government.

Great labor unions are just such centers of power and loyalty. Great associations of farmers, of men who own and manage industries, bar associations, medical societies—these are rivals of government for loyalty and influence. In the vigor of such associations we find assurance that some persons can win enough confidence among large numbers of people to effectively oppose those in government who might try to use their power to keep themselves on top and take over the country.

In the ever continuing effort to keep government subordinate to the people rather than wholly dominant over the people, public education and the giant agencies of communication play a most important role. If government controls the schools and the media of mass communications, those in the government have highly effective means for persuading the people to like what the officials wish to do rather than the other way around. What a regime can do when it controls the schools and the channels of communication is amply demonstrated by what goes on in Russia and China today and in Nazi Germany a few years ago.

We do not know enough about the facts of life in different parts of the world to permit any precise conclusions about how power and loyalty must be allocated in a society in order to make popular government effective and secure. How to measure individual and group autonomy, and how to fix the degree of autonomy necessary for popular control of government, are unknowns. We have seen enough of other countries, however, to justify the assertion that any nation that wants government by the people must prepare for it in social organization and social instruments that lie well outside the realm we ordinarily call political.

My views on the second commitment noted above, *equality,* were developed in the earlier discussion of democratic ideals. I placed considerable emphasis on the relationship of equality in economic welfare to the maintenance of equality in political participation. I must now note my supposition that the ability of a population to control their government is greatly dependent on concurrent experience in managing the associations and organizations that mark the pluralistic society. The literature of American history and political thought is in agreement that congregational control of the church in New England was indispensable to the success of the New England town meeting. I think we may presume with equal confidence that democratic government is nourished by a state of mind which takes it for granted that the policies of the medical association, the labor union, the Four-H Club, will respond to the demands of the membership. Such a state of mind, when supported by practical experience in expressing and enforcing demands, is of critical importance to the mobilization and expression of political demand. A common sharing in the control of an organization is possible only if all who share do so with some measure of equality. Disparities in the amount of influence are proof of domination by some individuals and domination is not a distinguishing characteristic of democratic enterprises.

The latter remark suggests the necessity for inserting a caveat at this point. In this book I do not presume that equality is first in a hierarchy of values which distinguish the democratic way. The appeal of equality often comes into sharp conflict with the appeal of personal liberty or freedom of choice. In case of conflict one may often, with good reason, conclude that equality should yield to liberty. The necessity of choosing between the two, and the need sometimes to put liberty above equality, is recognized in all thoughtful literature. But I must record my personal conviction that much of the literature evaluating the American political and social system ascribes an unwarranted priority to equality. Above the commitment to equality in the American mind, in my opinion, is the determination that this society shall free men for the realization of their greatest potential for making the richest possible contribution to the common good. The value placed on equality is brought to the fore when personal ambition and maneuvering become offensive. Conceptions of a rightful measure of equality thus become a brake on the aberrations and excesses of personal enterprise.

The third point in developing theory relating to social requisites for democratic government is the *commonalty* of commitment, the likeness of beliefs and determinations which prevails among the population. We have a considerable literature about this condition of life in free societies, usually offered under the heading "consensus." The conceptions that lie back of the word "consensus" vary greatly from writer to writer, and care in fixing particular definitions does not always remove meanings carried over from other uses of the word. To avoid unwanted carry-overs, I speak of commonalty rather than consensus.

I have suggested that some measure of autonomy and of equality must be prevalent in the life of a nation for the people to control their government. Autonomy and equality can have vigorous careers within any population only if they are secure enough to be taken for granted. There must be no constant struggle to maintain the required level of autonomy and equality. Vigilance may be the price of liberty, but liberty will be lost if its price is excessive vigilance. People must pay a price in alertness and stubbornness if they would preserve the minimal opportunities for personal choice, the minimal degree of equality, and the requisite level of attainment in all the other ideals and practices we have identified as concomitants of democratic government. The price stands a chance of not being too high only if a state of mind prevails under which onslaughts against the system are discouraged.

It is not enough, therefore, for citizens to have substantial holdings of relevant knowledge and personal conviction. There must be spread throughout the population great bodies of *common* knowledge, *common* beliefs, and *common* purposes. Many people must have substantially the same views about what government ought to do; otherwise government cannot please more than a few. Many people must have the same understanding about how government works and can be controlled; otherwise they cannot get together in a joint effort to control government.

Further attention will be given to requisite common purpose later in this book. A few things should be said now about common understanding of how government works and how it can be controlled. This concern is often discussed under the rubric: rules of the game. "Rules of the game" is a satisfactory label only if broadly interpreted; it must embrace not only the conduct of the players but the way they are recruited, organized and disciplined to behave as a team.

For a government to be controlled by the people, there must be among the population a substantial number of persons who for one reason or another want to hold public office, but who also accept the proposition that they must give up office when they are defeated at the polls. Competition for political power works much like business competition. Men who want to get into places of power identify and define the issues of the day in order to convince voters to support them; they point out the mistakes of those in power in order to make capital of them; to win elections they form organizations with sufficient common purpose to deliver a program of government once they get into power. Carried to an advanced degree this system of competition for power produces stable and effective political parties, without which a great nation would stand little chance of getting government to suit the people.

For this ultimate result, however, readiness to compete for public office is not enough. The competitors must play the game in compliance with restraints which assure the survival of the losers and the emergence of new competitors. The great mass of people who are aspirants, not for seats of authority but for the benefits that accrue from having friends in office, must reconcile themselves to occasional or even prolonged defeat while they lay their plans for victory at a later day. This they can be expected to do only if those who have won the places of power deal benevolently with those who lost in the contest.

Verbal descriptions are necessarily inadequate, and unless supplemented by imaginative flights by the reader, will be misleading. Unlike the picture, which enables the observer to comprehend the whole in one view, the verbal account must move from one statement to another. Collectively, the several statements do not present everything in the life situation that is being described. The fact that some things are mentioned and others go unmentioned creates a danger of misleading emphasis.

Such are the hazards infesting my account of the social requisites of democratic government. In specifying three requisites and separating them for special description and evaluation, I may give the impression that they stand apart from one another in actual social situations. They do not stand apart in reality; we only separate them in the mind for focused contemplation and discussion. The reader must combine them in his imagination. There are not three separable requisites for democratic government. There is a way of life in which men are accustomed to make choices and assume responsibilities; in which people accord deference to one another; in which one man's status in critical social relationships is essentially the same as that of all other men; in which men are relieved from suspicion of one another because they have common standards of behavior and share confidence that particular acts will excite certain expected responses. It is this way of life, defying exact description, that provides the environment in which democratic government can flourish. Indeed, it may be an error to characterize this way of life as the environment of democratic government. The conduct of people in providing for their self-government is not apart from but is itself an aspect of that life in which autonomy, equality, and commonalty loom up for inescapable attention.

# II

*Popular Government*

II

# 3. TWO SYSTEMS OF DEMAND AND RESPONSE

The proof that a government is effectively controlled by the people is found in the evidence that those who hold public office are obliged to exercise their authority in ways acceptable to the people or, failing to do so, are obliged to give up their authority. Where should we look for the critical evidence that public officials actually do respond to popular expectations in the United States? Two theses, derived from two principal interpretations of the American experience, are commonly offered. Recognizing the dangers of oversimplification, the two propositions may be stated this way: (1) Popular government in the United States is a consequence of equilibrium among groups who compete for control of government. (2) Popular government in the United States is achieved by an equalization of influence among individuals who press demands upon the government. We shall refer to these propositions respectively as the group competition and the equalization-of-influence theses.

These alternative conceptions of the genius of American democracy presume different systems for the organization of demands to be pressed on government, and for the mobilization of persuasion and force that induces response to these demands. Later I shall refer to the alternative systems as the pluralist demand-response system (emphasizing group competition) and the populist demand-response system (emphasizing equalization of influence).

## The Group Competition Thesis

Some observers of government in the United States find the explanation of its democratic character outside of the formal provisions for the people to select their officials and confront those officials with demands. They acknowledge that the formal provisions for popular control have some relation to final lodgment of power, but they think that those arrangements are not of first significance. Far more important, according to this view, is the comparative strength of groups who compete for advantage and even alter governmental forms in the process of competition. Government responds to the pressures put upon it. If one sector of the population acquires strength out of proportion to other sectors, government will respond to the demands of that dominant sector and become government by a group rather than government by the people. But if a population is aligned in many groups, each conscious of special objectives and all competing with others, there is a chance that government will execute policies in keeping with the wishes of many rather than a few. Finally, according to this view, if the groups wage a continuous battle for advantage, the equilibrium of power that results virtually guarantees that the policies and acts of government will approximate what most of the population think desirable. This happy result, runs the argument, is the proof that a government is democratic. In this view, the methods prescribed for choosing public officials have only a minor relation to the prospect that those officials will try to act in keeping with public expectations.

Persons who hold this view about the character of democratic government find confirmation for their position in the experience of the American people. What we actually have in this country, they say, is a set of arrangements that maintains equilibrium among sectors of the population that compete with one another for security or for advantage. People we identify as owners and managers of industry are aligned against other people we identify as labor. Farmers want more of something than city people are willing for them to have; and even farmers and city people are further divided into sub-groups for some purposes. People in the South stand pretty close together in support of demands that conflict with demands originating in the North, the Middle West, or the still farther West. Labor cannot get all it demands because owners and managers and a mass of people called consumers put up too much resistance.

Adherents to the group competition thesis argue that the structure and procedures of American government change as the competitors realign. Our two basic divisions of governmental authority —among national, state, and local governments on one hand, and among the legislative, executive, and judicial branches on the other—are elastic enough to permit a group that gets whipped in one forum to move over to a new forum for the next battle in its campaign. Further, the argument runs, our major divisions of power must be elastic enough to enable these groups to maintain their identity and keep fighting; otherwise we shall face the necessity of either reconstructing the government or seeing it go down under strains it cannot withstand.

Some people who believe that the foregoing account accurately portrays what goes on in this country say that this is the way it should be. Government which responds to group pressures gives the greater voice in decision making to those who command the greater resources, those who are most ready to exploit means of influence, those who are willing to make necessary concessions in order to unite with others in the exercise of influence. Such people, it is argued, ought to have the greatest influence in determining what government will do. They are, speaking generally, the people who possess the highest skills, manage the nation's wealth, direct the nation's greatest enterprises, and therefore have the greatest concern that government be used to advance the activities which assure a good life for the nation as a whole. These people, the argument runs, are not organized for the presentation of only one set of demands upon government; they are divided among competing organizations and they lay before government many sets of conflicting demands. As public officials resolve these conflicts, finding grounds for agreement and negotiating compromises, they give the nation a program of governmental activity which in the long run works out for the best interests of nearly everybody.

Such is the nature of democratic government according to those who offer the group competition interpretation. In giving us this account of American experience they describe a pluralist demand-response system.

## The Equalization-of-Influence Thesis

The interpretation of American experience recounted above is unacceptable to many people, both as a description of what gives our present system of government its democratic character and as a statement of an ideal to be more fully achieved. No doubt all careful observers will agree that our government does indeed negotiate compromises among competing groups. But, say the critics of the group competition thesis, so does the government of every country. Anywhere you look, people are associated in groups for the maintenance or advancement of common interests. These groups lay claims before public officials, who make decisions which in varying degrees respond to the pressures put upon them. Even the government of Russia changes its course from time to time because the demands of great sectors of the population have to be met. This is proof enough that response to group pressures is no guarantor of government of the people, by the people, or for the people. What we seek as proof of democratic character is evidence that government responds to the weak as well as the strong. We ask: How equally do men share in the advantages and disadvantages that result from governmental action? What institutions and ways of doing things give people assurance that everybody counts in their political system?

This criticism of the group competition interpretation suggests that the proof of democratic character is to be found in provisions for popular selection of public officials and easy access to the arenas of decision making. This is the position taken by those who adopt the second interpretation of American experience. A prime objective of the American political system and the aspect of its performance which proves its democratic character, according to this view, is the equalization of influence and the evening up of advantage. The guarantee of an approach to equality among individuals is found primarily in provisions for popular election of public officials and secondarily in the placement of governmental authority and the methods by which public policies are made and executed.

Government in the United States is in fact democratic, according to this second interpretation, because all but a very few adult citizens are invited to participate in the selection of public officials, because one man's vote carries the same weight as that of any other's, and because the officials who are selected in this way are under a compulsion to run the government the way they understand the voters want it run.

The central fault of the group competition thesis, in the view of those who take the other position, is that is shows little concern for the equalization of individual influence in government. The struggle among groups is a contest among centers of power that may bear little relation to the number of individuals involved. If big business enterprises win over small business men in a fight about regulation of prices or the letting of contracts for production of war materials, it may be that the spokesmen for big business represent the interests of many more stockholders, employees, and customers than the small business men do. But you do not know that. All you know is that big business had greater resources or used its resources more effectively than small business in this particular battle.

If you take the position that everybody counts in governmental matters and that one individual ought to have as much say as any other about what government is to do, you must make elections crucial in the control of government. There is no guarantee that all voters will enjoy equal influence in the selection of public officials. But an election where one man has just as many votes to cast as any other man is the closest you can come to a guarantee that individuals will share equally in control of government. Then if you provide that the candidates who get the most votes will take over the offices, and that men who take over offices in this way will have authority sufficient to do what those who elected them want done—in that case you have a sturdy assurance that government will be carried on to suit the most people. This assurance is vigorously reinforced by provisions for all men, the weak as well as the strong, to place their demands where officials cannot readily overlook them.

This is the distinctive character of democratic government and the genius of American political experience, in the view of those who accept the second of the two interpretations. They put their faith in a populist demand-response system.

In presenting these alternative accounts of how government is induced to respond to the demands of the American people, I stressed the relation of each to the ideal of equality. The group competition thesis makes little or no provision for equalization of influence; the alternative proposal puts so high a premium on equality that I named it "the equalization-of-influence thesis." The two demand-response systems also differ in their relations to autonomy and commonalty. It seems clear, on the face of things, that the group competition thesis and its pluralist demand-response system can be justified only if one supposes that both individual and group autonomy are highly developed in the society. If autonomy is essential for group competition to flourish, then it is reasonable to suppose that a flourishing competition among groups supports and reinforces autonomy. It is no doubt equally true that the alternative to the group competition explanation, the populist demand-response system, must also rest on highly developed personal and group autonomy; indeed, I asserted such a requirement when I offered autonomy as a requisite of democratic government. I think it probable, however, that a system based on the idea of group competition will put a higher premium on autonomy, at least on group autonomy, than will the system which stresses equalization of influence. As to the relation of the two theses to commonalty, I am not clear. Later I express my conviction that each demand-response system contributes effectively to the construction and maintenance of common mind and common behavior. On the surface, it would appear that the populist demand-response system, relying as it does on popular election of officials, is more dependent on commonalty than the group competition system, and that a robust competition among groups is more likely than the electoral process to disrupt such commonalty as already exists. A more penetrating examination of the two systems might alter these tentative conclusions, however.

## Demand and Response: Two Systems Related

Introducing the two interpretations of American experience, I acknowledged a danger of oversimplification. It may be that I have also offended by overstatement. It is unlikely that any thoughtful person embraces one of the interpretations so unreservedly as wholly to reject the other. Choice between them is a matter of emphasis; one thesis is seen to provide a better explanation of American experience than the other. A study of descriptive writings and statements of ideals and a critical appraisal of speeches made in the public forum leave no room for doubt that differences in emphasis are sharp and significant. This is what the argument is about when one man says that low-income people have the politicians by the throat and another man says that big interests are running the country, when one man says we have too much democracy and another man says that more democracy is the best cure for what ails the country.

The way to find out who does command attention and win favorable response from officeholders is to examine American experience, searching out the origins of demand for governmental action and relating the decisions of public officials to the different demands laid before them. The search is beset by difficulties, and competent investigators will come up with different findings in the future as they have to date. Nevertheless, the search must go on.

An examination of experience also will help one make up his mind whether response to group pressures or courting of voters in order to win public office offers the nation greatest promise of achieving the good life. However, knowledge of who said what and who did what cannot answer the question: Which structure of influence and which system of demand and response should I prefer? The answer to that question will hinge in large part on one's concern that the weak as well as the strong be listened to, and one's readiness or reluctance to take a chance that men who claim to speak for others are conscientious spokesmen for those they represent. Knowledge about what men do and the consequences of their acts can never be sufficient to bring all men to agreement on matters of this character. For such reasons the attractiveness of the two demand-response systems will vary from person to person and a choice between them must be a matter of personal preference.

I do not attempt, in this essay, to deal equally with the two contending explanations of how the American people achieve government by the people. My prime objective is to examine and explicate a set of arrangements and a system of behaviors that maximize the opportunities of the individual, as an individual, to press claims upon men in authority with some hope of a favorable response. Insofar as I refer to American experience, unless I indicate a different intent, I shall refer to institutions and practices that support the equalization-of-influence thesis. Before embarking on that special inquiry it is necessary to insert here a few paragraphs about the interrelatedness of the two views of American experience that were distinguished in the preceding section.

Close attention to the way government and politics are carried on in this country makes it abundantly clear that the American people are divided in attachment between the two ways of inducing response to public demands, and that they shift back and forth in placing major dependence on one or the other of the two ways. The fact seems to be that many people adopt conduct based on the conviction that equilibrium among competing groups gives us our greatest assurance that the policies and acts of government will actually prove satisfactory to the nation at large. It is equally clear that great numbers of people firmly believe that government for the people is best assured by popular elections and other arrangements that enable people to share equally in control of government. Finally, it must be said that the behavior of the nation as a whole shows vacillation between these two interpretations. At times the climate of opinion and conduct is such that legislators and other public officials feel little compulsion to make good on the promises that presumably won their election and, instead, pursue courses of action that balance the demands put upon them by powerful groups. At other times there is widespread denunciation of big interests, of selfish interests, of lobbyists and seekers of privilege. When this mood is strong upon the nation office holders are alert to the effect their acts may have on elections. Candidates for office try to find out what the voters want done and make promises in keeping with what they find out, and politicians generally keep their ears to the ground and do everything in their power to give the voters what they want.

Understanding of what we have chosen when we elevate one system of demand and response above the other may be advanced by noting two vignettes of American experience. The first, when government responded to group pressures for thirty years after the Civil War, is supplied by a leading textbook in American history:

In the three decades that followed [the Civil War], business interests sought to retain and extend their political influence on national, state, and local levels. They were willing to grant certain favors to farmers and working-men—homestead laws, for instance, and pensions for Union veterans. But, as was natural, the captains of industry were much more interested in obtaining government backing for their own projects and in heading off attempts to check, control, and regulate their enterprises.

On the whole, the businessmen succeeded . . . How did the industrialists, financiers, and other businessmen acquire and hold their political power? They were, after all, a small minority of the American people. . . . Part of the answer can be found in the weakness of the opposition. . . . the farmers lacked effective national organization for much of this period; differing party loyalties and the memory of the Civil War made it difficult to bring together western and southern agrarians. It was much the same with labor. . . . the unions reached only a small fraction of the American workingmen. Frequently there was dissention in labor ranks; and labor chieftains always found it hard to cooperate with farm leaders.

Other foes of big business were even less effective. These included white-collar workers, small merchants and manufacturers, and some professional people. Many of these groups had no organization whatsoever . . . Others organized for professional but not political purposes. All wished to improve their lot; but all looked down on workingmen and farmers, all were reluctant to join hands with labor and agrarian elements.*

The second vignette, drawn from a biography of Franklin D.

---

* Merle Curti *et al., An American History* (New York: Harper and Brothers, 1950), vol. 2, pp. 153-155.

Roosevelt, reports a sensitiveness to popular expectations that is strikingly different from the first one. The biographer tells us who commanded the attention of the President and other top officials during Roosevelt's first term of office and his first campaign for re-election.

A remarkable aspect of the New Deal was the sweep and variety of the groups it helped. Not only the millions of farmers and industrial workers, but great numbers of people in other categories had benefited from New Deal largesse. The Home Owners Loan Corporation conducted a vast rescue job, making over a million loans to mortgage-ridden home owners. The WPA put to work not only blue-collar workers but artists, writers, actors, teachers—and in jobs that salvaged their self-respect. The National Youth Administration helped thousands of hard-pressed high-school and college students to continue their education. Old people were looking forward to their pensions [guaranteed by the Social Security Act of 1935]. Bank depositors had a guarantee of the security of their savings. Businessmen gained from government contracts, broadened purchasing power, freer lending policies. . . .

Before a wildly fervent, chanting crowd in Madison Square Garden, Roosevelt . . . brought his campaign [for re-election] to a passionate climax. . . .

"This is our answer to those who, silent about their own plans, ask us to state our objectives.

"*Of course* we will continue to seek to improve working conditions for the workers of America. . . . *Of course* we will continue to work for cheaper electricity in the homes and on the farms of America. . . . *Of course* we will continue our efforts for young men and women . . . for the crippled, for the blind, for the mothers, our insurance for the unemployed, our security for the aged. *Of course* we will continue to protect the consumer . . . will continue our successful efforts to increase his purchasing power and to keep it constant.

"For these things, too, and for a multitude of things like them, we have only just begun to fight. . . ."

Roosevelt showed such a sure sense of popular moods and attitudes that some believed he had intuition or a sixth sense in this field. Actually, his understanding was rooted in solid, day-to-day accumulation of facts on what people were thinking. Roosevelt read half a dozen newspapers a day. He kept up a vast correspondence. Tens of thousands of letters came to the White House every week reporting people's views and problems. He got some understanding from crowds—the way they looked, how they reacted to certain passages in his speeches. As President he enjoyed special advantages. Through favored journalists he could put up trial balloons and test public reaction. He had special voting polls conducted, and he often received advance information on other polls. Administrators in regional and state offices sent in a good deal of information, as did state and local party leaders. A huge division of press intelligence clipped hundreds of newspapers and compiled digests.°

Any reader who has been alert to American public life during the decade beginning in 1960 can provide a third vignette that records a great sensitiveness of public officials and other political leaders to the demands of Negroes as Negroes, of Negroes and whites as poverty-ridden people, of small farmers trying to stay on their farms, of city people anxious to keep defense industries from being closed down, and many others.

Neither system for organizing demand and inducing response goes out of business when the other is in its heyday. Elections were held and campaigns for votes took place during the thirty years following the Civil War when historians tell us that industrialists and financiers came out best in a contest of the strong for control of governmental power. Industrialists and financiers won concessions from an unfriendly President during the period when the New Deal was admittedly a common man's regime. Decisions were made in the two periods with greatly different concern to satisfy demands expressed in two arenas—the arena in which spokesmen for powerful groups make clear what they want public officials to do, and the arena in which individuals enter the voting booth to replace officials who have not satisfied them.

Historians have done a good job of reporting the nation's reliance on the two demand-response systems. If it be the job of the political scientists to explain their coexistence and relate them to ideals that we cover by the term "democratic," then the political scientists are not well started on their undertaking. The search for explanation must be guided by theory, and theory comes in the wake of ground-clearing analysis that fixes orientations, firms up conceptions, and illuminates approaches to the citadel of unknowns that the scholar must attack. I can bring only a meager offering to the task of ground-clearing, or pretheory analysis.

It seems fairly clear that a turn to the equalization-of-influence (call it populist) system of demand and response is stimulated, fed, and boosted to its climax by the successes of the group competition (call it pluralist) system. The struggle for advantage makes it good strategy for the group to enlarge its base by coopting potential supporters, and at the same time to structure itself for a univocal expression of its demands in the forums of

° James M. Burns, *Roosevelt: The Lion and the Fox* (New York: Harcourt, Brace, 1956), pp. 267, 282, 283, 284.

decision. In reaching for support, the already powerful group gives strength to many persons who were previously weak. But in the process of fixing policy there is a rejection of some demands, and in the univocal expression of demands there is a silencing of persons who had urged a different array of demands. Gains for the many, which accrued from joining hands with others, are offset by loss of autonomy in fixing goals and expressing demands. The march of the group to success, accordingly, is accompanied by loss of adherents who made success possible. This sequence of events is not inevitable, but it may be typical. In any case, it certainly has been the experience of many competitors in the pluralist arena.

If the weak or the not-strong-enough are squeezed out of the organizations that compete with greatest chance of success, where do they go? These persons may attach themselves to other groups where they anticipate a better reception for their demands, or they may regroup in new organizations. But also, many who have been thwarted in their previous hopes despair of future success in the arena that pits group against group and turn their attention to the populist demand-response system.

Always on the scene are mobilizers of the electorate whose political organizations are going concerns. Many of them are allied in Democratic or Republican parties. Some of the mobilizers, with their followers, are appropriately labeled splinter groups; swollen in numbers or headed by determined leadership, the splinter group may be recognized as a minor party. Somewhere in this arena is a purposeful group, an incipient group, or a would-be leader ready to assemble a political organization to which the refugee from the pluralist arena can attach himself. Previously viewed as an apathetic voter or a casually involved member of the electorate, he becomes a more or less active participant in electoral campaigns. If his new strategy for influence is successful, he wins a hearing in the places where public policy is made because he has helped fill these places with men whose ears are attuned to what he has to say.

Populist movements have their downs as well as ups, just as we observed in the case of groups in the pluralist arena, and for much the same reasons. Only a shrewd and resourceful leader can hold a militant group together for long. Not only is he haunted by disaffection of great numbers who most dislike the position he espouses; he is confronted by rivals for leadership who stir up disaffection among others of his following. If the leader of a once determined and optimistic segment of the electorate sees his following disappear, he may note that they go in three directions. Some remain active in the populist arena, trying their luck in a new alliance under other leadership. Others drift into political apathy, investing little effort in either electoral activity or strategies for influence in the arena of competing groups. A third part of the disintegrating political movement desert the populist arena as a place for significant investment and carry their wits, their energies, and their resources to an appropriate spot in the pluralist structure, adding their strength to that of others in an effort to win concessions by a bargaining process.

If the swings between the two demand-response systems have been more or less cyclical, we have not plotted the regularity of the cyclical phenomena. Nor are we in a position to say that the phenomena of the past will recur in the future. We have entered a new era of communication. We have more knowledge than previously of how a man's mind can be invaded, greatly improved skills for planning the invasion, and unprecedented facilities for breaching the barriers. The political leader today uses polling and other devices to find out what voters want, how badly they want it, and what they may be willing to do to get what they want. He has expert assistance in formulating objectives and adorning them with appeals that maximize their attractiveness. And he, the leader, may be placed before the voters in an image scarcely recognizable to those who know him best. All this knowledge, skill, and communicating apparatus is available to the managers of groups in the pluralist structure, as it is to the demogogues and statesmen who mobilize voters in political campaigns. Uncertainty as to how this new potential will be used makes it foolhardy to predict that reliance on the two demand-response systems in the future will follow a course that it took in the past.

## Demand and Response: Two Systems Evaluated

Further comparison of the two demand-response systems is necessary. What are their respective utilities? Can we identify any aspects of the two systems that would indicate which ought to be preferred—at all times under all circumstances, or at particular times under particular circumstances?

A few general observations may help to guide one's thinking on this problem.

First, the populist demand-response system, depending primarily on popular election of public officials, admirably subserves the twin ideas that the many ought to share in control of government, and ought to share equally. The right to vote is defined by law, and the law now invites to the polls all but a few adult citizens. In the election of public officials, one man's vote is exactly equal to every other man's vote. Actual practice does not match statutory provision, but the gap between the two has probably diminished in recent years. Whether, and to what extent, it actually has diminished is one of the more important issues for research.

The pluralist demand-response system also invites great numbers of persons to share in exerting influence on those who make governmental decisions. But we have no way of knowing how many share, and no guarantee that those who are influential today will have a comparable amount of influence tomorrow. Furthermore, equality among participants is not a goal of the pluralist system. Indeed, it is keyed to the antithesis of equality. Victory in the struggle between groups goes to the strong, and in the absence of formal provisions to prevent it, one must suppose that influence within the groups responds to displays of strength.

It was posed at the beginning of this essay that the democratic character of a government is determined by the answers given to a three-part question: How many share, in how much of the critical decision making, with how much impact or influence? There are times when the voter can hardly doubt his power. There is a sweeping out of officials by great majorities, the officials who come to power turn the ship of state on a new course, and the voter later congratulates himself as the beneficiary of a new regime. For most voters, this good fortune can occur only occasionally. When some are winning, others are with the minority and lose. Frequently the voter feels he has no choice. The nominating process presents him with alternatives but the candidates look equally good to him, or he would like to reject both of them, or he simply cannot tell where either candidate stands in relation to his interests. Sometimes he makes the choice with confidence and later concludes that he helped put the wrong men in office. Many people, of course, count themselves out occasionally or for good by staying away from the polls.

We shall see later that the populist demand-response system affords the individual several means of influence other than voting. These significantly augment his power, but they are tactics that predominate in the arena of group competition and pay small tribute to the equalization-of-influence principle.

Second, the pluralist demand-response system encourages and fortifies oligarchy; the populist system imposes a brake on oligarchy.

The success of a group, when competition is sharp, depends not only on the numbers enlisted but on the plans for attack and the presentation of a solid front. Plans for attack and unison in attack are gifts of leadership, and leadership, concentrated in a few and firmly held, is oligarchy. Political parties are by no means free of oligarchy, but the party boss, sitting in acknowledged dominion over a political machine, is not the familiar figure he once was in America. The necessity of getting popular support in recurring elections gives the electorate some chance of reconstituting party leadership. The ability of the voters to influence party leaders is increased if they avail themselves of the opportunity, now provided in a number of states, to elect precinct committeemen and other party officials. It must be noted however, that many students of politics feel that provisions for popular participation in the nomination of candidates and election of party officials has burdened the voter with more responsibilities than he can carry and therefore multiplies opportunities for party leaders to make decisions of which the voter is unaware.

It is hazardous to make generalizations about how pluralist groups arrive at their positions on public policy. Top officials of great industrial firms speak directly to congressmen, Presidents, and governors. Lesser officials in big firms, and high and low officials in smaller firms, speak to public officials at many levels of government. Big business, small business, agriculture, labor, the professions—these and still other centers of common interest are variously associated to press demands upon national, state, and local officials. The business firm is oligarchical by design and no doubt of necessity. Trade associations, professional associations, and organizations created for the special purpose of influencing public policy differ in their authority structures. It is probable that most of them are headed by men who hold office by direct or indirect vote of the membership. It is not clear that incumbents can easily be displaced. In some organizations, at least on some occasions, the officers poll the membership before deciding on claims to be pressed upon public officials.

Contemplating the vast array of spokesmen for specialized interests, one suspects that consultation of the clientele before taking positions on public issues is unusual. Much more nearly typical, it appears, is the situation where men of power ostensibly speak for great numbers of people who do not know that a decision is being made and do not recognize the names when they read that someone won a victory for them. This is likely to have been the case, for instance, when the newspapers report that the President decided on a policy of supreme economic significance after a series of conferences with spokesmen for money, big industry, and small business.

Third, the necessity of going to the people for support in periodic elections forces political leaders to engage in a continuous process of educating the voters; in relatively few of the pluralist groups is the leadership confronted by a continuous need to address its clientele. In most of them the compulsion to consult is episodic, and for some of them the episodes are few and infrequent.

The quiet appeal, the debate, and the harangue that emanate from candidates for public office and other political leaders supply a large part of the copy for newspapers, radio, and television. We shall look further into this educative effort at a later point. Leaders of the competing groups address their respective followers through the media of public communication, through their own specialized publications, and especially through a communications network that moves ideas, appeals, demands, and instructions up, down, and across a hierarchy of leaders. The bottom layer of leaders connects this communications network with the membership of the organization and an even larger attentive population thought of as a non-member clientele. Study has not gone far enough to permit reliable estimates of the comparative importance of the two great educative systems—the address of political leaders and candidates for office and the address of leaders who speak for the groups that compete in the pluralist arena. Certainly they complement one another in preparing the American people to assume the obligations imposed upon them by a commitment to popular government. They combine to create that agreement upon purposes and the means to be used in achieving purposes which was discussed above under the label "commonalty."

Fourth, it is undeniable that the pluralist demand-response system is a mainstay of individual and group autonomy, a condition we identified above as requisite for government by the people. Indeed, the competitive life of groups which we have been talking about is proof that life in the United States is marked by a high degree of personal and group choice. The relations of the populist demand-response system to individual and group autonomy are not as clear. Some activities that figure prominently in the populist or equalization-of-influence system—e.g., letters to congressmen, attendance at protest meetings, marching and other demonstrations —not only are proof of autonomy, but contribute to the strengthening of autonomy. On the other hand, the wooing and buying-out process by which political leaders seek to bring the electorate into their camps is seen by many observers to reduce free choice. The political campaign tends to divide the electorate into two great segments and within each segment to take the edge off enterprise and bind the voters into a mass helpless to do anything but go along with the leadership that planned and administered their entrapment.

The proof of personal autonomy is in deliberate social displacement—changing employment, moving to another part of town, joining an organization. Ordinarily the reason for making the move is to improve one's position. If one sees himself as underprivileged or low on the totem pole, he will view a move for his betterment as an effort to achieve a closer approach to equality. If he thinks himself to be well placed already, he may see his upward movement as escape from a condition where he was the equal of too many. The norms or laws that govern life in the competing groups encourage disdain for unchanging status; influence in the counsels of the group comes as a reward for going forward according to tests of progress which prevail in the group. Upward movement on the economic and social ladders may be an asset for the man who hopes to rise in the esteem of the electorate, but this is not dependably the case. If he moves, physically, across the boundaries of a political jurisdiction, he may lose all the investment he has made in a political career. If his upward progress on economic or social tests is too rapid, he may be given a downward push on election day by his less fortunate fellow men who like to see their own kind in public office. The relation of the electoral system to economic and social enterprise in the United States has not since received a scrutiny as perceptive or as wise as that provided by a Frenchman more than one hundred years ago. Any reader who wants to know how our populist political system stimulates or depresses self-displacement in economic and social life will find no better way to start his search than by reading Alexis de Tocqueville's *Democracy in America*.

Fifth, and finally, I must emphasize the close interrelationship of the two demand-response systems. They are not wholly separable systems for expressing demand and inducing response. Voters act like members of competing groups when they put pressures on public officials; indeed, the members of the competing groups are part of the electorate, and the spokesmen of the groups may also be influential political leaders. Similarly, men who work most effectively in the pluralist arena freely invade the arena of political campaigns. Acknowledging that they speak for a group with known interests and a known membership, agents of the groups endorse and recruit candidates for public office. They contribute to the campaign costs of candidates they favor and harangue the voter. We have, from one perspective, not two demand-response systems in the world of American politics, but a single bifurcated system, which operates on differentiable fronts, for differentiable objectives, by differentiable methods. Granted that the differences are differences in emphasis, I find it useful to say that they mark the existence of two demand-response systems. By examining them separately we risk overlooking some significant interrelationships, but we also gain the advantages of a focused scrutiny.

# 4. THE CITIZEN'S ROLE

The principal means available to the citizen for exerting influence on government must be re-examined. Too much that is essential to popular control of government has been overlooked in too much of the literature. My effort to search out the attitudes and behavior essential to popular government in the United States has led me to array opportunities for exerting influence on government under six heads.

One, the people make the culture and the societal ways that envelop government, determine its structure and processes, and condition its product. This is a fact for all governments, but undoubtedly popular governments are most responsive to the underlying culture and societal ways.

Two, the voting population participates in fixing the content of the constitutions that establish and regulate our governments. If one thinks this overstates popular participation in adopting and changing the national constitution, he will admit its truth for our state constitutions.

Three, qualified voters approve or disapprove proposed public policies in referendum elections. We are in an experimental stage as respects national policies; we have, since the 1930s, given farmers the right to decide by referendum voting whether certain farm crops shall be subject to controls provisionally set forth by Congress. Popular voting on local government issues is common in many states and some states provide for popular approval or disapproval of statewide policies as well.

Four, the voters name the officials who will hold the authority of government, make the major public policies, and direct the administrative organizations that do the work of government.

Five, we subject our public officials, both the elected and the appointed, to continuous and insistent demands. If they do not do what you and I want done, we very soon make clear what we will do in retaliation.

Six, and last, we exert great influence by our attitudes and behavior which welcome or repulse a public policy. Public officials and political leaders read our minds and, influenced by what they find, decide whether to enact the law they are considering, modify the content of a proposed policy, reconsider the timing of their acts. After the law is passed, we make it effective by a friendly response, modify its impact by resistance, or nullify it altogether by refusal to comply.

It will be seen that some of these means of participation lend themselves to regulation, and that others do not. The act of voting can be regulated, whether the poll be for selection of officials, amending a constitution, or recording approval or disapproval of a referendum measure. We can define the issue to be decided, fix a time and place for the voting act, state in precise terms who can get into the polling place and who cannot, and specify a rule for deciding what the decision will be if voters disagree. We can do some things to regulate the appeals and pressures by which we induce officials to do what we want done. We can, for instance, require formal hearings, create advisory bodies, secure some representation of interests in the organizations that formulate and enforce public policies. But we cannot regulate the contacts of citizens with officials as we regulate the voting act; the official must have information which only citizens can supply, and the channels of communication that carry the information are heavily encumbered with demands for favors.

Concerning the sixth means of citizen influence that I mentioned, it is apparent that the public response that makes a law enforceable or renders it inoperative cannot be regulated at all. You can hardly say to the governed: you may violate this law provided you violate it only in these ways and to this extent.

It now becomes clear that standards of equality and majority rule can have only a limited application in our system of government. Where we can regulate the participative act, we can make substantial provision for equality. We can prescribe one man one vote, and we can count all votes according to the same conventions of mathematics. But we cannot wholly guarantee equality in the selection of public officials because we cannot, by law, control all the prior acts which determine who will survive competition long enough to be a contestant when the vote is taken, and we do not know how to keep one man from compounding his strength by influencing other voters. Similarly, if we wish to, we can provide for majority rule in every case where a vote is taken. Actually we do not provide for decision by majority in all cases where we are able to do so; most of our offices go to the man who gets more votes than any other candidate, regardless of how far he falls short of winning a majority of all votes cast.

Far more striking, of course, is our departure from equality and majority decision where participation takes any form other than voting. Think of the appeals we address to our public officials and the pressures we exert to make them do what any of us wants done. We suppose that the official will take some note of how many people are for and how many against an action he contemplates. But we know very well that he will not carefully count heads and make his decision according to his count. We expect him to respond to persuasiveness, to a show of strength, to a threat of reprisals. However, we know that effectiveness in these things is not evenly distributed among men. Decisions are likely to go in favor of those who bring the greatest resources to the struggle for advantage.

Consider finally the case where public officials abandon enforcement of a law in response to a ground swell of popular complaint or an organized campaign of resistance. Certainly the rule of decision by majority is wholly wanting in this instance, and the principle of equality is honored only in the sense that officials are unwilling to require a complaisant sector of the population to comply with a policy they know a rebellious sector of the population will successfully evade.

By such reasoning I conclude that much of the writing that puts emphasis on provision for equality and majority rule in the American political system strays a long way from reality. Generally, what is said about equality and majority rule is applicable only to the election of public officials and occasional voting on specific issues of public policy, but the writers do not make this clear. Little harm may be done if you and I are deceived a while longer; great harm may come if architects of democratic government in other countries are misled. The misrepresentation of our provisions for equality and majority rule in our literature can have deplorable consequences when read by people who seek in our experience a model to guide their own efforts to construct a democratic system.

The foregoing comments will indicate my conviction that the six avenues of popular participation just described are of unequal significance. Three of them—election of officials, appeals and pressures, and public reaction to acts of government—seem most important to continuing popular control. While I insist that appeals and pressures and public reactions to policy are essential instruments of the populist demand-response system, I think the popular estimate is correct when it gives prior place to elections. Popular selection, by an inclusive electorate, of officials who maintain close contact with different sectors of the population is the bottom level instrument of democratic government.

The attractiveness of popular selection of public officers lies primarily in the fact that the electoral process gives people their best chance to share equally in controlling their government. But the electoral process contributes other benefits to the political system. Four will be mentioned. Each of them will be recognized as an element of that general state of mind and behavior which I called commonalty.

First, a vigorous competition for elective offices, once it is established, creates a great compulsion to enlarge the electorate. Sooner or later there appears on the scene a man ambitious for public office who thinks that his chances of being elected would be greater if some sector of the population not now admitted to the polls were given the right to vote. When the managers of an organization important enough to be called a political party despair of a sufficient popularity with the present electorate, they look for promise of support among the nonfranchised, and sooner or later they come up with a campaign to honor the principle of equality by inviting an additional sector of the population into the electoral process. For a time, another party's management may oppose this extension of the right to vote. Our history to date shows that, over time, the champions of a more liberal franchise always win. Immediately after party lines became sharply drawn and office seekers decided that high pressure campaigning for votes was a worthy enterprise—I think of this as dating from the election of 1800—the property requirements limiting the right to vote began to tumble. The white immigrant from Europe was invited into the polls almost as soon as he got the salt water out of his hair. Women were admitted to the suffrage not because of a growing piety that could no longer condone injustice, but because calculating politicians figured out how they would get most of the women to vote right.

Where antagonism of the established electorate is intense and deep-seated, the right to vote is reluctantly given. The case of the Indian and the Negro illustrates the point, but it does not negate my thesis. The Fifteenth Amendment, asserting a right to vote regardless of race or color, derived a great part of its support from convictions that the Negro would vote the Republican ticket if given a chance to mark a ballot. And the increasing participation of Negroes in Southern elections during four decades after World War I was encouraged and defended by white politicians who made concessions and promises that assured them Negro support at the polls.

Second, a generous bestowal of the right to vote guarantees general public appreciation of the stakes of politics. This point requires little elaboration. If office seekers or party workers want a man's vote, they tell him why he ought to vote as they want him to. If a vote is important enough for one side to ask for it, it is important enough for another side to generate a counter-argument. In this fashion, political education starts. It is completed by the newspapers and other instruments of communication. When virtually all adults can vote, public affairs and political activity are high priority news. A man must be highly selective, indeed, in what he listens to or must close his ears entirely if he would escape a substantial acquaintance with main political issues in America today.

Third, the necessity of winning elections in order to get in office and stay in office chastens the office holder and the politician who is allied with him. They listen to the spokesmen for special interest, in part because this is a way to find out what the people want done, in part because this is a way to win support in the next election. But yielding to demands from one group of voters, or from an organization that can swing votes, may alienate another part of the electorate equally or more crucial to the office holder's re-election. Rarely, therefore, can he lend more than one ear to the message coming in from even the most powerful spokesmen for a special interest. One ear must be available for the counter-demands of opposing groups and for the rumblings of a general public that is only apprehensive because it has not made up its mind what it wants. Listening to many voices, the office holder and the politician must file the incoming intelligence in a number of boxes. Who want what, how badly do they want it, and how do they want it done? Who will support me and who will oppose me if I act this way or that? And always, is the general public ready for the proposed policy? Will cooperation be forthcoming from those parts of the population that will have to cooperate if the policy is to be effective? How much dragging the feet must be anticipated? Is the protesting part of the population so secure in the conviction that God has blessed its position and so determined not to let the Lord down in a fight that its dogged opposition to the policy will prevent successful execution? Here is challenge for the tolerant attitude, and here is confirmation for the complaint that American politicians tend to be all things to all men.

Fourth, near-universal adult suffrage, vigorous campaigning for votes, and a high priority on news about politics and public affairs—these conditions in a society all but guarantee a growing toleration of differences in political position. The office seeker, the political worker, and the public communicator all harangue the population on the point that not everybody can win. The most bitter campaign culminates with solemn declarations that today the people will speak and that tomorrow all will compose themselves to live according to the decision.

Together these four effects of campaigns and elections promote give and take, or toleration, which in turn tends to moderate demands and to mitigate attitudes that might eventuate in resistance. Elections are thus revealed to be central to the whole process by which the people control their government; the campaign for votes and the decision at the polls fix bounds for the other channels of participation and unite them to form a populist demand-response system.

The preceding survey of the channels open to the citizen for controlling his government prompts one to inquire: Who should be given a right to invade any one of the several channels? Who ought to be allowed to participate in the selection of officials, and who ought to be allowed to press claims upon public officials with expectation that his claims will be considered sympathetically? When we say that everybody counts, do we mean every man, woman, and child in this country? When we say that government must comply with the wishes of the people, whose wishes are we talking about?

We shall not attempt to answer all these questions in the pages that follow, but we may succeed in throwing some light on several of them. I have asserted a conviction that popular election of public officials is the prime instrument of democratic government. For that reason I fix attention first and most fully on the question: Who may vote and what are the conditions of voting? The examination of these questions about voting, which begins in the next chapter, will be aided by a quick survey of some preliminary considerations.

Obviously we cannot set up as a test for democratic government, that government must be run to suit everybody 100 per cent. If we did that, then government would be unable to forbid anybody to do anything he wanted to do, or to coerce anybody into doing anything he did not want to do. The best we can do is construct a system of government that will be obliged to operate with a degree of satisfaction to the people. As more people find some satisfaction with public policies and as the measure of their satisfaction increases we more closely approach the ideal in democratic government.

In trying to make our government as satisfactory as possible we have to watch for three things. What people are we going to take into consideration? What consideration are we going to give to the intensity of feelings which people express? What do we do when people are divided in their positions on an issue?

On the first of these points, we can surely say that we want our government to consider the interests of every man, woman, and child in our country. There are orphan children who have no parents to speak for them, and we certainly want our government to make provision for their welfare. There are foreigners transiently in our midst on business or pleasure, and we certainly want our government to protect their lives and property while they are here. But to say that we want our government to give consideration to their interests is not to say that we want orphan children and visiting foreigners to participate in controlling our government. In working out this problem of relations between government and the people, we must provide for different kinds of relations. Some people will be seen but not heard (little children and visiting foreigners); some people will be both seen and heard, but will feel strongly that no one pays much attention to what they say; other people will have a great influence in the control of government.

Our primary way of admitting people to share in the control of government is to give them a right to vote. Government in the United States is carried on by, or under the direction of, men who are selected for their offices by a decision at the polls. We determine what kind of government we shall get primarily in the act of choosing men for the key public offices. By re-electing the people already in office we approve what they have been doing and give them a green light to go forward along the same lines or along new lines that they have indicated in their appeal for votes. By turning them out of office and putting other people in we indicate that we want a change of policy and we authorize the new group to proceed along the lines they have proposed. While there are ways of influencing the conduct of government other than by voting, the right to vote is the basic assurance to any man that he can share in the control of government. A wide extension of the suffrage is, therefore, as we shall indicate more fully later on, essential to democratic government.

On the second question, concerning intensity of feelings on political questions, we must distinguish between what we formally provide and what we work out in other ways. We make no allowance, in the formal voting provisions, for differences in gravity of interests or strength of convictions. In any election each voter has one vote on each question that is to be decided; all votes carry the same weight, regardless of how concerned or how indifferent particular voters may be. We could work out a system for weighting votes according to the interests at stake and the strength of personal convictions, and we have taken some steps in this direction in voting on local issues.

Strength of conviction and intensity of feelings make themselves felt where they are not formally provided for. The man who has the greater interest in the outcome of an election, or who is more certain of his judgment, is more likely to go to the polls than the individual who neither cares about the outcome of the particular election nor distinguishes the merits of the opposing candidates. Persons with deeper convictions talk about the forthcoming election and influence the voting of other people. In this way they compound their strength. After the election is over and the newly elected officials are in office the voters who are really concerned about what the government is going to do are likely to make their wishes known to public officials and may try in one way or another to put pressure on them. These are ways in which variations of intensity affect governmental decisions even though not formally provided for in the arrangements for voting.

The third question is not so readily disposed of. What do we do when voters indicate different wishes in an election?—and of course they practically always do. If there are only two positions which voters may take—e.g., only two candidates for an office—the solution is easy. The greater number of votes wins over the smaller number of votes. That is the only sensible conclusion to reach, since we make no allowance for differences in intensity of feelings. But the situation is not always so simple. Frequently there are more than two candidates for an office. If we are voting directly on a local improvement program and how to finance it, voters would like to take positions scattered over a wide range of alternatives.

We make a considerable effort to narrow the voter's choice and secure majority decisions by eliminating alternatives before the final election. This is what party organization does. If there are only two parties with candidates in the field, the pre-election decisions in convention or primary election will turn up one candidate for each party, and the final choice can be determined by majority vote. But pre-election decisions do not always reduce the voters' job to a choice between two alternatives. Frequently there are three or more parties with candidates. In that case we may simply provide that the candidate receiving the most votes is elected, even though he gets far less than 50 per cent of the votes. In some states, the law provides that the leading candidate is elected if he gets a certain percentage of the total vote—say 35 per cent. Many states provide for a run-off election between the two candidates who led the field in the first election.

No matter what devices are used to reduce the number of alternatives before the voter, it is rare indeed that a majority of the voters obtain the result that they prefer above all others. I prefer the candidate of my party to the candidate of the opposing party, but I really wanted a different man in my own party who was eliminated in the primary election. I voted for the bond issue, and I am glad that it was approved by a majority vote, but I am still of the opinion that it is for a bigger amount than necessary and I wish that my advice had been heeded when they were formulating the proposal to be submitted to the voters.

It is considerations like these that necessitate caution in formulating a definition of democratic government and cause me to adopt indefinite language such as my statement that in democratic governments the public officials are obliged to act "within limits that are acceptable to the people." There are too many unknowns in the minds of the population, too many unknowns in the organization of influence, too many unknowns in the processes of decision to permit one to specify how many people must acquiesce in the acts of government and how comfortable those people must be in their acquiesence. These uncertainties, of course, lie not only in the complicated world of campaigning and elections; they pervade all the other means of exerting influence as well. Believing political life to be so befogged with uncertainties, I am forced to reject formulations asserting that democratic government is simply rule by the majority.

My definition, or specification in lieu of definition, was formulated with a view to experience in the United States. It supposes that the affairs of government will be put in the hands of selected men; that the people in the mass will not try to make the decisions of government. For that reason, there is emphasis on men who "possess the authority of government," and on the necessity of their exercising their authority "within limits that are acceptable to the people." If, instead of giving public officials authority to govern them, the entire American nation decided the critical issues of policy by listening to alternative proposals on the radio and sending statements of their preferences to Washington to be counted and converted into decisions, a more precise definition of democratic government might be possible. But we cannot be sure of that, for strategy designed to make democratic government secure would then be different from any we have contemplated. Means for providing people with knowledge would be a more critical problem than it is today; difficulties, now unforeseen, in framing questions for decision and recording statements of preference would emerge. We shall do well enough for the time being, it seems to me, if we can sharpen our perceptions of what gives the American way of government its democratic character. Our system, making the choice of public officials the citizen's critical act, greatly reduces the task of providing minimal civic education. The citizen who feels utterly incompetent when asked for a judgment on current issues of public policy may still participate intelligently in the electoral process by appraising the character and quality of contending candidates for office, or by deciding, after inquiry, to entrust the government to one political party rather than the other. If his vote records a choice between individual candidates or a preference for the roster of candidates offered by one of the political parties, the voting citizen will have accommodated himself to the regime of competition that was mentioned above. We must now examine that system of competition for political power in some detail.

# 5. THE RIGHT TO VOTE

Democratic government, as developed in the United States, is a regime in which a great number of men make public affairs their business and, in order to get ahead in that business, organize for concerted effort to capture public offices and promise courses of governmental action as rewards for electoral support. If placed in public offices they exercise authority with a view to retaining electoral support. This describes a vision of the American scene, but a vision that is in large part realized in fact. Let us view it as an ideal type. Democratic government, so viewed, is a system of competition for power that results in a conduct of public affairs that accords with the expectations of the people.

The electorate is the base of competition for political power; the approval of voters is what the political managers and candidates compete for. By giving their votes to one candidate or another the voters determine who wins and who loses in the competition for political power, and in determining this they make their impress on the policies of government. They have, in company with non-voting elements in the population, other means for influencing the conduct of public officials, but deciding who will occupy the seats of authority is the critical act in popular control of government.

If the number of people who can make an impact on government is a measure of democratic character, as posed near the beginning of this essay, then the electorate must be inclusive. The right to vote cannot be universal; no nation is likely to take on the difficulties of polling newborn infants. What parts of the population ought to be invited to share in the selection of public officials?

We have approached universal adult suffrage in the United States without a comprehensive theory of enfranchisement to guide us. Progress was accomplished by a process of accretion. Sectors of the population, first in England and then in North America, before and after Independence, successfully bid for a right to share in the selection of public officials. Each addition to the electorate was accompanied by its rationalization. Each proposed addition, if contested, produced some assertions of principle— that religion is irrelevant to political power, that possession of property is or is not an indicator of capacity to select for office men who will maintain and improve the political system, and so on. The requirements that one must meet in order to be admitted to the polls are set forth in the statute books of state and national governments, and they are recounted and justified or questioned in textbooks. But the textbook commentary does not include carefully worded statements about ideals to be achieved, most promising means for achieving alternative ideals, and the relation of varying ways of life to prospects for utilizing the suggested means. These concerns would seem to be central to any serious discourse entitled to be called a theory of suffrage.

## Qualifications for Voting

The tests for admission to the polls which are fixed in statutes provide a starting point for the theory maker but their utility for his purposes is limited. The usual specification of twenty-one years is not per se preferable to eighteen years (the requirement in a few states). In a debate as to which age requirement is best, the argument will turn on the probable relation of each point in age to a battery of more fundamental considerations. A specific age is fixed by law in order to facilitate a quick and defensible decision at the polling place as to whether the applicant to vote shall be given a ballot. So with residence requirements, such as that requiring the applicant to have resided one year in the state and sixty days in the county; the specification of fixed periods facilitates a quick and defensible decision, and the periods that are specified bear some relation to more fundamental considerations not mentioned in the law.

I do not undertake here to develop, or even to outline, a theory of suffrage, but I shall set forth some judgments as to what may be the fundamental considerations underlying the requirements for voting in the United States. It seems to me that six primary considerations have figured in such debate as we have had concerning a right to vote.

## COMPETENCE

This is ground enough for disqualifying newborn infants. It is also ground enough for a rule that great-grandpa may not vote if a doctor would have to be called in to rout him out of a state of coma sufficiently to make a mark on an absentee ballot. You might contend that a man should not be allowed to vote if he cannot find his way to the polling booth or remember which offices are to be filled. Perhaps such elementary tests of competence would have been examined in political debate if there had been confidence that readily administrable tests could be devised to differentiate competence at that level.

Concern about competence accounts for the period of prior residence required for voting in the community to which a man has lately moved. A period of thirty days may be thought sufficient for the would-be voter to apply for registration and for the registration authorities to determine whether he is indeed twenty-one years old, a citizen of the United States, and meets the other requirements for voting. But another month, or six months, or a year may be thought essential for the newcomer to learn what offices are to be filled, to develop a judgment on the issues confronting the people of the local unit or the state, and to appraise the candidates for office. As tests of competence, residence requirements are notably crude. The voter who moves from Indiana to Illinois is required to be in Illinois a full year before entering the polling booth, but this wait can hardly be justified so far as his voting for President is concerned. Ballots and voting machines can be designed so that the newcomer can vote for President after the month required for local registration, but be denied the right to vote for state and local offices because of doubt that he has been around long enough to have a judgment about the candidates. A movement to revise voting legislation so as to make residence requirements more neatly fit a test of competence seems now to be in progress.

A literacy requirement—proof of ability to read and write—appears on superficial inspection to be wholly defensible; further examination shows it to be debatable. Without question, the ability to read is closely related to acquisition of knowledge about offices, candidates, and governmental policies. Low rating on literacy tests correlates positively and significantly with low interest in and little knowledge of public affairs. On the other hand, talking about politics appears to give some people considerable sophistication about public affairs, and radio and television greatly augment their opportunities to learn by ear and eye.

If inability to make an intelligent choice on election day affected no one adversely except the voter who cast the unintelligent vote, we might drop tests of competence from further consideration. But there is reason to believe that uninterested and ill informed voters exact a price from the rest of the electorate, especially when they invade the polls in large numbers under the stimuli provided by party workers. The concentration of power in city bosses and the corruption that was ascribed to political machines during many decades of the last century were due in great part to the ability of party leaders to swap small favors for the vote of immigrants who had not yet learned how to use the ballot most effectively for their long-run benefit. Still it is not a foregone conclusion that the enfranchisement of uninterested and ill-informed voters, even when they invade the polls in great numbers, represents a net loss to the nation. Consider the case of the Negro immediately after emancipation. Surely it is a fact that few of the former slaves could have appreciated the opportunities that electoral participation afforded them; few of them, in the first decade of freedom, could have been expected to make an intelligent choice among candidates for public office. On the other hand, if the Negro had been assured a right to vote, the white man might have gotten busy with the Negro's civic education. Men who are hungry for office, in sharp competition for votes, and willing to pay a price for support at the polls can be very patient in explaining to the ignorant voter how government can serve him well or do him in. The necessity of winning the support of uninformed men can be the cause for ending their ignorance.

The issue is not a dead one, and the debate is as appropriate for today as for any time in the past. The adult Negro undoubtedly feels strongly that he wants improvement in his status and that political power must be an instrument for this improvement. But if the Negro has suffered as grievously from his former deprivations as we are told by Negro and white leaders alike, one must suppose that great numbers of adult Negroes have only a limited comprehension of how they can best use the ballot to advance their interests. If so, their feelings of helplessness increase the power of leaders who win their confidence. It may indeed be the case that Negroes with the least appreciation of the alternatives available to them will be the readiest to vote as a bloc, and because they vote as a bloc will have tremendous effect on what white politicians and officeholders decide they will have to do about Negro rights. With such a view of the future before him, one can take a position for or against literacy tests according to the social consequences he thinks likely to accrue from a disciplined Negro vote.

### INTEREST

A vigorous debate, in the early days of the republic, centered on conceptions of "interest," need for balancing interests in creating a government for free men, and questions about how a proper balance of interests could be secured by giving and withholding the right to vote. Viewed in certain ways, interest is only an aspect of competence. It is argued that a man should not be allowed to vote unless he knows what his interests are, has opinions as to what government could do to advance his interests, and is able to appraise candidates according to what they are likely to do to advance his interests if elected. These requirements are readily translated into conditions of competence. But, it is argued further, many people who are very clear about what they want will vote for the candidates who propose to do most for them right now. If such voters prevail, public officials may feel compelled to do too much too quickly and subject the social structure to strains it cannot absorb. Voters who put such demands on government may also be viewed as lacking competence if their behavior is thought to be an unwise balancing of long-run and short-run interests.

At the time of founding this political system there was a fear, shared by many of the new nation's leaders, that much of the adult population, if allowed to vote, would put short-run interests above long-run interests and bring the experiment in self-government to a quick end. More than a fear of incompetence went into their apprehensions, no doubt. Some of the leaders must have been fearful that certain elements of the population were only too much aware of where their interests lay. Some elements of the population, appraising their short-run and long-run interests very shrewdly, could be expected to use the ballot for ends which some political leaders thought incompatible with the general good or even destructive of free government.

Confronted by so dismal a prospect, which sets of interests ought to triumph and when ought the victory be won? Enfranchise all adults and fight the battle of conflicting interests in successive elections? Or restrict the suffrage and remove from elections those who might put too much strain upon the system? Those early leaders who spoke most earnestly in favor of balancing interests supported the second course. The most extreme of them contended that only persons who owned property or offered other evidence of a high stake in stable institutions and continuing public policies should be allowed to participate in choosing public officials. Faced with the necessity of compromise, they agreed to an inclusive electorate for some offices provided that other officers (e.g., one chamber of a two-house legislature) were selected by a process that responded to elements in the population (mainly property holders) whose interests dictated stable government and continuing policies.

The early decisions to restrict the suffrage in order to aggrandize certain interests and repress others have since been reversed in the main, but not altogether. During the depression of the 1930s there was a demand, of proportions to require notice, that people on public relief ought not to be allowed to use the ballot to insure the continuance of relief payments. The disenfranchisement of the Negro, where done by law or contrary to law, has been supported in large part by contentions that the Negro's interests are incompatible with those of the more numerous white population. Controversies about allocating seats in legislative bodies also arise in part out of determinations to advance the interests of some by repressing the interests of others.

It will be seen that the issue of interest as a test to be applied in fixing the right to vote must be tried in one's mind against a more basic question. That deeper question is: Who counts in a democratic society and who is to count for how much in the political life of the United States?

COMPLIANCE

The relevance of tests of compliance may be determined by considering three questions: May we exclude from the polls persons who attempt to disturb or impair the electoral process? May we exclude persons who give cause to believe that they will resist the electoral decision or refuse to comply with decisions made by the elected officials? May we exclude persons who make known their enmity to the political system that enables voters to select and replace their public officials?

Practice throughout the United States shows that we are ambivalent on the first question. Some of our states have enacted laws that disenfranchise for a period of years persons who are convicted of specified offenses related to obstructing voting, tampering with the ballot box, wrongly reporting election returns, etc. Pennsylvania, for instance, adds to the penalties of fine and imprisonment a four year period of disenfranchisement for any person convicted of violating the election laws. These evidences of public concern to protect the right to vote stand in sharp contrast to other actions, publicly condoned and abetted, that are specially designed to exclude lawful voters from the polling place. This has been notorious practice in the South where public officials unlawfully refused to register Negroes and where polling officials refused to give the ballot to Negroes who, by any fair man's judgment, had met all the legal requirements for voting.

A public policy that disenfranchises a man for stealing votes might appropriately disfranchise the man who refuses to vacate an office after the voters have elected another man to replace him. This, no doubt, we would readily do if we thought that resistance to the electoral decision lacked moral justification. The fact probably is, however, that persons who refuse to vacate public offices in this country nearly always do so because they think the polling was not fairly conducted and because they intend, by refusing to vacate, to force a judicial decision as to who rightly won the election. No doubt it will be generally agreed that, when the refusal to give up the office is a sheer act of usurpation, it is appropriate to impose severe penalties. These penalties might well include disqualification from further office holding and denial of the right to participate in electing officers.

Refusal to comply with the laws enacted by a popularly chosen assembly, if it is not a clear case of resisting the electoral decision, touches on the second and third questions posed above; it impeaches the wisdom of the voters who chose the lawmakers, and it displays notable disrespect if not enmity to the political system. It is customary, in the American states, to deny the ballot to persons in jail. Some states extend the disfranchisement for a period after release from prison, occasionally providing that the governor may shorten the period of disfranchisement as he might commute a sentence or give a pardon. One might approve disfranchisement, even for the remainder of life, if he believed that the crime disclosed deep-seated attitudes inimical to a regime of law and order, but object to disfranchisement even during the period of imprisonment if he thought the unlawful act had been done in protest against a public policy which the offender believed morally indefensible. Thus a present-day Thoreau would be given an absentee ballot if he sat in jail on election day; so would the religious zealot in jail for refusing to allow his children to be vaccinated; the Negro rightly imprisoned but claiming that he violated the law to make the white man inquire whether his laws are just.

At the center of public attention for several years has been the question of what to do about persons committed to the overthrow of government in the United States by force. At present neither the national government nor any state government disfranchises a person, otherwise qualified to vote, because he is known to have a firm purpose to assist in the violent overthrow of the United States government. A federal statute (The Communist Control Act of 1954) withdraws all legal protection and benefits from the Communist Party and the effect of this statute, making it impossible for persons to run for public office as candidates on a Communist Party ticket or under any pseudonym for the Communist Party, may be viewed as restricting the free choice of voters who would like to support Communist candidates. It has long been the policy of the United States to reject applications for citizenship on the part of residents who are judged to be at enmity with the American system, and for many years it has been the policy to reject such persons when they seek admission to the United States under our immigration laws. There seems to be no widespread objection to these exclusions in the naturalization and immigration laws. It seems a safe bet that some people would vigorously object if any state excluded from the polls all persons who are found, on sufficient evidence, to have a firm purpose to utilize force if necessary to terminate this experiment in democratic government.

## SHARING OF COMMON POSITION

Competence and interest appear to be basic tests for fixing the bounds of enfranchisement. Compliance may also be viewed as a basic test if one supposes that doubt about his loyalty to the white man's system was the reason for not allowing Indians to vote for more than a century. Some other tests are not designed to proclaim a right to vote but have as their purpose to withdraw the right to vote from some persons who fall within the bounds set by the more basic tests. Such a secondary test is implicit in the assertion that it is unnecessary to give the ballot to certain parts of the population because their interests are adequately reflected in the voting behavior of that part of the population which is already enfranchised. This was the standard reply to women during the many years when woman suffrage was an issue before the American people. The husband, it was said, adequately spoke for the special interests of his wife, and men in general adequately spoke for the interests of the female sex. Unmarried women above the age of twenty-one, especially if they had no father and no brothers, could ponder the implication that they either had no special interests or that the spokesmen for these interests were hidden where they could not find them. The present day demand that the voting age be dropped to eighteen years meets a response similar to that once made to women: that young people of age eighteen through twenty have no interests that are not adequately represented at the polls by older people. The contention that young men just a few years short of twenty-one have a concern about fighting wars that does not trouble the upper-age sector of the present electorate surely is true and worthy of serious thought. But one must not overlook the fact that it makes a poor argument for giving the vote to young women of the same age. And, of course one can push the age requirement on down, contending that boys of twelve or fifteen ought be allowed to vote today because the acts of today's officials will determine whether these boys are to risk their lives a few years later.

OTHER MEANS OF POWER

There appears never to have been at any time in American history a significant demand that certain elements of the population be denied the right to vote because other means of influence give them all the power they should have. However, some countries have sought to adjust voting power to other means of influence. For more than half a century Catholic priests have been denied admission to the polls in Mexico on the ground that their influence over other voters gives them voice enough in selecting officials, and perhaps a good deal more than they are entitled to. While we do not, in the United States, try to even up political power by withdrawing the ballot from the otherwise powerful, we have other policies designed to take the edge off certain peaks of power. Most notable of these efforts to even up advantage is legislation which limits the amount of money a candidate can spend on his political campaign, and limits the amount of money any individual can contribute to a political campaign. Such legislation is thought generally to fall far short of its purpose, but the purpose, undeniably, is to avoid the disproportionate wielding of power which a wealthy man can bring to the electoral process.

## SOCIAL COMPATIBILITY

There have been blanket denials of the right to vote in our history which cannot be accounted for on the preceding grounds, and which do not fit any other specific tests I have been able to hit upon. Throughout our history, in many parts of the nation, the Negro has been denied the right to vote, not because he failed to meet specific tests but simply because he was a Negro. Individual Negroes who offered proof of high intelligence, advanced knowledge of public affairs, and acceptance of the political system were turned away and the best reason given for refusing them the ballot was that they belonged to the wrong race. One who disapproves of the practice may condemn it as a breach of the vital test of democratic character—that everybody counts—and argue that no effort need be made to fit it into an array of tests for fixing the right to vote. Another man, favoring the exclusion of Negroes, might answer that Negroes had not, at the time of blanket exclusion, been admitted to the American society, and that the rule "everybody counts" no more applied to the Negro then than it applies today to the newcomer who has just reached our shores. Still a third position, and the one I find persuasive, is that the Negro was, by emancipation, admitted to the American society and thereby entitled to the benefits and assurances implicit in the democratic ideology, but that he was denied the right to vote for a package of undefined and in large part undefinable reasons. Not knowing what was wrapped up in the packet of undifferentiated prejudices, and wishing a term that might cover other cases than the Negro, I have chosen the label "social compatibility." Whether consistent or not consistent with democratic ideals, the American people have utilized a conception of social compatibility as a test for admission to the suffrage.

Tests for admission to the suffrage will be administered by that part of the population that already dominates the political process. It seems to me that there are conditions in which those who control the political process would be wise to apply a test of social compatibility and exclude from political power elements in the population that fail the test. Any of man's social contrivances can succumb to excessive strain, and a populist demand-response system can be brought to collapse by the incompatibility of demands addressed to public officials with excessive intensity and persistence. Anticipating such a result, the dominant part of the population may well think it premature to invite certain of the excluded elements of the population into the electoral arena. Such a decision may be viewed as a judgment that the amount of commonalty essential for the security of democratic government has not yet been attained. Elliott Arnold, in his *Blood Brother*, gives us a vivid picture of the civic condition of the Chiricahuas during a period when they were successively escaping from the reservation and being brought back within its confines. White men who had successfully evaded a scalping party on Monday could hardly be expected to invite their enemies to vote on Tuesday. Doubt about the extent of commonalty may justify the use of a social compatibility test by people who are trying to found new nations in our own time. The religion-like commitment to the democratic idea which prevails right now may have led contemporary nation builders to extend rights of participation to elements of the population that had better been made wards of the state than partners in management of the state.

## Administration of Elections

The most careful statement of who has a right to vote is nullified if legal requirements are ignored on election day. Election laws are an object of recurring attention by state legislatures, but it is nonetheless a fact that we have not solved the problems of honest polling in communities where elections are most bitterly contested. A good handbook of election law and procedure for any one of the fifty states is likely to run well above one hundred pages. This makes it clear that we can examine only a few main questions of election administration here. The following appear to be most worthy of attention: (1) What can be done to make voting easy and convenient for the voter? (2) What can be done to make sure that only people who are lawfully entitled to vote do so? (3) What can be done to assure honest administration of the polls, honest counting of votes, and honest reporting of the results of elections? All of these questions present challenges for theory making, but I shall undertake no more than a descriptive account of American practice in respect to each.

I exclude from attention those disfranchisements which are the purposeful act of the community. Rejection of the Negro at the polls in a state or community where dominant opinion supports his disfranchisement ought to be separated in analysis from those instances where the polling officials, acting surreptitiously or in flagrant violation of community expectations, hinder the effort of the community to record its wishes on election day. It is the latter type of offense that occupies our attention here.

## MAKING VOTING EASY AND CONVENIENT

A good deal of attention has been given to this problem in public policy. Voting districts or precincts are small. The mountaineer and his wife and the man who lives on the edge of a desert may have to drive a good many miles to the voting booth. The farmer who lives in a well settled area is not likely to have to go any farther than his children's high school. The urban dweller rarely has to walk more than a half dozen blocks. And when he gets there—mountaineer, farmer, or city man—the voting booth is pretty sure to be on the ground floor of a building with a roof on it. He does not have to climb five flights of stairs, crawl behind a furnace, or hold an umbrella with one hand to keep the rain off the ballot he is marking with the other. We make it easy for the man who is at home on election day to cast his vote.

It appears equally true to say that most states also make it easy for the man who will not be at home on election day to cast his vote. Most states have enacted absentee voters' legislation that enables a man to mark a ballot in secret but under general observation of a person authorized to administer oaths, and send it by registered mail to his voting precinct where it will be counted. Voting by this method is not subject to as close supervision as voting in a polling place which is under the management of half a dozen polling officials. Consequently some people think that the possibility of fraud—e.g., stealing ballots and marking them—is too great to justify provision for absentee voting. It is presumably for this reason that a few states make no such provision, and some other states limit it to particular situations such as voting by men in military service.

Americans have shown less disposition than some European countries to make public provision for getting voters to the polls. The polls are usually opened early enough in the morning and kept open late enough in the evening to let the working man stop in on the way to work or on the way home. Furthermore many states, possibly all of them, make some provision in law for employers to release the employee from work long enough to do his voting. But the housewife with children under her feet often finds it quite a problem to store them in safe places while she goes to the polls. Where the two political parties are strongly organized and engaged in a sharp fight, they may provide transportation to the polls and baby sitters to look after the children. In some places neutral organizations like the League of Women Voters provide a baby sitting service. Election day practices in some European countries indicate that they make more of a concerted effort than we do to solve the problems that keep busy men and busy women from going to the polls.

## DETERMINATION OF QUALIFIED VOTERS

Constitutional provisions and statutes are quite definite as to who has a right to vote, and where any man who is entitled to vote may do his voting. One of our problems in administering elections is to make sure that everyone who is entitled to vote does so at the right place. People must be kept from voting more than once in any election, and those who are not legally entitled to vote must be prevented from voting at all.

For a long time we depended solely on the officials sitting at each polling place to determine who could and who could not vote. Polling officials are usually residents of the precinct where they serve and they have sufficient personal knowledge to judge the qualifications of many voters. When a man's right to vote is challenged the polling officials can put him on oath and listen to his statements and those of other people who have something to say about his age, residence, citizenship or other qualifications. This arrangement probably works well in small and stable communities. The polling officials in a big city, however, do not know enough of the precinct's residents. When a truckload of ringers is driven in from a distant part of the city or another county, with a party worker to swear that he knows every one to be a resident of this precinct, the suspicious and honest official may lack the courage to hold out against other polling officials who are friendly to the party organization and want every man to vote if the right party brought him in.

A solution which has been worked out for this problem is registration of voters in advance of election day. In most states registration is permanent. When a person comes of voting age, or moves into a new community, he goes to the proper public official and fills out a form showing his age, his residence and when he started living there, and whatever else may be essential to establish a right to vote. Under some state laws he is required to indicate the party with which he is affiliated if he intends to vote in primary elections.

Some states attempt to purge the registration lists completely from time to time by requiring periodic re-registration. This has some advantages, especially in forcing eligible voters to restate their residences when they move. But periodic registrations seem to discourage neutral people from examining registration lists and demanding that they be cleaned up, with the result that the records are packed with more unqualified voters under periodic registration systems than is the case with permanent registration.

Where there is a well-organized political party that is pressed to get all the votes it can, party workers try to find out who can be counted on to vote right, and do what they can to get these people registered. They may also manage to register some people who do not exist and some real people who are not legally quali-fied to vote. While they are doing these things, of course, they examine the list for names of people who are friendly to the other party and demand removal of names that are wrongly on the list. Where there are two vigorous and sharply contesting organizations, therefore, we have the greatest assurance that lawful voters will be registered, that attempts will be made to register people who are not lawful voters, and that an effort will be made to purge and correct the lists before election day.

Such rivalry may or may not procure a reasonably clean list of voters. In any event, this result is not achieved in all jurisdictions. There is a clear need for neutral citizen groups to arrange for and carry out systematic examination of the registration lists from time to time. Where leaders in civic affairs have made up their minds to have accurate lists of voters ready for each election, the evidence is that they get just about what they want. There is also ample evidence, however, that the civic leaders in most American com-munities have done little or nothing to clean up the registration lists. A movement, apparently under way, to carry the act of regis-tration to the voter's home or place of employment, increases opportunities for fraud and makes even more imperative close scrutiny of the process by persons who are devoted to honesty in elections.

## RECORDING THE VOTES

The American ideal is that every man shall cast his vote in secret, that ballots shall be counted as they are marked, and that votes shall be added up and reported in keeping with customary arithmetical procedures. We have not attained the ideal in all parts of the country on any one of these points.

In every state the laws provide for voting in secret. This is a fairly recent innovation. In the early New England town meeting voting was usually by voice. After paper ballots came into use, they were frequently of a publicly distinguishable character (e.g., different colors of paper for parties or candidates) and they were marked or deposited under circumstances which enabled other people to tell how any man was voting. This made bribery, intimidation, and the minor punishments of ridicule and insult easy. About 1880 the states began to provide by law for voting in secret. This involved ballots printed in advance and carrying the names of all candidates, and a closed booth where a man could mark his paper (or later, fix the levers on a voting machine) without being observed by anyone else. Forms of ballots differed then, and differ today. Candidates for all offices—national, state, and local—may appear on one piece of paper, or they may be printed on separate sheets of paper. Most states arrange candidates in columns under a party label so as to facilitate voting in support of a particular party; a few states have an office column ballot which is intended to discourage voting a straight party ticket. The same effects can be obtained by the arrangement of offices and candidates on the face of the voting machine.

While all states provide by law for voting in secret, that right is not always enjoyed. Reports of several years ago indicated that there were a few places in the South where a man could vote in secret only if he could spread his coat out far enough to hide his ballot. Booths were not provided; instead there were simply tables where a voter could lay his ballot while he marked it. Other people might stand and watch if they wished. Such practices are tolerated, of course, only where there is general agreement among community leaders that all good people are going to vote the same way and that the community ought to know about any people who vote differently.

It is unlikely that one will find any boothless voting places in the North and West, but he can easily find places where certain people will not be permitted to vote at all or where their votes will not be counted correctly if they do vote. Each polling place is managed by a small number (probably four to six) of officials. They have authority to decide who is eligible and who is not eligible to vote. They can ignore the registration records or read them wrongly if they are determined to. They can let me vote twice if they are all agreed to do so, and they can tell you that you have already voted and threaten to arrest you if you show up to vote. In most states, the officials who manage the polls also count the votes. If all the officials are bent on stealing the election for the same party (or the same candidates in a primary election) they can tear or disfigure ballots, ignore them, count them wrongly, and even ignore the ballots altogether, reporting whatever vote they think the candidates they favor will need in order to be sure of winning. Voting by machine does not eliminate these opportunities for trickery. If the fraud-proof voting machine has been invented, it has not been generally installed. Indeed, many experienced observers of the voting act view the voting machine as a positive aid to fraud. Where the polling officials are in collusion, they can make the machine report in keeping with their wishes with less chance of detection than was ever the case with paper ballots.

There are many American people who want none of these things done. If people who are determined to have honest elections dominate in any community they can have them. They can get them without much trouble in rural areas and smaller cities. They will have a bigger job of organization to secure honest elections in big cities, but they can win their objective there too if they will settle down to a hard fight.

The first essential for honest elections is a good election law. The law determines who will have authority to name the polling officials, fixes the procedures which they are required to follow, and specifies what recourse the citizen shall have if he thinks he is mistreated or the election procedures are not honestly applied to others. Some states operate under an election code that has been very carefully worked out; other states have election laws that seem to invite corruption.

The most difficult problem in planning an election law is who to put in charge of elections. There must be election officials for the state, for a smaller jurisdiction such as the county, and for each polling place. The state authority must decide who has legally announced his candidacy for state office, see that ballots are correctly printed and distributed, receive election returns from all parts of the state and add them together, and finally announce who has been elected to (or nominated for) state and national offices. In some states this responsibility is given to an administrative official, often the Secretary of State; in other states a special election board is created. We hear little complaint about the way these state officials do their work. They do not directly supervise the polling so that they escape blame for most of the skullduggery that takes place.

Much closer to the actual conduct of elections are the county (in some places municipal) election officials. The responsibilities of this election authority vary, of course, but here or there they include the following: register voters and purge registration records, fix the boundaries of voting precincts, direct the printing and distribution of ballots, provide and care for voting machines, appoint officials to manage elections at each polling place, hear complaints and issue instructions as questions arise in the course of voting, and (if they live up to their obligations) do whatever they can to see that elections are conducted in accordance with the law.

Clearly those who manage elections—the county election authority and the officials at each polling place—ought to be committed to a system of honest elections. But how do you find men and women who will put the democratic ideal above the advantage of particular candidates? In some states the judge of a court is designated county election official. Often the judge picks the polling officials carefully and is in his office on election day to do what he can to secure honest election management. In other communities the judge takes this assignment too casually. Here or there, it appears, the county or district judge has actually converted his office of election official into an important cog in a vote stealing machine.

Dissatisfaction with the single officer, whether judge of a court or administrative official, has led to the creation of a bipartisan election board in some states. Indiana offers an illustration. The chairman of the Democratic county committee names a man, the chairman of the Republican committee does the same, and these two men with the clerk of the circuit court manage all elections in the county. One of the jobs of this board is to name persons to man the polls in each precinct. These appointments are also controlled by the bipartisan principle. The Indiana statute says that the chairman of the county committee of each of the two leading political parties shall nominate persons to serve as election officials at each polling place. If these nominations are made and the county election board finds the nominees legally qualified, these persons and no others are to be appointed to manage the voting. Each polling place will then be presided over by two groups of three people, each of which groups is charged to make sure that nothing is put over on it by the other group.

Acknowledging that no conclusive study of election administration has been made, it seems safe to say that the bipartisan system has worked pretty well for general elections where each of the two parties has a lively organization. Adherents of one party maintain a pretty effective check on the agents of the other party. This system breaks down, however, where agreement to conduct a crooked election is reached between leaders of the two parties. The Democrats may agree to a miscount of votes in favor of the

Republican candidate for mayor if the Republicans will allow a miscount in favor of the Democratic candidate for sheriff. It breaks down also in the primary election. If each of the two party organizations is highly concerned about the nomination of certain candidates, the Democratic members of the election board may be so busy miscounting votes in the Democratic race that they have no time to shame the Republicans for the stealing they do in their primary.

Granting that the appointment of bipartisan boards is not an adequate solution to the problem of securing honest elections, it appears to be the best arrangement we have hit on yet. Some Southern states, where bipartisanship cannot be resorted to, have authorized each candidate for nomination in a primary election to suggest one person for each polling place where his name will appear on the ballot. The proper election official then chooses by lot from among these names, thus composing a group of officials for each polling place who will be as diverse in their loyalties to particular candidates as chance may determine.

A good election code is essential to a system of honest elections. Vigorous rivalry between two or more well organized political parties provides a device for setting up groups of men who can be counted on to protect their political interests from one another. We cannot be sure of honest elections, however, unless there is dominant in the community a wish to have honest elections and willingness to go to a lot of trouble to secure them. If community leaders in Sweet Potato County are determined to know how everyone votes and to punish anyone who votes the wrong way, the few independent persons who are bold enough to stand out against the community are pretty sure to take some punishment. If no one but party workhorses pays any attention when Democrats make a deal with Republicans in Chicago, candidates will continue to be sold out and elections will continue to be stolen. On the other hand, if leaders of the Chamber of Commerce, the American Legion, the local Federation of Labor, and the League of Women Voters make up their minds that they are going to have honest elections they can get them. The big question is, when are the people who dominate this country's affairs going to resolve that elections must be conducted in a democratic manner?

# 6. THE CITIZEN'S EDUCATION

The citizen can participate in political life with some confidence only if he has the materials needed for constructing confident judgments. He must be able to find out what public officials are doing, what the issues are, and where men who seek public office stand on these issues. This process of making a voter competent to express his wishes starts with his upbringing as a child; it is continued in the gamut of his relations with other people until the day when he ceases to observe and comprehend.

If a nation has not developed a system of general education for its young people, it has little prospect of developing a democratic government. The educational system, however, must be supplemented by a great system for the collection and distribution of information and opinions. If there are no organizations and news reporters to collect information; no newspaper, radio, and magazines to distribute information; no getting together of the people to talk over and argue about what they read and hear—if a nation is devoid of these or equally effective arrangements for communication, it can have no assurance that the people will be able to find out what is going on and be able to relate what they find out to their interests.

If people do not have a basis for confident judgments on matters relating to government, they have no basis for choosing between candidates for office, and the whole system of competition for political power breaks down. If a secure and vigorous system of competition for public approval is once established, however, the likelihood that information and opinion will flow through the population is greatly increased. The necessity of convincing voters that their interests lie in a particular direction induces those people who wish to run the government to feed out the information and arguments that support their case and injure that of their opponents.

Two principal needs must be served by the nation's educational and communications system: first, the individual must be equipped for judgments; and second, the commonalty that we considered earlier must be established and maintained. Any person who expects to speak his own mind about government, politics, and public affairs must be able to identify his own interests, long run as well as immediate, indirect as well as direct. He must be able to see the relation of alternative public policies to his interests. And he must be reasonably sure where different political leaders, public officials, and candidates for public office stand in respect to the public policies and governmental actions that are under consideration. This conception of need is not likely to excite either doubt or opposition. But doubt and opposition quickly appear when one speaks beyond the vaguest of generalities about the need for a common mind and about beliefs and attitudes that ought to be held in common by the people who compose a self-governing nation. I shall not extend here what was said earlier concerning the content of a sufficient commonalty. It may be well to note, however, that success in achieving commonalty may lead to a degree of conformity that is widely deplored in our own day. But it is equally important to note that without a very substantial amount of conforming there must be either no government or a government that is imposed upon the population by some process other than popular agreement.

Most discussions of the preparation of the citizen for participation in political life focus on formal education and communication by the mass media. This emphasis discounts too greatly the fact that personal observation and common talk are pillars of any system of public enlightenment and common understanding. Personal observation gives the citizen much of the information he needs about public affairs and provides much of the basic understanding that enables him to evaluate information coming to him in other ways. Personal observation plays its greatest role, no doubt, in enabling the individual to judge what his interests are so far as government is concerned. I know, without being told or reading a newspaper, whether I have running water in my home or not, or whether I want it, or whether I wish to have the service improved. The experience that enables me to determine what my interests are also tells me what government is or is not doing to advance those interests; I have firsthand knowledge of the character of the city's water service. It will readily be seen that if urban renewal, slum clearance, and city beautification programs are to be carried out with sympathetic attention to the sentiments of people whose interests are most intimately affected, the managers of those programs will have to deal with attitudes formed mainly by personal observation and common talk.

Only the most self-sufficient—perhaps we should say narrow-minded—person is willing to make up his mind about any significant issue of public affairs exclusively on the basis of his own personal observations. Most of us want to hear what other people have to say, tell them what we think and see how they react to what we say, check our knowledge with theirs, and rely in part on their judgments in making our own judgments. Just as common talk enables us to check our observations and helps us fit them together into conclusions, so it extends our knowledge far beyond what we have had opportunity to observe. I do not know the candidate for office; you do, and what you tell me gives me the basis for a judgment about him. You tell me about the excellent treatment, or lousy deal, you got at the city hall and my conclusion about the character of a public official or the quality of city government as a whole is affected according to the confidence I have in you.

The importance of personal observation and common talk is greatest in the smaller units of government, where firsthand experiences are most easily compared. But personal observation contributes substantially to evaluation of government at higher levels also, especially in the case of facilities and services affecting citizens directly. Farmers know what they like and don't like about the federal government's soil improvement program without any help from schoolteachers and broadcasters. They need advice from people with a broader outlook before they pass judgment on programs for disposal of surplus farm products. The inadequacy of personal experience and the judgments of neighbors increase as the impact of the policy becomes more distant (e.g., a law forbidding adulteration of drugs), and as the issue for evaluation becomes more inclusive (e.g., whether the Democratic candidate for governor would provide a more friendly administration than the Republican candidate). But the contribution of common talk to judgment on these distant and generalized questions can easily be overlooked.

The great organizations for communication—press services, newspapers, radio, etc.—are like the arterial system of the body. The arteries distribute blood to parts of the body and the capillaries carry it to the tissue. The nutrients in the blood, destined for the body's cells, are delivered by a process of osmosis which puts no dependence on fixed channels of flow. Talk—explanation, argument, gossip—is related to the great organizations for communication as the capillaries are related to the arteries. Talk picks up the information where the newspaper and radio drop it. The scandal in this morning's paper and the address on TV last night enter into the knowledge of great numbers of people who neither read the news account nor heard the speech. A process of osmosis or seepage is at work and conversation is our name for that process. Common sense tells us that and recent studies of political behavior confirm it; common talk is found to be a vital factor in the formation of personal opinions and decisions about voting.

The analogy of the circulatory system can be extended by noting how talk delivers convictions and knowledge of events to reporters who start its flow in fixed channels of communication as the substances that exude from the tissue are attracted into the veins and get on their way to the centers of the circulatory system.

Educational institutions, the press, and the broadcasting industry are the nation's principal means for widespread dissemination of the knowledge, ideas, and convictions that are requisite for government by the people. Each of them is a complex of organizations, processes, and specialized functions. Each complex originates, collects, and scatters knowledge, ideas, and convictions. Each serves the individuals faced with making a judgment, and each contributes to the construction of a common mind and common behavior. Each is subject to considerable discipline by the public it serves, and some of that discipline is expressed in governmental regulation. The policies that have developed to regulate these special worlds of education and communication are not mere vagaries of American experience. They are crucial for the effectiveness of the voter on election day, for the quantity and quality of influence on government exerted by the people in all the other ways available to them, and for the development of the equality, autonomy, and commonalty which I believe to be requisite for a system of popular government. We shall examine each of the three great media of education and information and then consider the prospect that people in public offices may use them to win consent for what they propose to do.

## Education

Parents have the primary responsibility for starting their children on the road to understanding. We have law that limits what parents may do in respect to training their children, but the law gives the parents a wide range of freedom. They may bring the child up to trust other people or to be suspicious and fearful; to embrace a particular religious faith or to be an atheist; to be opposed to the expansion of governmental authority or to be a socialist; to be a loyal Democrat or to think that the Republican party has a monopoly on political wisdom. They may not, however, start the child forward overtly on a criminal career; the child may be taken away from the parents if it is legally determined that they have exceeded certain bounds which the law prescribes.

When the child reaches school age, the parents lose some of their special advantage in forming his mind and character. The youngster goes to a school for instruction which, in its essentials, is the same for all children in the United States. Instruction is essentially the same for all children within any state because state law and state administrative authorities attempt to maintain a uniform educational program. Education in each state resembles education in every other state not because of a national legal requirement, but because of such factors as the following: during the settling of the country ideas about education were carried from one place to another; state lawmaking bodies copied provisions from the statutes of other states in making their own laws; teachers trained in a particular college, university, or school of education scatter out to teach in all parts of the country; teachers and school administrators in all parts of the country read the same professional journals and belong to national professional associations; and people generally throughout the United States share common views about what the schools should do because we move from community to community, travel and observe, and read a common body of literature.

Some persons have expressed fear that a common school system will lead to a nation with one set of beliefs, and deprive us of opportunity to examine alternative ways of achieving the good life. We have set up in our educational policies certain safeguards against any such dire eventuality, notable among them being the following:

First, we do not require all children to attend public schools. Parents may send their children to a private school if it meets certain standards set by law and state school officials. Catholics take advantage of this permissive attitude in all parts of the country, doing so at the cost of paying for education in their parochial schools and paying taxes for the maintenance of public schools which their children do not attend. We are currently engaged in a reconsideration of the relation of parochial education to state and federal tax policies and to the distribution of public funds for educational purposes.

More troublesome than the fitting of Catholic schools to the basic system of public education is the accommodation of demands posed by certain groups that seek to withdraw generally from civil society. The Amish illustrate. The Amish do not ask, as the Catholics do, that they be allowed to manage an educational system that is wholly compatible with the minimum requirements of state law; rather, they want to remove their children from the kind of education the state requires. It seems fair to state that we have not yet faced up to the challenge that the Amish and certain other groups lay before us. For this reason it would be idle to speculate as to what compromises may be made between the demands of the smaller groups and the convictions that fix public policies about education.

Second, local school authorities have considerable choice as to the nature of public school education in the communities under their jurisdiction. In one community the teacher may be permitted to question or even to cast aspersions on generally accepted ways of doing things; in another community such a teacher will promptly be fired on the charge that he is a troublemaker. At one time a particular school may include some teachers who reveal their left wing leanings in the class room; after a school board election some of these teachers may be replaced by others who reveal just as strong a bias toward conservative beliefs.

Third, we try to keep the schools out of politics. In about forty states there is a state board of education with some measure of authority over public education; in all of these states the board is expected to keep the schools from falling into the hands of those in control of the state government. Every state has a superintendent of public education and in all but a few states he is either elected at the polls or appointed by the state board of education; in any event, it is expected that the superintendent will not use his authority to further the purposes of any political group. By one device or another, but mainly by special elections of school boards, we try to divorce the schools from the rest of government. The most superficial knowledge of how the schools have been used in Nazi Germany and Soviet Russia to make the oncoming generation into firm supporters of the regime in control of the state should make abundantly clear the significance of our insistence that the schools must not be wholly controlled by any group that controls the rest of government.

Fourth, no educational institution or school of educational

thought is given a monopoly on the training of teachers. The requirements for a teacher's certificate in any state may make it somewhat easier to qualify for a certificate by attending training institutions in that state. But in every state there is more than one institution for teacher training and in every state there are many teachers who went out of the state for some or all of their training.

In view of these safeguards against too much uniformity and coercion in the education of young people, one may ask why the nation should continue to depend primarily on public schools. Why should we not provide a school fund by taxation, but distribute this money to schools managed by nongovernmental groups or corporations that collectively provide a wide range of emphases in education but in every case meet minimum requirements fixed by law? It seems likely that we are on the threshhold of an audible demand for movement in this direction.

In contemplating what may be the best policy for the nation as it marches into a style of living that we cannot now even dimly foresee, it is important to keep in mind three primary concerns which our educational policy must serve. The society has an obligation to guarantee to all young people a fair chance to equip themselves for full realization of their natural abilities. The society must also assure that the growing-up years are used to prepare the adult to take care of himself, and to be neither an excessive burden upon the society nor an unduly abrasive element in it. Finally, if we are to continue to enjoy government by the people, the educational system must do a considerable part of the job of preparing the population for self-government.

Earlier I endorsed the idea that certain social conditions must be present in order for popular government to flourish, and suggested that these might be related to individual and group autonomy, equality, and commonalty. If one presumes that there are social requisites of democratic government, I think he is obliged to acknowledge that they can be furthered or impeded by the preparation that young people receive for citizenship. If one presumes that autonomy in personal and group behavior is essential for self-government, then he must insist that the educational system prepare young people for autonomy. The same thing must be said about preparation for the requisite amount of equality. Even more apparent is the critical relation of the education of young people to the states of mind and the behaviors which I labeled commonalty. The educational program must prepare the young to function successfully as adults in anticipating social strains, withstanding strains, making concessions and adjustments that reduce strains. Equally certain, they must be prepared to avert the development of conditions that result in strains which the society cannot ameliorate, subdue, or live with. Strains that cannot be withstood arise from demands that are truly incompatible. It is too much to suppose that an educational system can condition the population so that no incompatibilities will arise in the political demand structure. But by developing common tastes, common values, and common suppositions as to how demands can be satisfied, the educational system can lower the incidence of incompatibilities. In fulfilling this social need, the educational program skirts the boundaries of an excessive conformity. This is an old and apparently inescapable dilemma: how to produce a population with that respect for order which permits creativity to flourish without constricting the range of individual choice which provides the impulse to creativity.

Everything I have said about the usefulness of education and the difficulties of fitting the educational program to significant differences in value positions and social goals is sternly called to our attention by the Negroes' drive for equal treatment in our society. In the case of *Brown* v. *Board of Education* (347 U.S. 483), the Supreme Court ruled that segregation in school denies to children of the minority race the equal protection of the laws which the Constitution requires. Chief Justice Warren cited as the main reason for that ruling the Court's conviction that segregation works an immediate injury upon Negro children, generating "a feeling of inferiority as to their status in the community that may affect their hearts and minds in a way unlikely ever to be undone"; and (quoting from another judge) having "a tendency to retard the educational and mental development of Negro children." Going beyond this immediate cause for the decision, Chief Justice Warren noted the importance of school attendance to preparation for citizenship and participation in a democratic society. He spoke of "our recognition of the importance of education to our democratic society. It is required in the performance of our most basic public responsibilities. . . . It is the very foundation of good citizenship. It is a principal instrument in awakening the child to cultural values. . . ."

Admitting, as we surely must, that the Chief Justice is right about the relationship of the schools to political efficacy and impregnation with societal and cultural norms, we are challenged to ponder rather than take for granted the terms on which Negro children enter the public schools. The Negro has a right to send his children to a public school dominated by a white school board, a white teaching staff, and a white student body if he wants to. But may the white population assume, and try to induce the Negro to comply with the assumption, that Negro children should be educated in schools that respond mainly to the white man's societal and cultural norms? The adult Amish community withdraws its children from the public schools because it wishes them to escape entrapment in the worldly values and beliefs that are inculcated by the public school system. Catholics maintain parochial schools not simply because they believe they can impart useful knowledge more efficiently than the public schools but also because they wish their children to be taught values and beliefs that would not be implanted by the public schools. So the nation faces the issue: Is the Negro to be remade in the white man's image, and is a public school system which in the main is bound to respond to the preferences of the more numerous whites to be used for this purpose? Or, are Negroes who wish to preserve something distinctive, which we may call a Negro culture (or subculture), to be encouraged to do so, even if this is possible only in schools under Negro direction and attended by few white children? This issue, clearly stated and clearly understood, is now the subject of debate among Negroes in the United States. It seems likely that it will become the subject of debate among the whole population.

## Publication and the Press

The educational system prepares the citizen for the intake of knowledge about a vast world that he cannot see, and for adjustment of this new knowledge to what he already knows and believes. The unseen world is mainly reported to him by the printed page, radio, and television, either directly or through the remarks of other people who also read, listen, interpret, and add emphasis. Judged by the quantity of material carried and the quality of thought that goes into its preparation the printed page is by a wide margin the most significant of these media. This will be readily perceived when one thinks of library collections, the hard cover and paperback books in bookstores and supermarkets, the magazines designed for the general public or for groups with special interests, and the newspapers.

Books, magazines, and newspapers, like the schools, make two kinds of contributions to democratic government. They equip the individual to play his roles in popular government, and they help build and maintain that commonalty in belief and behavior that is requisite for government by the people. No nation has been better served by its press than the United States, and we have secured this result with a minimum of government assistance and regulation. Our fundamental policy toward publication is freedom of the press. We trust that the enterprise of writers and publishers, competition for attention, and reactions from those who buy and read, will assure a wide range of attention, enough truth to offset falsehood, some depth in penetration, comfort and challenge for all points of view, and a fair balance between calls for innovation and respect for what we have tried. Freedom to print has not been unrestricted at any time in our history, however. The considerations that must be weighed in fixing restrictions are discussed at a later point in this book and will not be further noticed here. The ground level policy of a free press is supplemented by three other public policies. Official records of government at all levels are open to inspection, and public officials readily disclose information to professional reporters; reduced rates for mail service are given for virtually all kinds of printed materials; and copyright laws protect the interests of writers and publishers in what they have put in print for a considerable number of years.

The freedom from governmental control that the press enjoys in the United States is exceptional rather than typical of the world today. The subordination of the press to public policy in the communist countries is well known. But it is also true that in many noncommunist countries one or more of the principal newspapers are the official voice of the government. When political control is not so complete, all or most newspapers may be so dependent on financial support from the government that they are effectively restrained from serving the people as newspapers are expected to serve the people of the United States. Awareness of this experience in European and Latin American countries partially accounts for the meager support given to the occasional proposals to correct some of the shortcomings of newspapers in this country. One reads from time to time that a nation that goes to the trouble of building a free public school system cannot afford to let its newspapers fall into the hands of a particular class of people, or allow the content of newspapers to be determined by a businessman's judgment as to what will attract the greatest number of readers, increase sales of space to advertisers, and produce the greatest profit for the owner. It is said that if we continue to let newspapers be run as business enterprises, we ought to require those who manage them to report news objectively and impartially and give space to those people who can most effectively present the many points of view which surround a controversial public issue.

It is easily seen that it would be most difficult to formulate legislation likely to advance us toward these objectives, and harder still to enforce it. The dangers attendant on public regulation of newspapers and the press services can hardly be overstated. The people of a democratic nation depend primarily on newspapers for facts about their government which those in power would like to conceal. Newspapers also provide an audience for those who criticize the acts and policies of public officials and spread the message of those who are trying to oust the party in power. If we try to regulate the newspapers through government, we run the risk that those who control the government at any time will use their regulatory power to perpetuate their control of government. They may enact laws and pursue enforcement policies that keep newspapers from reporting what the opposition has to say and destroy its capacity to tell the people what the government is actually doing.

Regardless of whether anything is likely to be done or can be done about such matters, it seems appropriate to note certain conditions of American journalism that have special significance for popular government. They impose limitations on the scope and reliability of the newspapers' content which are likely to be overlooked. Three of these limiting conditions will be briefly examined.

First, events in public affairs become subjects for investigation and reporting by newsmen only as they seem important in relation to all the other things pressing for the newsmen's attention. As a consequence the newspaper is likely to let sleeping dogs lie. The newsman may know that his neighbor hates his wife but he does not run a story that the community should be on the lookout for a murder. Similarly, he fails to keep the people informed that the orphans' home is a fire trap; that policemen are taking more bribes than formerly; that the county recorder's office is understaffed and falling behind in the preparation of its records. He waits until a crisis converts into "news" something that he already knows has public significance. The newspaper tells us about the hazardous condition in the orphans' home after it has burned down, or more happily, when a civic organization or prominent person issues a statement that only the kindness of providence has so far kept it from doing so. So also, when the grand jury starts to investigate bribe-taking by the police, or a candidate for public office complains about police corruption, the newsman has an occasion for making disclosures without being charged with simply stirring up trouble.

This statement is too generalized to be strictly true, of course. Everything connected with the President of the United States has news value, and enterprising newsmen may write more words about what the President is likely to do than they write later on in telling us what he did do. The correspondent in a foreign capital or a war theatre is expected to anticipate the future and mix with his account of today's events his apprehensions as to what is building up for tomorrow and years ahead. In "breaking news" about local affairs, the larger newspapers feel safer than the small ones. Some metropolitan newspapers have a policy of occasionally exploring and reporting conditions that have not yet been brought to public attention by overt incidents. The small town paper, on the other hand, is likely to wait until news is created for it. Its resources are inadequate for investigations, and the owner-editor ordinarily has no wish to invite hard feelings on the part of people among whom he must live. These tendencies to play safe are affected, of course, by the extent to which the management of the paper is devoted to the interests of a political party. If the paper is violently partisan, it may become highly aggressive in efforts to tell the people how they are being sold down the river when the opposite party is in power.

Second, the treatment given to many events is greatly affected by what the newsman is told by other people, what he views as safe to print, and what he supposes his readers want to be told. Practically everything in the society section of a newspaper may consist of items supplied by people who want their lives exposed to public view. Much political news comes to the newspaper in the same way. The candidate running for office is likely to be the principal reporter of his own campaign, giving handouts with quotes from his speeches and announcements of where he can be seen and heard in the days ahead. The official who needs a defense for what he has already done or public support for what he is about to do asks the newspaper to send a reporter, and if he has been disappointed with previous reporting may have a story readymade for the reporter when he arrives. Much of the copy about the ideas and acts of our highest officials—President, governor, congressman—is quoted directly from their speeches and other public statements.

What comes to the newsman in these ways is selectively printed and much of it may be rewritten. If the newsman doubts the accuracy, authenticity, or reader-interest of a story, he will reject it altogether. But the fact remains that a great deal of what gets his attention is called to his attention by others. During most days of the year he is a collector of news, not a spy or detective who noses out news from people who try to conceal it. His detective work is confined to occasional salient events or crises in public affairs. This characterization of newsgathering appears to apply to the reportorial staffs of the great press services (AP and UPI) as well as to the reporters of individual newspapers. In contrast, certain columnists who specialize in depth reporting or the sensational peep behind the scenes carry on considerable personal investigation.

The way he gets his news forces the newsman to be wary about what he prints, even if he collected the information and is writing the story himself. A man can be certain that he knows what has been going on, and be equally certain that he could never lay out the proof that events occurred as he is sure they did. When he is less than certain that he knows all that is going on, he may be reluctant to disclose the facts that he is sure of; if he prints what he knows, events may take a different course and then he can anticipate charges of misleading the public and injuring innocent people. Once a political leader becomes a public figure, it is safer to continue expanding the image that is first projected than to try to substitute another that the newsman thinks a truer summation of the great man's actual behavior. Once his pollsters and press agents and television consultants have gotten over the hump in fixing a favorable image for the would-be great man, the newsman who questions the image too sharply risks a reader reaction that he is trying to destroy an admirable person. A supposition of goodness and greatness reflecting far more imagination than reality can be removed from the public mind only by evidence that can be footnoted and for that reason may be very hard to come by. This prospect of confirming the expected applies in some degree also to the reporting of a continuing course of events. If the press as a whole is telling one kind of story, the newsman who sees it differently may think it necessary to array an overwhelming display of evidence in order to refute a supposition that arose out of fancy rather than fact in the first place. If the facts which the deviating newsman offers are likely to encounter an opposing array of facts, he had better be doubly sure that he is reporting things that actually occurred.

Third, the press has critical power over the emergence of groups and causes that have been removed from public attention. Standing alone against its adversaries, a minority group often wages a losing battle; it may hope to win if a greater public comes to its support. The press, including radio and television, determines whether the attention of the larger population will be captured. The population that is alerted by the press, not consciously involved in the issues that are at stake, can view the struggle with greater objectivity than can the adversaries. A finer morality of distant contemplation thus intrudes to contradict and ameliorate the harsher morality of immediate confrontation. Recent experience of the American Negro illustrates this process.

The first organized protests by Negroes in the South after the Segregation Decisions of 1954 and 1955 were designed to alter conditions at the time and place of action: a boycott of buses in the city of Montgomery, Alabama; a sit-in at the lunch counter of a department store in Greensboro, North Carolina; spontaneous rebellions at various places in the South, fitted to no longrun plan of action. The attention given to these events by the nation's press and the sympathetic response of people throughout the nation to the Negroes' complaint made it apparent that the time was ripe for a comprehensive planned campaign for liberation. Leadership for such a campaign appeared, and the leadership recognized that its audience was white and Negro people in all parts of the country. A message was to be carried not only to the partisans—Negroes on the march and white segregationists arrayed for defense—but to the sympathizers and the indifferent onlookers as well. Such an audience can be reached only by the nation's newspapers, magazines, radio, and television. The civil rights march on Washington in 1963 had all but accomplished its immediate objectives before it happened, because its approach had been front page news for weeks. Subsequent marches and other dramatic demonstrations have been scheduled with an eye to coverage by newspaper and television. Something may be gained by a march on Jackson which excites no conflict because the city fathers supply maps of the city streets and promise open house for both races in every eating place in the town; far more will be gained by a march on Selma if the public officials promise a reception with firehose and dogs. More is accomplished in the latter case because the press is forewarned of business for reporters and photographers. If the Negro leadership has been shrewd in scheduling the event and diligent in its press relations, the newsmen and broadcasters will be on hand at a cost which may run close to a million dollars for the news agencies.

These few remarks give some indication of the Negro's dependence on the press for the success of his efforts to win improved

status in this society. What political leaders do is largely determined by their readings of the public mind, and the success of
judges in securing compliance with their orders is greatly affected
by the strength of public support. Furthermore, if the American
people can be put in the appropriate state of mind, they may
yield to the Negro most of what he demands without the intervention of officials and judges. The Negro leader, therefore, may
well believe that the managers of mass communication have more
power to impede or advance the Negro cause than do the officials,
politicians, and judges. If this is a correct estimate of the importance of their contributions to the political process, we are required
to raise these men and their work to a prominent place in our
theories of democratic government.

## Broadcasting

Enough has been said about the contributions of radio and television to public understanding of political affairs, but attention
should be called to some aspects of public policy that regulate the
terms on which this service is supplied. Broadcasting falls between
education and publication in respect to degree of subjection to
governmental control. We do not have a system of radio and television stations financed by public funds and managed by public
authorities comparable to our system of free public schools. Neither
are broadcasters allowed the autonomy in managing their communication service that is accorded to newspapermen and other
publishers.

The justification usually given for public regulation of broadcasting is a supposed natural limitation of frequencies suitable
for transmission. The premise was certainly sound in the early
days of radio, but technological advance, extending the range of
usable frequencies, has since brought it into question. When
public licensing was initiated, about 1910, the nature of trans-
mitting equipment was such that only a limited number of frequencies could be used for broadcasting. Consequently, there
were more applicants than frequencies, and the licensing authorities often had to decide which of many applicants should be
allowed the use of a particular frequency. This in turn led to the
establishment of standards to guide the licensing authorities in
deciding who would get a frequency.

The complexities of the licensing process and the electrical interference that plagued radio transmission made it seem best for

radio to be regulated by the national government. Today the Federal Communications Commission allocates bands of radio frequencies for AM, FM, and TV broadcasting; police and other safety communications; communication services by telephone and telegraph companies; industrial, transportation, and other private communication systems; and many additional uses. For transmission of frequencies within each band, FCC issues licenses for all radio transmitters except those owned and operated by the national government, these being licensed by the President on the advice of an interdepartmental committee.

Our interest here is in broadcasting which is received in the American home—AM, FM, and television. The policies governing broadcasting, as fixed by statutes and the FCC regulations, may be summarized as follows:

There is an effort to provide a fair and efficient distribution of broadcast facilities among all the states and communities of the country.

There is an attempt to maximize the number of individuals and firms that communicate to the American people. This is accomplished by limiting the power of transmitters and fixing the direction of antennas so that stations in different parts of the country can use the same frequency; by allowing any one person or organization to have only one station of the same class (AM, FM, or TV) in the same listening or viewing area; by favoring a new applicant over one already engaged in broadcasting; by limiting the total number of stations that will be licensed to any one person or firm; and by preventing the establishment of network monopolies by affiliation arrangements and other practices that, in the view of the regulatory officials, might improperly control the distribution of programs. The basic theory underlying these policies stems from our policies relating to publication and the press; we think that control of what enters the minds of the American people should be divided among many people rather than concentrated in a few.

This policy of diversification of control is carried to the relationships between broadcast stations and newspapers. The newspaper is tied into the great network of one or more press services and is staffed with reporters and news analysts. These advantages may help win a broadcast license for the newspaper in any community which has a number of radio stations. However, if there is a scarcity of broadcast outlets in a community, FCC prefers to license an applicant who does not already have access to the public through a newspaper, rather than add the radio station to the facilities for communication which the newspaper owner already has. In every case where there is a contest for the license, however, FCC must weigh all considerations that are relevant to the character and quality of service, and give the license to the applicant deemed best qualified to serve the local public.

There is a limited amount of public control over the content of broadcasts. Profanity, obscenity, and suggestions of pornography are forbidden. Information relating to lotteries or helpful to gambling operations may not be put on the air. Efforts are made to limit the frequency and length of commercial announcements. If one candidate for public office is given time on radio or television, other candidates for the same office must be given equally advantageous time on the same terms. When a broadcast licensee permits his facilities to be used to air a controversial issue of public importance, he must afford reasonable opportunity for the presentation of contrasting points of view. If the industrialist is allowed to give his account of a controversy with labor, spokesmen for labor must be given an opportunity to present the other side of the issue. If one civic group is allowed to discuss a community problem, a fair hearing must be given to other groups with different viewpoints. But a thorough airing of one public issue or community problem does not obligate the broadcaster to give time to people who would like to bring another and equally important issue to public attention.

The policies of station operators on these and similar matters are taken into account in issuing and renewing licenses, in assessing fines against licensees, and (when the offense is extraordinary) in rare proceedings to revoke a license. When competing applications for new stations are under consideration, FCC will try to find out which of the applicants is most likely to deal fairly and impartially with all issues and events of importance to the radio audience. When a license expires (usually at the end of three years), FCC inquires into the conduct of the station during the license period and asserts a right to refuse to renew the license if the station's record shows that it has not adequately served the needs of its community or has not treated significant issues and events with sufficient impartiality. Several station owners who used their frequencies mainly for personal advantage or in a manner not consistent with the public interest have been taken off the air, but the impact of FCC's authority for the most part has been to cause station owners to refrain from major abuses because of fear that they may fail to win license renewal.

The authority of FCC to influence the character and quality of radio and television broadcasts is constantly challenged as an interference with freedom of expression. This issue came to the fore prominently at the end of World War II. After extensive study and an anxious if not agonizing search of their minds, the seven members of the Federal Communications Commission, in 1946, issued a comprehensive statement of the kinds of programs they thought ought to be put on the air. The document, entitled *Public Service Responsibility of Broadcast Licensees,* was commonly called the *Blue Book* because of its blue covers. In the *Blue Book,* FCC cited the promises as to character of broadcasts which a number of applicants made when they applied for licenses; then showed by how wide a margin they failed to live up to those promises after getting their licenses. The *Blue Book* then announced a number of standards for radio service which would be considered in granting and renewing licenses—carrying sustaining programs (programs not paid for by commercial sponsors); permitting appearances by people in the community (locally produced plays, performances by local musicians, programs sponsored by the schools); discussion of public issues; and limitation of advertising excesses.

The *Blue Book* was addressed especially to problems of radio broadcasting, television then being only at the dawn of its career. However, in practice FCC did not press for realization of the standards it had set forth. The *Blue Book,* therefore, is not a reliable source of information as to the standards for service which have actually been applied since its issuance in granting and renewing broadcast licenses. It will be helpful, however, in clarifying one's views about the fundamental questions of who is the best judge of what the American people want to see and hear in their homes and who ought to decide what they will be able to see and hear. Station operators and network managers argue that they cannot get a listening audience and consequently cannot sell time to commercial firms unless the people like what goes on the channels. For that reason, they insist, they have a greater compulsion than anybody else to find out what people are interested in. To this contention, critics of the programs that are now being supplied make two answers. They say that during much of the broadcast day network programs are not shown and station operators put on the air what costs them least (phonograph records and antiquated movies) and what brings in the most money (commercial announcements). They make the further point that preferences of the mass audience should not be a controlling test of good programming because a main objective of broadcasting ought to be the elevation of public tastes and the enlargement of public appetite for fuller understanding of the world we live in.

The issue of who is to have power to determine what will go on the air is as much alive today as it was when the *Blue Book* was presented at the close of World War II. The commissioners who decide whether broadcast licenses will be issued or renewed appear to agree that the preferences of the listening public ought to determine what will be put on the air. They are also of the opinion, though perhaps not unanimously agreed on this, that the full range of public preferences is not satisfied by giving the audience what it listens to most eagerly. In a public notice issued in 1960, five of the commissioners (one did not participate and one dissented) called attention to the Act of Congress which requires them to issue and renew licenses only when they find that a license would serve "the public interest, convenience or necessity" and then went on to say that the broadcaster's principal obligation is to make a 'diligent, positive and continuing effort . . . to discover and fulfill the tastes, needs and desires of his community or service area, for broadcast service." In order to fulfill their obligation, the commissioners stated that henceforth in considering applications for new stations and renewals, they would require the applicant to show "(1) the measures he has taken and the efforts he has made to determine the tastes, needs and desires of his community or service area, and (2) the manner in which he proposes to meet those needs and desires." Further, the applicant's thoughtful speculation about public tastes, needs, and desires would not satisfy the commissioners. "What we propose is . . . first, a canvassing of the listening public who will receive the signal and who constitute a definite public interest figure; second, consultation with leaders in community life—public officials, educators, religious, the entertainment media, agriculture, business, labor—professional and eleemosynary organizations, and others who bespeak the interests which make up the community."*

Many of the most influential spokesmen for the radio and television industry vigorously rebutted the statements of policy and the arguments presented in the *Blue Book* and the 1960 *Report*. Many broadcasters have shown great reluctance to probe the interests and wishes of the expected audience and community leaders. Newspaper owners and editors may have as much at

* The report *Public Service Responsibility of Broadcast Licensees* was published by the Federal Communications Commission (Washington, D.C., 1946). The statement of 1960, *Report and Statement of Policy on Programming Inquiry*, is in *The Federal Register*, vol. 25 (1960), p. 7291.

stake in this controversy as do the networks and broadcasters. There are far more radio and television stations than newspapers in the country. The American people have more choice in selecting a radio or TV program than they have when they select a newspaper. Any thoughtful argument in favor of a broadcaster giving proof that he will make a diligent effort to "fulfill the tastes, needs and desires of his community" is surely applicable as well to the men who provide newspaper service.

# 7. POLITICAL ACTIVITY AND ELECTORAL BEHAVIOR

Man is a gregarious animal and he needs little prompting to get together with his fellows and talk about the things that relate to his well-being. But special arrangements are required to bring people to that measure of agreement that is necessary for effective participation in public affairs. This is the job of political organization. Men who are interested in public office get around to see people. They ring doorbells, pass out handbills in the subway station, and invite people to congregate for public speeches. As this competition for public approval sharpens, men seeking different offices find it profitable to work together. Cliques grow into factions and factions into formally organized political parties. Men who seek no elective office nevertheless extol the merits of candidates and solicit votes, because the party organization makes it worth their while to do so. All this activity that we call politics is a demonstration of that competition for political power which is as essential to popular government as competition among businessmen is to a capitalist economy. Competition for control of public offices is essential to popular government because it identifies men in relation to public issues and enables the voter to make his vote for a candidate an indication of the things that he wants his government to do.

Political activity which is directed toward elections must serve two ends. Its immediate and conscious purpose is to manage the effort of the citizenry to control their government. It has also a long-run purpose, which may or may not be consciously recognized—to contribute to that condition of belief and behavior which I have labeled commonalty. Political organization and the activity we call politics has long been a prime point of attention in writings about American government and politics. It is not necessary, in this book, to supply a description of the prevailing organization and activity. Our objective in this chapter will be two-fold: first, to show in broad perspective how our association in political parties contributes to a peaceful choice of public officials and a common mind about the purposes and methods of government; second, to inquire into the prospect that the American electorate can exert a significant control of government through elections.

Let us, for convenience in expression, use the word compromise to cover the complicated process of achieving common mind and instituting concerted action. We shall open our inquiry by noting some social conditions that hinder arrival at compromise, embarrass our efforts to understand how compromise is achieved, and delay or prevent our recognizing it when it is achieved.

## Organization for Compromise

It must be said at the very beginning that what we are going to examine under the label "compromise" is an exceedingly complicated aspect of life, defying adequate description. The process of achieving compromise is intricate, and the state of affairs that results from compromise—revised expectations and altered moods relating to further concessions—is viscous rather than solid, ever-changing rather than stable. We can examine the process and the result only by fixing our minds on an ideal type or model, a simplified view of a world too complicated in reality for exact description. The model which we shall examine suggests that nearly all people know where they stand on political issues, whereas actually most people are uncertain about their position on many things and a good many people seem to know their minds on very few things. It suggests that people trouble themselves to find out what others want, readily acknowledge the necessity of making concessions, and scurry about in activity designed to form alliances —suppositions that we know to be far removed from reality. Granting this, it is useful to fix our minds on an idealized situation in order to see what is fundamentally involved; thereafter one can take his bearings anew and address his analysis more closely to what really takes place.

Certain sets of interlocking circumstances are readily identifiable as largely responsible for the complexities we encounter in examining compromise. Each of them helps to make the process of effecting compromise devious and difficult to trace; collectively, they obscure the results of the bargaining process and make it difficult to tell what agreements have been reached on what matters for what period of time. Four of these controlling conditions will be mentioned.

First, we are born into a world that is already highly organized for politics. The Democratic and Republican parties are going concerns. One or the other of them will capture the Presidency, and these two parties will win nearly every seat (if not all the seats) in the two houses of Congress. In some states it is foreordained that one (and not the other) of these two parties will run the state government; and in all the other states only these two parties stand a chance of winning the state offices. The same is true for most local governments.

Clearly this limits the opportunity of any voter to help form a working organization that will be committed to his particular set of objectives in public affairs. He can choose between the two great political parties, voting for the candidates of the one that comes nearest to satisfying his wishes. He can work within a political party, trying to get candidates he likes nominated and trying to influence office holders after they are elected. If he works intelligently and persistently at this over a period of years, bringing great resources to his campaign, he may succeed in bringing one or both of the political parties to a position that he likes very much on one or a few issues.

Few men can claim credit for the emergence of a new political party or a significant change of position by one of the existing parties on an important national issue, and those few are likely to be remembered by historians. Always the man who gets the credit is aided by uncounted other persons who can never be identified when credit is being assigned, though occasionally one of the little men can say with good reason that he made a personal impact on the mobilization of demand and response in the public life of his community. In many city governments elected officials are chosen on a nonpartisan ballot, a main reason for removing the regular party labels being to facilitate free-lance political activity by persons who otherwise would be smothered by the regular party organizations.

Second, the process of concession and compromise is complicated by unevenness of perception of personal interest, understanding of the political process, and readiness to accept leadership. Some people know what their interests are and can relate them to specific issues and specific candidates for office; others know what they want but do not know how to get what they want; still others appear not to know what they want. Some, feeling a moral obligation to participate in elections, claim that they vote without confidence in the choices they make; others solve the problems of uncertainty by staying away from the polls. Where perception of personal interest and understanding of the political process is unquestioned, readiness to participate in organized effort may be lacking. Some people get an early attachment to one party and vote for its candidates even when they claim to like almost nothing the party stands for. Others jump from party to party in a series of elections and give no better reason for it than that they distrust the leaders in both parties. The contributions which these two classes of voters make to the continuing processes of compromise are certainly different and presumably far less significant than the contributions of two other classes of voters: those who adhere consistently to one party because they like what it persistently stands for on main issues, and those who move from party to party according to the respective platforms in each election.

Third, compromise is complicated by government structure. You and I may be wholly in agreement on certain major issues confronting the national government, but in complete disagreement on major issues confronting one of our local or state governments. This limits our willingness to work together for the nomination and election of a slate embracing candidates for office in the several governments. This fact is a major reason why each of our principal political parties constantly shifts ground on questions of public affairs. Political leaders who are enthusiastic co-workers when the national election is their big concern, fall out when an issue of state or local politics becomes uppermost. And many voters who are deeply interested in public affairs can be neither faithful Democrats nor faithful Republicans because they support one party in national politics and the other in state or local politics.

Fourth, the most committed and the most foresighted citizens make compromises that are far from compatible and sometimes cancel each other out. I may enthusiastically support a candidate for President because I like his recommendations on public policy, but in the same election support a candidate for Congress who makes it clear that he takes a dim view of those same recommendations. There is a marked tendency to enlarge the opposition party's membership in Congress in non-Presidential election years. This practice must draw some support from a widespread belief that it is a good thing for the President to be bold in urging legislation and a good thing for Congress to be reluctant about enacting it.

A common practice of working out compromises today and undoing them tomorrow is easily observed in the support given to "non-political" organizations that speak for particular interests. The staunchest supporter of the President may contribute money to one or more organizations that are doing their best to thwart the President. Doctors who favored public health legislation and voted accordingly in recent years nevertheless felt obliged to pay dues to medical associations that used income from dues to oppose public health insurance. Many working men know that some of the money they pay into their union will be used to defeat candidates which the same working men personally prefer. The part that interest groups play in American politics is more fully noted later in this book.

If the foregoing remarks fairly describe the conditions under which compromise must take place, one can hardly aspire to a full understanding of the part played by political parties in securing government that is reasonably attentive to the many differing desires of a great nation. In spite of persistent scrutiny of this sector of the political process by many scholars, little can be said with confidence about the consequences of party activity for advancing agreement on issues of the day and establishing more securely the common mind and common behavior that contract the boundaries within which agreement must be negotiated. We shall attempt nothing further here than a few observations about three components of political parties that make special contributions to the process of continuing compromise. They are the voters who habitually support the candidates of the party, the men who stand for office on the party ticket, and a corps of workers that coordinate party activities, supply leadership in party affairs, and carry on the work that keeps the public aware that the party is in business. It will simplify language if we make the term "party organization" cover all persons whose activities make them a part of this third component, embracing not only the men and women of recognized position and influence but also the vast numbers of persons who occasionally volunteer for work. It should be noted also that the three components—loyal party members, candidates, and party organization—overlap. Some persons serve in two or more capacities and specializations of role are not always clear.

The contribution of the loyal party members consists of a set of instructions which they give to the party's candidates and the party's organization, and an assurance of dependable support in case those instructions are heeded. By their proven loyalty the millions of voters who are firmly attached to the party advise the party leaders that they must pay due respect to certain central expectations which are thought to be at the core of that party's ideology or program. They advise the leaders further that if they satisfy the membership on this minimal requirement they may proceed with wide discretion to offer the concessions that promise to bring into camp the additional voters whose support is necessary for the party's success on election day. They give the party leaders a firm assurance that if they heed these instructions, the party will remain intact in the wake of defeat and the leaders will have another chance to work out a set of compromises, attract enough uncommitted voters to win an election, and eventually take over the seats of authority.

The party's candidates for office (including those who try for nomination and fail and the successful contenders who sit as public officials) are the principal architects of compromise. In the ever-changing array of men and women who confront the voters in the contest for electoral support are some who staunchly defend the party's present position and others who think boldly about the need for change. These are the men and women who present the alternatives of choice to the electorate. It is the party's candidates who tell the voters what the government will do if the business of governing is turned over to the candidates of that party. It is the eloquence and bearing of the candidates and the cogency of their reasoning that enable the uncommitted voters to judge the sincerity of purpose behind verbal promises. Finally, of course, it is the party's nominees who have won elections and sit as public officials who prove what the party will actually do if entrusted with the power of governing.

The last of the three components of political parties to be considered here, the party organization, is the least visible and therefore the least understood of the three. It is also the least universal in appearance. Loyal party voters and candidates for office are found in all parts of the nation but party organization appears only in spectral form in some sections. The power of the party organization is overestimated by those who think the nation is in the grip of political machines. It is underestimated by others who think that political parties stand for nothing and therefore will move in any direction at any time on the chance of picking up a loose vote. We shall not attempt an estimate of power here, but will try to show that the party organization makes highly significant contributions to the process of compromise that is essential to government by the people. It is probable that nearly everything these people do in the political realm has some bearing on public understanding of political issues and in some measure affects the voter's opportunity to make an impact on the character and quality of his government. It will not distort reality too much, however, if we differentiate four principal contributions of party organization.

First, the party organization tries to hold the party's basic clientele, assuring the continued loyalty of the loyal. This is accomplished in large part by personal contact. The voter who is committed to a particular party is rarely held or lost solely by his choice among competing party platforms. He identifies with a given party on a broader range of concerns. Prominent among them, for many people, is a feeling that they are wanted in the party, that their support is appreciated, that they do belong. This assurance of truly belonging is bolstered by displays of personal attention coming from men recognized as important figures in party affairs. It may be strengthened by an invitation to attend a meeting that the voter would not otherwise think of attending. Loyalty may be deepened by the fact that a friend knows a leader of the party and testifies to his intelligence, honesty, and good will.

There is good reason to believe that issues are becoming more important to the voter's decision to stay with the party he has long supported or to move to the other side. There is equally good reason, however, to believe that the efforts of the organization to reinforce their loyalty influence great numbers of voters to stay with the party of their former preference. To the extent that a party organization succeeds in overcoming the attractions offered by the other party, it enlarges the opportunity of candidates and other party leaders to fashion appeals that bring new support to the party.

If I am right about its first contribution, a second contribution of the party organization becomes indisputable. The organization is not solely concerned with the party's devoted membership, it seeks also to bring others into the fold. This necessitates a continuous mixing with all elements of the adult population. Every party leader and active worker thus becomes a listening post attentive to expressions of satisfaction and discontent with governmental policies and their execution. If anybody knows, these functionaries of the party know the temper of the electorate: what the people like, dislike, and are fed up with; the intensity of feelings; what classes of voters are ready to turn the present government out of office; what appeals might augment the tide of revolt; and what changes in policy might enable those in power to replace discontent with toleration or satisfaction.

Because they have dependable knowledge and are interested in the success of the party, respected men in the party organization become prime determinants of what office holders and candidates for office will say and do. I have said that it is the candidates, including the successful ones who are in office, who persuade the voter that the party is attentive to his interests. Candidates turn to respected men in the party organization for counsel in preparing their appeals and planning their action. Candidates have their own ears to the ground, but the men and women who constitute the party organization have their collective ears to the ground more nearly everywhere and all of the time.

Their continuous circulation among the population makes all but inevitable the party organization's third contribution to the process of compromise. Party workers have a keen eye for men and women who can help them do their job. Vote getting is not wholly a matter of persuading voters one by one. It is accomplished in large part by winning the support of men who have influence with other men. The party organization thus becomes a recruiting office for new political leadership. Among the political leaders they recruit are young men and women who sooner or later will stand for public office. Where party organization functions at its best the leaders are continually searching for young people who can make successful appeals at the polls. When would-be candidates present themselves, the leaders slate some for active support, encourage others to keep up their hope, and discourage or crush those who do not have the look of winners.

In deciding which men will be groomed for public office, party leaders lay a heavy hand on future statements of party position. Men are selected for candidacy because of belief that they can make successful appeals in political campaigns, and the selections will not be made until the leaders have decided what kinds of appeals must be made to bring the party to victory on election day. The process of concession and compromise is in full operation.

The fourth contribution of the party organization to the process of compromise and the establishment of commonalty is a readiness to sacrifice principles for votes. It is due mainly to the bureaucratic character of party organization.

A party's organization is made up in part of people who are engaged because of principle. They have some clear and firm ideas about what government ought to do and they are involved in party affairs because they want to see those ideas operative in public policy. The devoted partisan of organized labor who gives freely of time and effort to the Democratic party is one example; the businessman who bitterly opposes further advance toward the welfare state may be his counterpart in the Republican party. But ideological commitment accounts for only some of the activists in each of the political parties. There is also a bureaucratic element. These are the people who are involved in party affairs for no better reason than the fact that they get personal satisfaction from the involvement. They like people and they like to be helpful to people. They want to be influential when decisions are made and they get pleasure from a reputation for influence whether they have any influence or not. They like a fight and they exult in victory.

The non-principled party man is a natural-born broker of compromise. For enough votes to swing an election he will readily give away a principle that brought some of his colleagues into the organization. This disposition to bargain promise for vote, to exchange principle for power, is strongly condemned as lack of conscience. It is seen as the underlying corruption of American politics. Viewed in a wider perspective, this placement of a low price on principle may appear to be an overriding virtue of the American political system. It accounts for the absorption of elements of the population into the electorate who would have been left outside much longer if only men of principle had determined party policy. Not many men whose goals for public policy and standards for public administration excite admiration would have invited into the polls the newly arrived immigrant who neither understood the design of our government nor was able to understand the debate which told him what his vote could accomplish at the polls.

The Negro who fled from the South decades ago could vote in the North. This was not because men of principle in the Northern cities offered him an opportunity to live wholly as a free man. While both principled and unprincipled men restricted the Negro in his abode, his employment, and his enjoyment of social amenities, unprincipled Northern politicians invited the Negro to the polls and perhaps dragged him there when he did not report willingly. It is poor politics to enter a false count on the polling books if people can be found who will mark the ballots the way you want the votes to be reported. The right to vote has not made the Negro's status equal to that of the white in northern communities but it has given him something to bargain with, and he has used his voting power to win concessions of some significance. In the South, an overpowering determination to maintain white supremacy placed disabling obstacles before the politician who would gladly have helped Negroes to the polls if he could be sure that they would vote him into power. It may be that if Negroes go freely to the polls in the South in the near future, it will be primarily because white people in the rest of the nation have decided that Negroes have a right to vote. But secondarily, the ability of the Negro to vote in the South will depend on the readiness of white politicians to encourage him to vote. If a welcoming hand is extended, it is most likely to come from those politicians who need more votes to assure their political success and who see a good prospect that the Negroes will give them those votes.

I warned at the beginning that I would present a simplified view of the processes by which compromise is achieved in our political system. This I have tried to do, hoping to disclose the main conditions, relationships, and practices that give to the world of actual politics its fundamental character. It may seem to the young person who is only beginning his observation of politics that the account I have given is far from simple. Be that as it may, far more happens than is brought to attention in these few pages.

If I have succeeded in illuminating some things that are fundamental, I may still have left unnoticed as many that are equally fundamental. My remarks can at best only guide one's first steps in an inquiry that may occupy his thoughts for a lifetime and leave him still doubtful that he understands much that goes on. At the risk of appearing presumptuous, I offer an overthought or central idea that may dispose one to patience in his investigation and evaluation of the political process. This is that the amount of agreement necessary for government by the people can be realized only if the negotiation of agreement is important business for some people; that the people who make this their business must be joined in organizations where they learn who can and who cannot be trusted and are able to anticipate what their associates will do; that every enduring organization exacts a price for its maintenance, and that the price for maintaining political organizations appears inescapably to require men of good intentions to obscure and straddle issues in order to win contests immediately confronting them; and finally that the deal which seems to sacrifice a principle, on closer inspection sometimes and perhaps often promises to yield a gain that can be credited to another and equally valued principle.

## The Critical Role of the Electorate

I have asserted that voting is the critical act in a participative democracy, and that the electorate must be inclusive. I offered some tests that may be useful in deciding who should be allowed to vote and who may rightly be excluded from participation in choosing officials. The utility of the tests is subject to debate, and the debate must turn on beliefs about what voters can do, are likely to do, and can be induced to do. In recent years the debate has centered especially on the two following questions: Is the voter intelligent enough and sufficiently informed to play the role assigned to him in the populist demand-response system? Does he display the amount of concern to improve his lot that is required for policing the competition for power we depend on to make government responsive?

It is frequently said that it makes little difference who can vote because the voter is so much a victim of propaganda and pressures that he cannot express his own free will when he does vote. If there is any truth in the last half of this proposition, it still does not prove the first half.

Of course the voter does not exercise his own "free will," if exercising his "free will" means expressing wishes that are in no way influenced by other people. We live in a society, and a society consists of people who influence one another and respond to one another. We talk to one another in order to make our beliefs and wishes known, to cause other people to see things as we see them and do what we would like them to do. The voter cannot escape the influence of others and he can rarely know how many of his convictions are imposed upon him by others.

Equally certain is the fact that much of the propaganda and pressure is founded on deceit and many voters will be fooled by it. This condition is not peculiar to the United States or to modern times; neither is it peculiar to politics and public affairs. All accounts of life in the Garden of Eden agree that one-half the population of that place fell victim to arguments and inducements that proved disastrous for the whole population. We may presume that every generation in every part of the globe has been beguiled by many kinds of serpent, offering many kinds of apple. In our own time and place the serpents try to get us to buy things we do not want and deceive us as to the quality of things they have to sell; they induce businessmen to make bad investments; they cause young people to depart from the ways of their fathers. We can never protect ourselves wholly from the deceiver because we do not know we are being deceived until we act on the advice and find out whether we are pleased with what we did.

The moral of this parable about the serpent is clear enough. Democratic government is not based on a presumption that each voter will live in isolation from other people and express preferences that are free from the influence of other people. Democratic government presumes that every voter will be constantly bombarded with proposals, arguments, and inducements. It presumes that the voter has the capacity to evaluate these appeals and to act according to what he concludes to be in the best interests of himself and other people whose interests he wants to advance. Obviously one's standards for a sufficient intelligence in voting must be considerably lower than what he thinks ideal. One may even argue that an ability to reach sound conclusions is irrelevant in fixing the right to vote. Whether the American people are bright or dumb, they are the only people we have in this country; and if government is to be broadly responsive to the population it must consult such people as are here.

Whatever the level of capability, we ought to elevate it. Knowledge and concern about one's political welfare and the will to improve it must be objects of attention in any attempt to increase the voter's effectiveness in controlling his government. There appears to be no disagreement on this point, but there is great difference of opinion as to the minimum levels of political awareness necessary for effective voter participation. Evidence obtained by survey research methods indicates that relatively few voters have sophisticated definitions of their own interests, understand how their interests may be furthered or hindered, or have more than the vaguest idea as to what governmental policies the principal candidates stand for. We do not know how to evaluate these findings.

In the first place, such inquiries are tests of articulation. Many a woman who cannot describe an article so the clerk can find it is able to point to it on the shelf and say, "That is just what I want." So it may be that the typical voter who yields no verbal evidences of political understanding, even when asked only for *yes* or *no* answers, nevertheless on election day shows a considerable appreciation of the candidates' awareness of his needs and concern for his welfare. How are we to know whether this is the case if the voter cannot translate his feelings into words that the pollster can make use of?

In the second place, the significance of the survey findings is in doubt because of unresolved questions as to what the voter must take into account in order to make his vote an instrument to advance his personal welfare or the welfare of the community. The most thorough inquiries into voter attitudes and voting behavior are by the University of Michigan Survey Research Center. [*] These studies differentiate three principal orientations of the electorate: the issue oriented voter, the candidate oriented voter, and the party oriented voter. Voters who think it important to have judgments on issues and to vote for candidates who support the solutions they favor are generally looked upon with approval today. Undoubtedly their views about priorities among issues and their judgments about preferred solutions enable the issue oriented voters to influence the content and emphasis of speechmaking at campaign time. Undoubtedly the preferences revealed by the issue oriented voters inform the candidates as to public moods and limits of public toleration, enabling candidates to hold forth the promises that seem likely to attract the greatest support. It is a striking fact about our politics that candidates, at least for the Presidency and Congress, tend to move to a common ground of proposed policy when leaders in both parties see genuine hope of winning the election. This conduct appears to be a response to readings of the public mind, and the minds that are most influential are those of issue oriented voters. Surely this is a great triumph of the democratic idea; it is proof that the populist demand-response system is indeed in operation. But it is not proof that the issue oriented voter, on the day when he casts his ballot, has voted "more intelligently" than the candidate oriented voter or the party oriented voter.

In calculating the wisdom of voting on the basis of issues, evaluation of candidates, or party preference, how ought one treat considerations like these? Was anything said in the campaign of 1960 to indicate that, when a Bay of Pigs issue should arise, Nixon with a Republican cabinet and a Republican leadership in Congress would have acted differently than Kennedy? If the answer to that question is—"Yes; the thoughtful, issue oriented voter could have predicted that Nixon would have acted differently than Kennedy did"—then what is the answer to the next question? Could the issue oriented voter in 1960, confident about what the

---

[*] The list of publications is extensive. Perhaps the best item to start with is Angus Campbell *et al.*, *The American Voter* (New York: John Wiley and Sons, 1960). An abridged version in paper covers and by the same publisher appeared in 1964.

two candidates would do on a Bay of Pigs issue, have confidently predicted which of the two solutions (Kennedy's or Nixon's) would have minimized the likelihood that a missile crisis in Cuba would later emerge? If problems of international policy, involving acts of persons out to surprise as well as thwart us, are thought not to provide a good test of ability to vote wisely on a basis of issues, then consider the prime problem of domestic policy in 1960. For all Negroes and for many whites, the big domestic issue was one of civil rights and improved status for the Negro. John F. Kennedy and Lyndon B. Johnson were the two principal contenders for the presidential nomination on the Democratic side. Contending for the Democratic nomination, Kennedy stated where he stood on this issue; Johnson said little. Reading the available signs as to what each would do if President, could the issue oriented voter have predicted with confidence that Kennedy would act essentially the way he did act when he later confronted Congress with proposals for civil rights legislation? Could he have made a confident forecast that Johnson would spur the drive for the Negro's advance that we have since observed?

To all of this it may be answered: "So what! Of course the issue oriented voter cannot enjoy uniform success in predicting what candidates for high office will do if elected. But does the candidate oriented voter or the party oriented voter stand as good a chance of selecting men who, once in office, will run the government the way he hopes to see it run?" There is no prospect that this question can ever be answered satisfactorily; we never know what the defeated candidates would have done if they had won. The following observations may guide one's speculation, however. A man who is alert to issues, and who notes what the candidates say about issues, nonetheless may claim that his vote is determined by an evaluation of the men rather than their positions, and offer the following rationale in support of his act. Many of the issues that will confront the official during his term of office are unknown when he is running for office and the issues that can be identified in advance cannot all be talked about in the time allowed for campaigning. If the candidate says enough about a few issues to make clear where he stands on each of them, he leaves so much unmentioned that he is free as an official to pick his course un-encumbered by promises. Able to pick and choose among many things the issue oriented voter would like him to talk about, the candidate puts up a package of proposals which offers something for nearly everybody but fails to lay down a strategy of action that gives anybody assurance that important advances will be achieved. The wiser the candidate, the more tentative he may be about his promises. He knows that solutions cannot be decreed but have to be worked out. Support has to be won and the price for support will not be known until the bargaining is done. The price for getting a good piece of the candidate's platform accomplished may be agreement by the official to let some of the most important pieces be forgotten or even to pursue a course of action which the official, as candidate, had denounced during the campaign.

The candidate oriented voter may argue, therefore, that political platforms are a slippery foundation for a confident vote. Far more dependable is the character of the candidate. Read his record of achievements rather than his promises of future actions. Study his face, his words, and his record to see if he is a man who will consult widely and ponder deeply before he acts, and when he acts will be careful that his mistakes are not irrevocable. Study also the men around him, for the strength of his entourage will augment the strength of the official and the flaws in the character of his closest associates are tipoffs to weakness in the candidate. These are inquiries that voters can make and they produce materials that facilitate judgments. If the man appears to be right—intelligent, energetic, properly confident and properly humble, possessed of courage, and devoted to the public welfare—such a man, if he is surrounded by other men of worthy qualities, can be trusted to find solutions for problems as they emerge. To ask such a man to announce in advance what he will do later on is to invite him to put shackles on his arms. To ask him to commit himself to particular policies is to demand that government act to suit one segment of the electorate rather than pursue the middle path that enables everybody to feel that his interests were considered.

The party oriented voter avoids the difficulties and responsibilities of evaluating the competing candidates and their respective positions on public issues. If he is a thoroughgoing party man, he delegates his vote to the persons or to the processes that select a party nominee. The party oriented voter may be alert to the issues of the day, may have sized up the contending candidates with great shrewdness, may know where each of them stands on the main issues. He may feel amply rewarded for the effort he put into his inquiry. But if he is a staunch party man his findings will have little effect on the way he votes, for he is committed to support his party's candidate.

This describes the party man of extreme type. But the issue oriented voter and the candidate oriented voter were also presented as ideal types in the discussion of the past several pages. There must be very few voters who, in choosing public officials at all levels of government, always or even usually are guided solely by the positions that candidates take on issues, attaching no importance whatever to the personal qualities of the candidates. Quite as unusual must be the voter who never allows position on issues to draw him away from the candidate who seems the superior man. Much more frequently encountered, one suspects, is the man who votes the straight party ticket regardless of the personal qualities of the competing candidates or the positions they take on the issues of the day.

All three methods of deciding how to vote are functional for the political system. It may be that popular control of government would be much less vigorous if any of the three orientations ceased to figure importantly in the electoral process. The party oriented voter contributes stability to the political system. He makes minimal demands on the party leaders who groom candidates for public office and write platforms that say what government will do if those candidates get to office. A party's leaders, knowing their basic following, recognize bounds beyond which they cannot stray in selecting candidates and promising governmental action. If, however, they keep within the bounds of expectation and toleration fixed by the party's basic following, they have a sure vote of calculable proportions. This sure vote, running into many millions in the case of a presidential campaign, can be ignored in fixing the marginal conditions of the campaign. Making a choice from among several men who are acceptable to the party rank and file, the leaders are free to select for candidate the man who will make the greatest appeal to candidate oriented voters; in writing a platform that loyal party followers can accept, the leaders dress it up with proposals thought likely to attract the greatest number of issue oriented voters.

In our two-party system, the leaders of each party have a wide range of choice in grooming candidates and writing platforms. As long as they stay within the limits fixed by the party's loyal membership, they can direct their campaign strategy to those elements of the undecided electorate that seem most ready to heed their appeal. Their ability to shape strategy with confidence is in inverse proportion to the number of voters loose on the electoral market. When millions of voters are safely corralled in the two party camps, it becomes possible to inspect the demands of the lesser numbers of voters who may move to either side. Imagine the predicament of party leaders if, each presidential year, they could view no part of the electorate as safely in camp; if instead of picking candidates and writing platforms to attract as many as possible out of perhaps 15 million uncommitted voters, they had to develop a strategy that would attract a majority of some 70 million voters.

The contributions of the three classes of voters may be summarized as follows. The need to win support from issue oriented voters forces political leaders to survey popular satisfactions and unrests and commit themselves to public policies that seem promising to these voters, and, when in office, to avoid policies that seem likely to bring about electoral retribution. The candidate oriented voters force party leaders to nominate for office men of a character that invites public confidence. The party's faithful membership fixes bounds beyond which its leaders must not stray in choosing candidates and writing party platforms; the issue and candidate oriented voters fix the directions in which party leaders will move when they exercise the discretion their loyal followers permit them to have. Collectively the three groups of voters subject the nation's party leadership to a severe discipline.

In trichotomizing the voters of the United States, I purposely oversimplified their motivations and overstated their independence to make clear an analysis of our political behavior which seems to me fundamentally correct. The fact that great numbers of voters feel a substantial degree of loyalty to a party but at the same time move toward the candidate who inspires their confidence or toward the candidate who seems most nearly right on issues does not lessen my conviction that the three orientations combine to discipline political leadership and guarantee a vigorous competition for political power. Neither am I required to modify my thesis because the behavior of many voters is guided by a low grade of intelligence. They adhere to a party only because their ancestors identified with that party; they vote for a candidate because he has a winning smile; they know exactly where they stand on the issues but they are a mile off as to what the issues are. There is as much reason to believe that these three kinds of ignorance counterbalance each other as to believe that their ill consequences cumulate.

Neither does the fact that great numbers of people stay away from the polls, either by choice or compulsion, contradict my thesis. There may be good reasons for wishing that all qualified electors would vote and for encouraging them to do so. But a near universal turnout on election day is not essential for an effective policing of political leadership and the electoral process.

It is only required that enough voters with certain voting attitudes, strategically placed about the nation, go to the polls with some consistency. We may speak of this segment of the voting population as a "critical electorate." How many voters are enough to compose a critical electorate will depend on how well they meet the tests of voting attitude, strategic placement, and consistency of participation. The function of a critical electorate can best be disclosed by an analogy drawn from the economic realm.

Consider the purchase of automobiles in a specified price range, which we may identify as Chevrolet, Ford, Plymouth, and Rambler. Our attachment to a free-enterprise system is justified by the supposition that, in order to maintain or increase his sales, each of these four producers will try to find out what the buying public wants and will try to put before it a product at a price that will be more attractive than the offerings of his competitors. The American car-buying public is expected to police the production of cars by choosing among the different automobiles put on a competitive market. It is a fact, however, that many people who want a low-priced car are committed to one brand name and will not consider another. It may be that this part of the buying public knows nothing about the comparative merits of the four available low-priced automobiles. It may be that no amount of advertising, sales talk, or advice from automobile mechanics will move one of these committed persons to buy any car other than the brand he has been using for many years.

Does this stubborn, nonreasoning, choice-rejecting behavior of automobile buyers defeat our expectation that automobile producers will improve their product or make more attractive the terms of purchase? And is our hope for improvement defeated by the fact that at any time when new models are offered many habitual buyers of low-priced cars will not be on the market? Not necessarily. The expected consequences of competition may accrue if the following conditions are met: (a) If in any year of new models a substantial number of persons will buy automobiles in this price range. (b) If among this buying public are many people who do appreciate comparative merits of the automobiles available and comparative advantages of the different terms of sale. (c) If many of these buyers purchase cars on the basis of judgments about merit and price. (d) If these judgment-using buyers are of sufficient number to cause the producers to improve their offerings in order to capture a part of that market. Given these four conditions, since automobiles are marketed in standard models with recommended prices, it follows that all purchasers

of the four low-priced brands will profit from the improvement
of prices and terms of sale. The improvements that were arrived
at to please a critical buying public will also benefit the buyer
who was born into a Chevrolet family and the buyer who picks
a car to go well with a new mink coat just as certainly as they
benefit the limited number of critical buyers.

Now apply the analogy to voting for public officials. Many
voters fail to go to the polls in an election year, and many of the
absentees rarely or never go to the polls. Many who do vote are
committed to one party and deny themselves the opportunity to
choose between contending candidates. Many who go to the polls
without commitment do not know what they want, or are unaware
that government could do something to satisfy their wants, or
have no notions about what the competing candidates would do
if elected to office. None the less, all these absentee and noncritical voters profit from the voting acts of that part of the voting
public who were alert to issues, observant of candidates, thoughtful in relating candidates to issues, and free to choose among the
candidates according to promise that one rather than another
will run government the way the voter wants it run. The analogy
is good, even when it is pointed out that great numbers of non-
voters and noncritical persons who vote will be most unhappy with
the kind of public policy that the critical electorate prefers. These
people are in a position similar to that of automobile buyers
who do not want any of the offerings in the low-priced range. If
men who prefer luxury automobiles, or ten-ton trucks, or earth
removers yearn for a disciplined manufacture and sale of the
commodities they want, they can create their own critical buying
publics. The same occurs with all sectors of the population who
feel they gain nothing—i.e., do not get the kind of governmental
performance they want—from the response which political leaders
make to the present-day critical electorate. These non-gaining
sectors of the population must crowd into the present critical
electorate, or compose separate recognizable critical electorates,
or find means other than participation in elections to force
response to their demands; otherwise they must remain outside
the competitive political life of the nation. It may be noted further,
in pursuance of the analogy, that both producers of automobiles
and political leaders, feeling the need for sales or voter support
in order to beat their competitors, strive constantly to bring
additional people into their respective critical markets.

The automobile market supplies a useful model for understanding how voters discipline political leadership. But there are dif-

5

ferences between the automobile market and the electoral arena
that limit the utility of the model. The market for cars is always
divided among the competing producers; public offices may go
*en bloc* to the candidates of one party. While changes in model
and price tend to be made once a year, they can be made in the
midst of the buying season; candidates are offered to voters, however, on a fixed schedule determined by the length of official
tenures. Automobiles are purchased every day; all votes are cast
on certain days specified by law. These differences between the
two arenas challenge us to caution but do not strip the analogy
of its usefulness.

For varying periods of time, buying habits may be fixed
and the sales of different automobiles may show little response
to the attractions provided by the competing manufacturers. But
improvements in automobiles are not called to a halt at such times
if manufacturers are confident there will soon come a day when
a sector of the public worth going after will be loose on the market
and will buy on the basis of product differentiation. In like manner,
for a series of elections voters may support the candidates of one
party regardless of their performance in office and regardless of
the promises made by the opposing party. This fact, standing by
itself, does not force a conclusion that officeholders and other
political leaders are likely to do just what they please and that
the electorate has no influence on public policy. Both households
of political leadership—those who have public offices firmly in
hand and those who are discouraged by repeated shutouts—may
be most attentive to public demands if they suspect that in the
near future a number of voters, sufficient to turn an election, will
again be free on the market and make their choices according to
the attractiveness of the offerings. Common sense suggests that
the period of voter indifference must not run too long, certainly
not so long that political leaders forget their experiences and lose
their skills in probing demands and fashioning platforms. It is
for this reason that I inserted in the concept of the critical electorate a requirement that voters with the indicated attitudes must
go to the polls with "some consistency."

More disturbing to the utility of the automobile market model
than anything mentioned so far are certain aspects of governmental structure and certain formalisms of the electoral process.
These structures and formalisms may also affect one's confidence in the thesis of critical electorates which I proposed above.
Consider first the fact that on the same election day we choose
national, state, and local government officials, and that for the

national government we choose President and Vice President, senators, and members of the House of Representatives. The intermixing of campaigns for office at three levels of government greatly complicates the strategy of selecting party candidates and writing party platforms. It sometimes happens, for instance, that particular party leaders appear more concerned to win top offices in their own states or cities than to make a good race for the White House; fixing the priorities in this way, they press for national candidates and national platforms that will appeal to uncommitted voters everywhere, even at the cost of reduced attractiveness to the critical electorates. The special problems of men who aspire to capture or hold seats in Congress add to the aggravations that ensue from ambitions to carry state and local elections. The former appear, on the whole, to be less disturbing to a party's presidential strategy than the latter. It regularly happens that several seats in the House of Representatives, from Southern and border states, will be put in jeopardy if the Democratic candidates for President and Vice President are especially objectionable to substantial numbers of voters in those districts. In that case influential Southern Democrats will oppose for nomination to the two top offices any of the aspirants thought likely to move voters over to the Republican side in the districts regarded as precarious. And in doing so, they may recognize that the candidates they oppose would draw more support from the nation as a whole than the men they recommend in their stead.

The constitutional requirement that the President and Vice President be chosen by special electors, and the custom of permitting a statewide victory of one party to capture all of that state's electoral votes, is the electoral formalism most likely to impeach the validity of the critical electorate thesis. Under the present method of choosing presidential electors, the presidential and vice presidential candidates who get a majority of the popular votes in Colorado will get 6 electoral votes; the candidate getting a popular majority in New York will get 43 electoral votes. If both parties think they can win in both states, but win only with special effort, they will go after loose votes in both states but they will make a bigger investment in New York than in Colorado. They will make a bigger effort in New York even if there are more uncommitted voters and therefore more capturable votes in Colorado than in New York—a strategy that would be irrational to the automobile producer who is as eager to sell a car in one part of the country as any other. Because of this varying value of popular votes, party strategists are alert to identify free elements of the voting population in any states that may be characterized as prime targets. If they can devise a campaign that will capture these voters they will also capture enough other voters to carry the state. If it happens that the same elements of the electorate become the prime targets in several states with large electoral votes, candidates will be chosen, platforms will be written, and money will be spent primarily to win the support of this limited sector of the voting population. There have been elections in which farmers constituted the prime target groups, and the presidential campaign was fought mainly on issues of concern to farmers. One can imagine a future election in which Negroes, Puerto Ricans, and poverty-ridden whites of continental birth are the prime targets in several states with large electoral votes. If this should be the case, it is conceivable that these voters may virtually dictate the campaign strategy of both political parties.

It will be seen that the critical electorate, if this reasoning is sound, is not simply a substantial number of alert and uncommitted voters scattered here and there about the country; it is made up of alert and uncommitted voters who are strategically placed in different parts of the country. The conditions of an appropriate strategic placement of uncommitted voters will greatly complicate any effort to construct a theory of critical electorates.

# III

*The Structure of Authority*

# 8. THE ELECTIVE PRINCIPLE

We terminate here our inquiry into the electorate and the conditions under which the voters attempt to control the government by election and replacement of officials. The exploration of this vast and complicated area of political life was only begun. In leaving the subject at this point I exclude from examination many of the most interesting and most important aspects of popular control—for instance, the conditions under which vigorous party organization and competition may come to existence and flourish, the routes by which men rise to public attention, alternative ways of designating party nominees, the management and financing of campaigns, and so on. Most of the important features of political organization and the nation's most striking experiences in achieving popular control of government are examined at length in the leading textbooks and a steadily growing list of special studies dealing with the electoral process. My ambition will have been satisfied if the analysis I have supplied clarifies for the student the basic rationale of popular government in the United States and in some significant way advances the thought of scholars who have not scrutinized the American system from some of the perspectives I have adopted.

The sector of the political system next in line for attention in a full treatment of democratic government is the decisional apparatus. The people (i.e., an inclusive electorate) choose public officials; the elected officials make policies and exercise control over appointed officials who carry on the day-to-day activities of government. The structure of offices and the placement of authority in the several offices is the decisional apparatus of government. If the elected and appointed officials who exercise significant authority are truly responsive to public expectations, then government by the people is secured. Understanding how authority is distributed among offices, one will then be prepared to study the limitations which, in democratic systems, are imposed on the officials who are the core of the decisional apparatus.

I shall not undertake a comprehensive examination of the structure of offices and the placement of authority, even in a summary fashion. The reasons for so deciding are these: An analysis comparable even to my treatment of the electoral process would make this a large book; I have expressed my basic convictions in other writings; and I am now engaged in research and thought that will require me to develop my views further at a later time. In the present essay, it will be enough to alert the beginning student to a few problems that suggest how pressing is our need for development of a more comprehensive body of theory. We start that analysis in this chapter under two heads: distributed self-government, and the elective office.

## Distributed Self-Government

Distributed self-government provides an easy transition from the electoral system to the decisional apparatus. By distributed self-government, I mean the national-state-local division of governmental authority. Political scientists customarily differentiate the national-state relationship from the state-local relationship by noting and emphasizing the degrees of autonomy assigned to the lesser partner in each of the linkages. The national-state relationship, as originally conceived and called federalism, envisaged separate areas of authority for the two governments, each protected against inroads of the other by a constitution superior to both. The state-local relationship, in contrast, assumed that the state could assign, alter, and withdraw the authority of local units.

Governments at the three levels differ significantly in the authority and autonomy enjoyed by each; they are alike in that at each level the principal officers are elected at the polls. At each level, by requirements of national and state constitutions, we provide for popular control of government. Hence the term "distributed self-government" which I have adopted as a means of identifying government going on simultaneously at three levels, as the term "federalism" identifies the relationships of the national and state governments.

The extent to which the American system of distributed self-government embarrasses the theory-maker is not likely to be exaggerated. Theory provides an imagined description of what, in the judgment of the theorist, will be found when a careful exploration has been executed. The kind of theory that I have been concerned with in this essay tries, by setting forth an imagined description, to show how the people make their wishes known and induce officials to comply with their wishes. The reality is most intricate, and therefore the theory must deal with baffling complications, when each citizen is invited to address his demands to several governments, when officials of several governments are in a position to pass the buck from one seat of authority to another, and when voters are exhorted to show discrimination in choosing officials for governments with widely different grants of authority to deal with public problems.

The readiness and the competence of voters to make judgments for the many offices that must be filled is a main center of attention for political scientists today. Empirical investigation and revision of theory have brought us a good distance forward since World War II. The ability and willingness of the voter to make discriminating judgments is, however, only one aspect of a system that creates several centers of authority and charges the citizens to exercise control over each. Equally important is an inquiry into how experience in self-government at one stratum of government sustains or impairs successful performance at the other two levels. A few remarks about the relation of local self-government to popular control of government in Washington should indicate the kinds of problems that will be encountered in a fuller inquiry.

There was throughout the earlier period of our history a strong conviction, shared by scholars and other shrewd observers, that the success of the American effort to control government in the national capital derived mainly from experience in managing local governments. In the United States, said the most respected of all observers, "the people reign without impediment." This they were able to do, he declared emphatically, because of the vitality of their local political institutions and practices. The citizen, he wrote, "takes a part in every occurrence of the place; he practices the art of government in the small sphere within his reach; he accustoms himself to those forms without which liberty can only advance by revolutions; he imbibes their spirit; he acquires a taste for order, comprehends the balance of powers, and collects clear practical notions on the nature of his duties and the extent of his rights."* This was Alexis de Tocqueville, a Frenchman who visited the United States in 1831-32. In the sentence I quote, he

---

* Alexis de Tocqueville, *Democracy in America* (New York: Vintage Book, 1956), vol. 1, p. 71.

referred especially to New England, where government was conducted in town meetings, but he indicated elsewhere in his book that in all parts of the country local self-government had underwritten national self-government.

It may be, as some political scientists assert today, that de Tocqueville saw more democracy in America than existed, and that he imagined a firmer connection between local self-government and national self-government than was warranted. Presuming that de Tocqueville was an accurate reporter and a wise analyst, the significance that he attributed to popular government in the community may since have spent itself. It may be that local elections and the effort of officials to please local electorates are not required for keeping alive a regime of popular control over national government that could not have come into existence without that local experience. Severe scrutiny, by imaginative and exacting analysts, of the relationships between active involvement in local government and the development of citizenship and political leadership will surely pay off in theory that sets priorities for further investigations.

Selecting officials is but a part of the total enterprise of maintaining popular control of government. The citizen lays demands before the officials, criticizes the service they provide, chafes at the regulations they subject him to, and drags his feet or openly rebels when he thinks that authority has reached beyond its proper bounds. In local public affairs especially, nongovernmental organizations intrude into the forums of decision and the day-to-day administration of public policies. These expressions and actions are instruments of the pluralist (or group competition) demand-response system, but they must be viewed as an integral part of the populist demand-response system as well. Indeed, the vigor of local self-government would ebb and the contributions of voluntary cooperation to the good life would diminish if the two demand-response systems were not united in the community.

The relation of our three-level distribution of governmental authority to widespread civic awareness and the vigor of political leadership has been the subject of intensive study, both speculative and empirical, by political scientists and sociologists. Who gets what, when, and how in the political life of urban communities has especially attracted scholars. If we honor as theory all of the recent speculation, it must be acknowledged that theory has roundly encompassed the spheres of influence and arenas of power that fix the character of local government in the America of our day. The research findings reveal astonishing variety in the distribution of popular influence over local policy and disclose great variance in the importance of social structure, public offices, and political culture as determinants of popular influence.

Rich as the recent contributions are, the construction of needed theory about the interrelationships of popular government at all three levels has scarcely begun. Three centers of uncertain knowledge will illustrate my point. First, division of authority among national, state, and local governments has been justified as a sure and efficient way (efficient in that it minimizes social abrasions) of providing for adjustment of public policies to varying special needs. The entire nation wants to reduce traffic accidents, fire hazards, and the incidence of crime and disease; it can hardly be doubted that these national objectives are most likely to be realized if local officials are allowed to develop policies and practices that seem to them most appropriate to local situations. But the assignment of any sector of public affairs to fifty states and a few thousand local governments does not guarantee that policies and practices will be carefully fitted to local perceptions of need. Our experience with public education, briefly summarized above (pages 85–90), illustrates this point. The converse, that national policies and national administration can be made to comply with great variance in local needs, is also true. There is probably no better illustration of this than our experience in supporting prices for farm crops. Congress and the President announce national policies in the form of statutes; farmers who grow a particular crop decide in a referendum election whether that crop will come under the national policies. Farmers also elect local committees (for counties and sometimes lesser areas) that have limited, but still significant, authority to fit the broader policies of Washington to the special needs of their respective localities. This is a system of highly decentralized national policy making and administration.

A second center of uncertain knowledge is the relation of distributed self-government to the consolidation or fragmentation of political power. If one is confident that the people now exercise effective control over the elected officials in Washington, and confident that the elected officials effectively control the great administrative bureaucracies—in that case one is tempted to reject the time-honored contention that liberty would be lost if the power seated in state and local officials were consolidated with the power seated in Washington. But he ought not succumb to the temptation too quickly. It may be that the subsidiary seats of power—in city halls, county court houses, and state capitols—provide many of the challenges, administer many of the checks, and mobilize much of the public expression that disciplines the national officials. As we shall note later, there is growing apprehension that Congress may become unduly submissive to the President and that both may become less sensitive to sectors of the public that express misgivings, disgruntlements, and outright antagonism. We do not now have the knowledge required for confident judgments that substantial emplacements of authority in state and local capitals are or are not essential for the security of government by the people in Washington.

A third nest of concerns for which theory is presently inadequate may be referred to as choice between conflicting majorities. The Negro, fighting for equal status with the whites today, forces Americans to consider a question that steadily confronts all European countries in which mutually suspicious and antagonistic ethnic groups are combined to form a single polity. When sizeable elements of the population take opposing stands on an important issue and maintain their respective positions with emotional fervor, how is the issue to be resolved? If only Jews lived north of the river and nobody but Christians lived south of the river, authority to fix public holidays could be consigned, by a federal arrangement, to the respective populations and conflict might be avoided. But if the antagonistic populations are mixed together as is the case with whites and Negroes in the United States, conflict is a continuing prospect regardless of where the authority to fix public policy is placed.

The Negro, suffering from discriminatory policies enforced by several of our state governments and confident of more just treatment by national authorities, has every reason to demand that the national government assume authority to regulate employment, public accommodations, and other social matters in which discrimination is practiced. This position is dictated by practical politics, not political theory. There was a time when the black man stood to profit more from state authority than from national. During a period when Congress enacted fugitive slave laws and presidents issued orders for their enforcement, the antislavery states of the North were havens to which runaways fled to escape the authority of the national government as well as the states where slavery was lawful. It is conceivable that the Negro at some future time, having won equal status by national intervention, may turn to other social objectives such as redress of past grievances or equalization of bargaining power in the market place. In that case he may see a chance of winning victories in certain state capitals that are impossible in Washington, and so become a proponent of state authority.

It should be taken for granted that when the stakes are high and people are determined to win victories over equally determined opponents, each group of contenders will favor that placement of authority that gives its cause the best prospect of winning. That is the nature of politics. But the fact that strategies will be determined by practical considerations does not invalidate the judgment that theory is badly needed. The protagonists may pursue their respective ends with utter disregard for what the theory-makers have said. But people who are neutral in the midst of conflict may control the decision as to which authority shall deal with the controversy. The neutrals will need something more than a politician's judgment to guide them; it is a function of theory to supply that additional guidance.

## The Elective Office

The elected public official is a key instrument in any government that makes a pretense of being democratic. The American plan of distributed self-government, depending on many elected officials, makes special demands for clear thinking about the authority of elected officials, the conditions of choosing them, and provision for their continuing attention to public expectations and demands.

If we elect too many officials, we have too many candidates to pass judgment on when election time comes around. But if we elect fewer officials, we encounter other problems of providing for firm control of appointed officials. If we elect many officials, we assume a risk that men with authority will feel independent of one another and governmental policies will not be well coordinated. But the greater unity of policy that we hope to get by reducing the number of elected offices forces us to assume other risks in giving the power of decision to officials who are not exposed to criticism and discipline in campaigns for re-election.

For what term shall we elect an official? If the term is too short, the official does not have a fair chance to deliver on his promises and the voters do not have an adequate basis for judging how good a job the official is doing. If the term is too long, the official can do a lot of damage before the voters get him out. There used to be a common saying, "Where annual elections end, tyranny begins." In recent decades there has been a marked trend to a four-year term for all offices, this sentiment having produced a considerable demand that the term for the national House of Representatives be increased from two to four years. Some states have provided for a recall arrangement that enables the electorate to pull a man out of office at any time they make up their minds to do so.

If we elect a new group of officials we want the old crowd to get out. We take this for granted in the United States but it is not taken for granted in some countries, where defeat in an election may do little more than inform the crowd in power as to how many people they may have to fight if they decide to resist the election. The people in such a country may manage to get what they want by supplementing their elections with armed revolt, but that is clearly a resort to force to achieve a result that could not be achieved by a democratic process.

How does a nation develop an understanding that its officials will bow to the will of the people? It is an understanding that must be so firmly held by the population as a whole that the most arrogant and determined man-on-horseback will think it futile to resist the verdict at the polls. It is therefore an understanding that must grow up over a period of generations. The instruction that people get on this point will come from those individuals who are concerned about public affairs and have given thought to the consequences of resistance by force. These people are in large part, if not in the main, the politicians themselves. They have had the experience of being out and wanting in, and they appreciate fully the pain of losing by force what was fairly won by a count of heads. Like men in every sector of affairs dominated by competition, they formulate the elementary rules that govern their competition. A secure and vigorous system of competition for political power in this country is undoubtedly our principal guarantee that unsuccessful candidates for office will yield to those who win in a popular election.

The obligation to retire, because of defeat at the polls or removal by a superior officer, is universally acknowledged, and failure to comply cannot be concealed. Reluctance of men to quit office, consequently, has not contributed significantly to our frustrations. However, giving up office is only one evidence of compliance with popular demand. We expect officials to be alert to changes of mind and new expressions of public wishes. The prospect for such alertness is regulated by the vigor of competition among those who seek to gain and hold on to public office. If those desiring political power are constrained to keep their ears to the ground, heeding the appeals and pressures directed to them and studying public reaction to their acts, then the populist demand-response system is fulfilling our highest expectations. The obligation to give up office when the voters elect another man is the sanction that induces the public official to do everything possible to read the public mind.

This neat picture of how the people can make their wishes known and how the electorate forces compliance with those wishes is so attractive that one regrets to mar it by painting in some disconcerting realities. The fact is that rarely does any one elected official have all the authority required for instituting and carrying through a public policy of substantial importance. Not only are several officials involved in fixing the content and securing the enforcement of a policy; these collaborating officials usually have been chosen by different electorates and are subject to removal by them. Acknowledging that the electoral arrangements give some segments of the electorate extraordinary power in the selection of the President, we think of the chief executive as the choice of the whole nation and answerable to the whole nation. Members of Congress, on the other hand, are chosen by the electorates of individual states or of congressional districts. No individual member of the Senate or House of Representatives answers to a nationwide electorate. Collectively the members of Congress may be in their places by virtue of a public mood that was not in ascendancy when the President was elected. Willmoore Kendall has written with great perception about two majorities, concurrent and in collision; the people may indeed elect a chief executive to suggest, to lead, to spur, and to act boldly on some matters, but on the same election day elect senators and representatives who will respond reluctantly to the President's urgings and put a brake on his forward thrusts.* State and local officials are also instruments of national policy in many important areas of public affairs. They may, with full approval of the local electorates, delay, distort, and sometimes nullify a national plan of action that was approved by a President and a majority of Congress who believed that they were responding to the expectations of a more inclusive electorate.

Any person who is at the start of his career as an observer and student of American politics may well be struck with wonder at

---

* Willmoore Kendall, "The Two Majorities," *Midwest Journal of Political Science,* vol. 4 (1960), p. 317, reprinted in Willmoore Kendall and George W. Carey, eds., *Liberalism versus Conservatism* (Princeton, N.J.: Van Nostrand, 1966), p. 156.

how an elected official in the United States can figure out who expects him to do what. Sheriffs, governors, congressmen and sometimes presidents confess to the same puzzlement. But elected officials and the politicians who advise them make a continuous reading of the public mind their principal business, and some of them manage to stay in business for a long time. A good share of those who attain longevity in public life will tell you that they stayed in business not because they eluded the people who made demands, but because they had enjoyed a measure of success in estimating the numbers of persons on the several sides of a controversial issue and calculating the intensities of conviction and determination behind each opinion. Politicians, including the high-minded ones we call statesmen, fix their attention on particular publics and particular electorates. It is to be expected that their strategies and contrivances for survival will enjoy greater success than will the efforts of scholars to explain how the survivors did it. This is no reason for scholars to abandon their search for explanations. Dogs have a much better record of finding their way home after being dumped in faraway places than scientists have of explaining how the dogs did it. But a student of honey bees is believed to have found out how the scout gives the rest of the colony detailed instructions for getting to the place where he made his strike. So there is ground for hope that students of political science may someday give a convincing account of how the American people push their expectations and preferences into the minds of their officials, induce them to respond, and make a replacement when the response is not as prompt or as satisfying as the voters think reasonable.

It is possible that all of our formal provisions for elective offices are the consequences of clear thinking; it is certain that the literature of political science does not adequately discuss the considerations that must be taken into account in making formal provisions. We enter now upon a general survey of needs for more elaborate theory relating to elective offices. The survey starts with attention to the legislative assembly and the chief executive and the relation of these two sets of elected officials to the administrative organizations that do the work which the elected officials assign to them. That inquiry into the constitution and interrelationships of principal offices will be followed by a consideration of needs and provisions for limiting the authority vested in the elective branches. Judgments about the constitution of offices and placement of authority necessarily are affected by convictions about needs for restraining the exercise of power that is granted. For that reason, the survey that starts in the next chapter should be prefaced by brief mention of certain problems that must be kept in mind at all points in our inquiry. These general observations point out four significant deficiencies in the theory now available to us in political science literature.

First, what authority should be placed in elected officials? An office is a lodgment of authority, so this question may also be put this way: what public offices should be filled by popular election?

No doubt political scientists are in general agreement that, in order to run the government effectively, elected officials must be able to enact the legislation that fixes the fundamental policies of the country, allocate money among governmental activities, determine how much money will be raised and by what means it will be obtained, and select the major administrative officials who will manage the operations of government. Beyond this, it is doubtful there is much generally accepted theory. Witness to such a shortcoming is recurrent argument about whether the American people would have been better off with a parliamentary system of the British style than with a separately elected chief executive, and the recurrent assertion that our literature concerning state administrative organization and forms of city government is mainly dogma and not carefully reasoned theory.

A second deficiency in theory relating to the role of elected officials centers about delegation of authority. A great deal has been written, most of it by lawyers and law professors, about delegations of authority by elected officials, and about the attitudes and actions of judges in respect to delegations of authority. We have not, however, developed theory that answers questions about whether an area of decision making is suitable for delegation; about what are suitable instructions for the appointed official who is to exercise the delegated authority; about how to judge whether the official to whom authority is delegated lives up to the expectations of those who conferred the authority upon him; about how elected officials can effectively recall the grants of authority that are not being utilized in accordance with their wishes.

We suffer from lack of theory on a third point relating to elected officials: what are proper limits to the efforts of elected officials to direct and control the appointed officials and employees who carry on the day-to-day operations of government? Granted that the elected branches should fix the fundamental policies of government, where are the boundaries that separate the fundamental from matters that ought to be left to executive officials, or sectors of the bureaucracy, or judges? Where is the line that differentiates effective direction and control from the detailed specifications that handicap administrative officials in doing what they were instructed to do? Intervention in day-to-day administration by elected officials may have the exemplary effect of causing administrative officials to enforce vigorously and impartially the policies laid down by the elected branches of the government. Or it may have the opposite effect of causing administrative officials to abandon impartial enforcement of policy and deal in special favors, special advantages, and special privileges. This is a point to which political scientists have addressed a great deal of expostulation but little analysis likely to prove a foundation for theory.

Finally, existing theory relating to the role of elected officials in government suffers from inadequate attention to the limitations imposed by a society unwilling to give its government too much power. Limitations placed on government as a whole, and therefore restraining the officials chosen by the people to run the government, are expressed in two essentially different ways. Some limitations are imposed by the culture without explicit formulation; some are written in constitutions. I am not aware of any significant body of theory designed to guide study of the limitations on governmental power inherent in the commitments and behavior patterns we call culture. We do have a substantial literature relating to constitutional limitations on government and judicial enforcement of constitutional limitations. But even here, theory to guide imaginative study is partial. Almost all the study of judicial enforcement of constitutions that has come from American scholarship has been directed to the national Constitution and to the decisions and opinions of federal courts. We have made only occasional forays into the political thickets that surround and entrap the higher courts of our fifty states. Our state courts are differently placed in the political structures that contain them. They are differently exposed to pressures originating within and outside the boundaries of party politics. There can be no doubt that fuller understanding of how state judiciaries are related to the political arena would greatly improve our ability to construct theory about how constitutions are made controlling upon governments.

# 9. THE LEGISLATURE AND THE EXECUTIVE

## The Representative Assembly

A representative assembly is the principal institution in the decisional apparatus of any democratic government. There appears to be no exception to this rule in countries with a large population. In all such countries, where government has proved responsive to demands arising from all parts of the population, the basic policies of the government are made in a representative assembly. It follows that persons who are genuinely concerned to preserve or improve the democratic character of their government must have tests for evaluating the character and performance of their lawmaking body. It is a major function of theory to provide suitable tests. Guidance of evaluation is not the only use of theory, but it supplies the *raison d'être* of the remarks in the next several paragraphs.

A persuasive evaluation of a representative assembly must be addressed to three principal areas of concern: the authority of the assembly, its fitness to exercise the authority given it, and the answerability of its members to the population.

The first concern, the authority of representative assemblies, will not be discussed at this point. I have noted the critical power of lawmaking bodies heretofore. I discuss the relation of the legislature to administration in the next chapter, and later chapters are concerned with limitations on the exercise of authority vested in lawmaking bodies. It seems unnecessary to summarize those remarks or extend them at this point.

The second concern, the fitness of the assembly to exercise the authority vested in it, poses three questions of prime importance.

Does the assembly attract men whose personal qualities are appropriate to the power they will wield? Are the members of the assembly representative of the population? Do the organization and procedures of the assembly facilitate inquiry, encourage deliberation, and provide for decisive action?

I am sure that some useful statements can be made about the qualities and the commitments that make a man worthy of carrying the responsibilities of a legislator. I am not prepared to do more than recite the obvious. Intelligence and honesty are not enough. Courage and capacity for sustained work are also essential attributes. Beyond the qualities that determine the character of the whole man are convictions and moods that are significant for public service. These include a readiness to sacrifice personal advantage for public benefit, a facility for negotiation, and a temperament that permits graceful accommodation to ends and means that fall considerably short of one's ideal.

I have more confidence in my judgment when the questions are about how to select and retain men thought well suited for legislative service. A full inquiry into this subject would look first to the health of the electoral system. If citizens are alert to their opportunities as voters, if ambitious men provide leadership for competing political parties, and if men of exemplary qualities aspire to hold public offices—if these evidences of alertness, interest, and vigor prevail in the political system, then the stage is set for the recruitment and retention of legislators worthy of their great responsibilities. To secure this result a further provision must be made. The position must carry the compensation that makes it possible, in a capitalist society, for men of the desired qualities to abandon other means of making a living. On the first point of inquiry—the health of the electoral system—I have already said as much as I think appropriate for this essay. On the second point, I think it fitting to say only that the relation of compensation for public office to readiness to seek and remain in public office calls for imaginative study. In my opinion there is promise for exploration of this subject in the methods pursued by economists who develop theories about the disposition of goods and services in various types of market.

Legislatures are composed of many people for two reasons: to assure knowledge of, sympathy for, and determination to do something about claims on government arising from all parts of the population; and to assure that open discussion and bargaining will precede decision. The intended result of these two conditions is the enactment of major public policies that in great degree respond to the expectations of the population as a whole.

Representation is the name for the first of these conditions. An element of the population is represented in the lawmaking process if one of the legislators understands the needs and wishes of that part of the population, and does something to satisfy them. Popular election of legislators by voters living within defined geographic areas (legislative districts) is the American way of providing for representation, but there are other ways of doing it.

There is a voluminous literature relating to representation, yet we have hardly crossed the threshold of understanding how it may be surely achieved. I shall do no more than identify a few of the many important points at which knowledge is insufficient. A bare citation of these baffling puzzles will make evident the pressing need for theory to guide research.

Start with a public that wants to be represented in Congress— the Black Muslims. If a district were specially created to impound their voting strength, the Black Muslims might succeed in putting one of their adherents in Congress. This would not secure the enactment of a law to clear the territory they want for a Negro nation-state, but it would give one of their spokesmen a platform from which to address a national audience. Ought a system of representation, in order to meet a reasonable test of democratic character, make some special provision for giving a hearing to all sizeable elements of the population that are certain to be ignored when special provision is not made? It may be answered that a legislature is for making laws, not for debating and educating the people. Taking this view, one may contend that no claim on government, no matter how intensely espoused, need have a representative in Congress until its adherents are numerous enough to command the attention and sympathy of candidates in districts that are drawn without concern to favor particular elements in the population. To this it may be answered that districts are rarely drawn with total unconcern for the varying interests of the population that is to be distributed among several districts. Voters are strategically distributed in districts to maximize the strength in legislative elections of the political party that controls the district making; high income suburbs are put in districts that the high income population can always control; Negroes may be inundated by whites in every district where Negroes are found. We have writing that condemns gerrymandering for party advantage, but we do not have thoughtful inquiry into strategies for advancing particular objectives of representation by a planned architecture of legislative districts.

Turn now to the legislator. How is he to decide which demands to honor when demands conflict, and whom should he represent when he knows that he cannot represent everybody? Was his district created to identify a constituency that he is supposed to speak and vote for? Or are districts only electoral devices to assure that a cross-section of the electorate can select a congressman from a list of candidates they stand a chance of knowing? If the latter, then the legislator may think that he ought to speak for the whole nation or for some element of the population (e.g., all working men) who lie mainly outside his district. If, on the other hand, he supposes he was chosen to represent the people of his particular district, then what part of this limited population, what part of their interests, and how balance their competing interests?

One can imagine that several hundred legislators, each determined to do what he thinks will prove most satisfactory to the entire nation, will come as near to doing this as an equal number of legislators, each trying to please the people of his own district. But it is as easily conceivable that an assembly of legislators who view the whole nation as constituents may widely miss the mark in trying to figure out what the whole nation wants. In any event, it is certain that the system of single member districts that now exists was not designed to return or remove legislators according to their success in pleasing the entire population. Common sense, as well as observation of what happens, tells us that the voters of a district will reward or punish the incumbent according to whether he pleases them; they are not likely to throw out a man who fought for their interests on the ground that he ought to have done more to please somebody else.

Who are they—the voters of a district who effectively decide that a congressman will be returned or replaced? The discussion of critical electorates and target groups (above, pp. 118–23) is applicable here. If in any district workingmen traditionally support candidates who favor labor legislation and businessmen and farmers vote for candidates who oppose labor legislation, then it may be that Negroes, by bargaining their support, can secure the election of a candidate who promises to fight for civil rights even though there is not a handful of friends for civil rights in the entire white population of the district.

It may seem that I have tried to make the provision of representation in legislative assemblies appear more difficult than it actually is. The opposite is the truth. I have tried to facilitate comprehension of a few perplexing problems by removing from attention other things that account for the perplexities. The life of a legislator, genuinely concerned to sort out his obligations and meet them, is far more complicated than I have suggested. We have not yet introduced complications that result from the character of the forum. If any aspect of the public interest is to be effectively represented in lawmaking it must have a spokesman on hand at various stages in the lawmaking process. This is because legislators have more to do than represent. They must decide, enact, and that means agree on the content and the wording of public policies. Action is expressed by voting in which, with few exceptions, a majority of those who take sides on the question determine what will be done. Debate is not simply an effort to win votes for or against a bill; it is also an effort to secure changes in the bill. The negotiation that produces compromises is not simply a strategy to win votes for the bill before the chamber; it may be bargaining for support or opposition to other bills, for support or opposition to a whole party program, or even for a credit card in good will that can be cashed in at an unknown date for support of a cause not yet foreseen. The vote that appears to have sacrificed the interests of a constituency may in fact have made possible victories for the constituency on other issues more important to them.

Debate and negotiations take place on the floor of the chamber, in committees, in the White House, and everywhere else that legislators meet with one another or with other people who are in a position to exert influence on the outcome of an issue. All of the extended arena in which legislators confer, persuade, bargain, and commit themselves to action is the forum in which lawmaking occurs. Surely all of importance that occurs in the forum must be taken into account by the student who seeks to explain how laws are made, how aspirations for legislation are thwarted, and how equality of bargaining power for all elements of the population may be approached most surely in the construction of assemblies and provision for election of individual members. A simple rule of equal numbers in the composition of legislative districts may have small consequences for the output of legislatures if the committees with critical power are composed without regard to representation of the interests that compete for their approval.

It is unnecessary to comment especially on the third concern of theory relating to the representative assembly—the answerability of its members to the population. In thinking about representation we think about answerability for failure to represent.

A full inquiry would attend also to the exposure of the legislative process (openness of debate, access to committee proceedings, publication of important acts), lengths of terms of legislators, and the electoral process (including the prospect that those who hold office may use the office to prejudice public evaluation of their acts).

The preceding spotty commentary on needs for theory relating to the legislative assembly and the lawmaking process was concerned principally with representation. This is the heart of the matter. We are well on our way to understanding all aspects of lawmaking if we understand how interests are distributed in the population, how the division of people into districts affects the presentation of their claims at the seat of government, how much supplemental representation any group picks up because their interests are shared by people in other districts who have managed to elect a diligent spokesman for those interests, and so on. Representation has been for centuries a problem of prime concern to scholars in all western countries. Yet, as I said above, we are only on the threshold of understanding how representation can be surely achieved. There is, therefore, a temptation to drop the idea of systematic analysis and formulation of comprehensive theory, and retreat to the plane of the practical politicians. That is the method of practical men. They divide the population with some attention to equal numbers, some attention to existing political organizations, some attention to the vested interests of men who are influential in the decisions about district-making, some attention to various things that are pressed hard by men that have to be listened to. Men can be aware of interests that they cannot define in precise language; they can be certain that a position has a rational foundation even when they cannot provide the explanation that exposes its rational basis. So men who are motivated by a fair amount of good will and restrained by a fair amount of respect for one another may lay out a set of districts that are generally thought to provide a fair amount of representation for all the interests of substantial importance. They can do this, as they have been doing it, without the guidance of comprehensive theory. The scholar is thus invited to put off the systematic study that might ultimately produce a comprehensive theory and, instead, engage in criticism of existing arrangements and promotion of practical formulas to aggrandize particular values. This predilection for obvious needs and easy solutions seems to account for the almost unanimous approval of the equal numbers requirement for district-making currently espoused by the Supreme Court. A disposition for the neat formula and the easy solution may also explain why so many political scientists justify the expanding power of the President with the declaration that a single person elected by the nation is bound to be a better representative of the whole population than 500 plus congressmen can be, when those congressmen are elected by states and lesser one-member districts.

## The Chief Executive

A major preoccupation of American political thought is commonly referred to as Separation of Powers and Checks and Balances. More than separating powers and relating them to one another is involved in the literature that carries this title, however. It embraces the attributes of power to govern, considers how powers may be meaningfully differentiated and appropriately distributed among different branches of government, and evaluates various arrangements for the holders of power to check one another.

To this day, nearly two hundred years after the writing, we quote *The Federalist* as the principal American exposition of this subject. Yet the treatment in *The Federalist* is far from complete. It is excellent on the need to differentiate powers, distribute them among different offices, and provide for checks and balances. But it is meager in its definitions; we are not given good accounts of the character, the content, the attributes of the several kinds of power that are differentiated.

Our conceptions of three major kinds of power have developed over the years, but no one has yet produced a systematic and comprehensive statement that can be viewed as a theory of separable powers and their distribution in democratic government. If one may say that we operate today under practical or *de facto* definitions of three powers, it must be said that the definitions and redefinitions that have evolved since the American system was founded have resulted in tremendous enlargements of the executive and judicial powers and the retraction of the legislative. The judicial power, originally thought to be that of settling disputes by ascertaining the applicable law and applying it, has grown to embrace a capacity to say finally what the Constitution permits, forbids, and requires, and to enforce its interpretations upon the other branches of government. I think it will be generally agreed that this capacity to interpret now includes the right to "find" and incorporate into the Constitution permissions and obligations which the architects of the system did not contemplate but which seem to the judges likely to advance the objectives of government stated in the preamble to the Constitution. The expansions of the executive power, with which we are concerned in the following pages, may be even more momentous.

I do not intend to describe or even to bound the present power of the Presidency. I propose only to comment on an apprehension that the office is becoming, if it has not already become, too powerful for the comfort of a people devoted to the ideal that all of its officials ought to answer to the population for their important acts. An understanding of what is feared and why people fear it necessitates some indication of the character and magnitude of the President's power and the course of his rise to ascendancy in the system.

The termination of the War of 1812 found the American people in a mood to re-evaluate their political system, and Congress in the lame duck session following the election of 1816 launched a re-examination—what for many congressmen was a soul-searching inquiry—of the nature of legislative power and the relationships of Congress to the other branches of government and to the American people. "Of all the powers with which the people have invested the Government, that of legislation is undoubtedly the chief." So declared a committee of the House of Representatives which had been instructed to bring in a report on the proper compensation of congressmen. "The members of the House of Representatives are the special delegates and agents of the people in this high trust. They, and they alone, proceed immediately from the suffrage of the people. [Senators were then elected by the state legislatures.] They, and they alone, can touch the mainspring of the public prosperity. They are elected to be the guardians of the public rights and liberties." John C. Calhoun of South Carolina, in the debate following the committee report, asserted that in the structure of our government the prevailing principle "is not so much a balance of power as a well-connected chain of responsibility," and then went on to say:

But what mainly distinguishes the Legislative and Executive branches, as it regards their *actual* responsibility to the people, is the nature of ʼheir operation. It is the duty of the former to enact laws, of the latter to execute them. . . . How can the community judge whether the President, in appointing officers to execute the laws, has in all cases been governed by fair and honest motives, or by favor or corruption? How much less competent is it to judge whether the application of the public money has been made with economy and fidelity or with waste and corruption? These are facts that can be fully investigated and brought before the public by Congress, and Congress only. Hence it is that the Constitution has made the President responsible to Congress. This, then, is the essence of our liberty; Congress is responsible to the people immediately, and the other branches of Government are responsible to it.*

This was the time in our history when legislative authority was most highly extolled and the President's office was in lowest esteem. I doubt that more than a few men in the Philadelphia convention would have endorsed Calhoun's statement without qualification. But Calhoun was in the mood of the men who, thirty years before, had constructed and launched the new political system. Hamilton in *The Federalist* (No. 73) spoke of "the superior weight and influence of the legislative body in a free government." His prime concern in several essays was to establish how energy could be provided in the executive arm of the government and to prove that the Constitution made ample provision for energy in the presidency. It is clear that he thought the need for energy to arise from the President's duty to execute the laws. His explanation and justification of the veto power in No. 73 permits no one to believe that he expected the President to play a leading role in the enactment of legislation. Fisher Ames, I think, stated the view of the President's place in the system that prevailed when the Constitution was adopted, when he said: "The executive powers are delegated to the President with a view to have a responsible officer to superintend, control, inspect, and check the officers necessarily employed in administering the laws."†

The early conception of the President's assignment as that of executing and supervising the execution of the laws bears little resemblance to the dominion of the President today. Admitting that the authority varies with the man in the office and that thoughtful observers differ as to how much response any of our former presidents did in fact command, it must be agreed that every one of our recent Presidents dominated the formation and expression of our foreign policy, initiated and exerted great influence on the enactment of legislation during his time in office, made a great impression on public policies by selecting, instruct-

* The committee report (December 18, 1816) and Calhoun's speech (January 17, 1817) are in *Annals of Congress,* 14th Congress, 2nd session, the quotations at pp. 317 and 575–76; reprinted in Charles S. Hyneman and George W. Carey, eds., *A Second Federalist* (New York: Appleton-Century-Crofts, 1967), pp. 148–151.
† In the House of Representatives, June 16, 1789; *Annals of Congress,* 1st Congress, 1st session, p. 474. In Hyneman and Carey, eds., *op. cit.,* p. 165.

ing, and counseling key administrative officials, and was the principal interpreter to the American people of what his administration was trying to do. Read into each of these four notations of his power all that the words can stand and you will conclude that I have not exaggerated the position of any President since 1932; construe each of them as narrowly as the words permit and you must still acknowledge that the presidency is a powerful office. The transformation of the office from what the founders envisaged has come mainly since the announcement of secession introducing the Civil War. All of the "strong" Presidents contributed to the grandeur of the office. And it appears indisputable that they did so largely by two courses of action, one of which the architects of our system did not anticipate and the other of which they did not approve: a liberal use of the veto; and the use of the appointing power for purposes other than filling offices.

The primary reason for giving the President the right to veto legislation, said Alexander Hamilton in No. 73 of *The Federalist,* is "to enable him to defend himself. The case for which it is chiefly designed [is] that of an immediate attack upon the constitutional rights of the Executive." The opportunity to protect the community from bad laws, he said, was a secondary reason for giving him the power to veto. Hamilton did not mention a third possible reason for conferring the veto power, viz., to give the President a lever with which to pry compliance out of congressmen who oppose him on legislation and other policies. The following instances, taken from a leading commentary on the Presidency, give an indication of how far we have now departed from the original plan. Herbert Hoover, after failing in repeated conferences to persuade leaders of his party in Congress to provide for "flexible tariff" rates: "I wrote out the provisions I wanted. I sent word that unless my formula was adopted the bill would be vetoed. The result was a complete victory." Franklin D. Roosevelt "was known to say to his aides, 'Give me a bill that I can veto' to remind legislators that they had the President to reckon with." Harry S Truman "vetoed a string of measures . . . peppering his sentences with vivid expletives like 'dangerous,' 'clumsy,' 'arbitrary,' 'impossible,' and 'drastic' not so much for the legislators as for the public."*

Powers were separated in designing the government in 1787 because the men who made the design believed that if certain

---

* Louis W. Koenig, *The Chief Executive* (New York: Harcourt, Brace and World, 1964), pp. 11, 139.

powers (capacities to act) were given to an official or to a group of men who could easily come to agreement, abuse of power would likely result. Undue or improper consolidation of capabilities for action would turn the system from republican government to tyranny. Checks and balances were intended to block the abuse of power; they were not intended to enlarge a capacity for abuse on the part of the branch of government that exercises the check. That this was the intention in providing for the appointment of ministers, judges, and other officials is attested in Hamilton's contributions to *The Federalist* (Nos. 76 and 77). The requirement of confirmation by the Senate would lessen the likelihood that unfit persons would be appointed. The risk in requiring Senate approval was that the President might be tempted to "corrupt or seduce" the senators.

It appears that surrender to temptation began very early. Senator Josiah Quincy of Massachusetts, speaking in the Senate in 1811, said:

with some highly honorable exceptions, it has been true in all past and will be true in all future Administrations, that the general way for members to obtain offices for themselves or their relatives is to coincide in opinion and vote with the Executive. . . . On every question which arises and has relation to Executive measures, in addition to all the other considerations of honor, policy, justice, propriety, and the like, this also is prepared to be thrown into the scale: that, if a man means to gain office, he must coincide with the Executive.*

Today we take it for granted that the President will use his power to appoint not simply to fulfill his executive obligations but to cause other men to further his ends in the discharge of their obligations. The public expects the President to name men to office less with a view to competent discharge of the office than with a view to securing enactment of legislation that would not be passed if inducements little short of bribery were not offered. Franklin D. Roosevelt may have been extreme in his resort to patronage for such ends but his behavior differs from other Presidents only in degree. During his first year in the White House, according to one of his immediate associates, Roosevelt held out in filling jobs until

the job seekers' principals had "delivered." Farley's talents [as manager of appointments] were stretched to capacity, but they proved adequate

---

* *Annals of Congress*, 11th Congress, 3rd session, pp. 847–848, January 30, 1811. In Hyneman and Carey, eds., *op. cit.*, pp. 178–179.

to their tasks. His formidable organization spread throughout the government, and its first assignment, the unpleasant one of standing fast until the emergency laws were on the books, making promises but making no deliveries, was efficiently carried out. By June matters had cleared so that the job-giving could begin. There was a feast to follow the fast. And Democrats in streams entered Washington's marble doors to disperse into the clerkships among the desks of the offices where the assistants to the assistants worked.*

The fact that the builders of our present political structure departed from the design of the original architects is not sufficient reason for concluding that the departures were unwise. We cannot be certain that the system would have survived if the original design had been adhered to closely. But it is equally true that general satisfaction with the system as it stands today is no guarantee that later generations will be content with what may have evolved between our time and theirs. For, unless one can find in the system some brake on its further evolution, he has to assume that circumstances not now foreseen will challenge political leaders as yet unborn to resort to acts that are not now contemplated. It would be a clear case of public foolishness to proceed on an assumption that because past innovations in the system produced no disasters, future innovations will not lead to disaster. It is the function of civic education, checks exerted by thoughtful and public spirited men on other men of power, and constitutional declarations to which men can appeal in times of dispute—it is the function of these three elements of a constitutional regime to preclude a march to disaster. And it is the function of political theory to provide textbooks in civic education, suggest principles of action for men who exercise power, and clarify objectives that may be attained in writing the language of constitutional documents.

In my opinion it is imperative that we do anew what the founders of this system did in the debates in constitutional conventions, in explanatory and polemical documents such as *The Federalist,* and in congressional debates during the formative years. We need again, and even more comprehensively and more systematically than the founders, to state clearly the manifestations of power to govern, ascertain how capacities to act may be meaningfully differentiated, calculate how the differentiable capacities to act may be distributed among offices (or branches of

* Rexford G. Tugwell, *The Democratic Roosevelt* (Garden City, N.Y.: Doubleday, 1957), p. 299.

government) with the twin results that government deals effectively with social problems and men restrain other men from abuses of authority, and to test every choice we have in constitutional structure against the necessity that those who exercise authority will answer to the people for what they do with their authority. The voluminous literature dealing with the Presidency elaborately describes what Presidents have done and clarifies the relationship of the executive to the other branches of government. In evaluation of those relationships, it tends to be polemical, making a case for enlarging the President's capacity to cause all branches of government to do what he wants done. One finds in this literature very little about the values (and how to maximize the values) of consultation and decision by agreement or compromise among men who are not subject to bribery or coercion by one who sets the terms of agreement or compromise.

Even more notable for its underdevelopment in this literature is severe analysis of the evidences that the people regularly or occasionally hold the President accountable for his performance. The act that pleases a voter is a claim for his support in the next election; when a balancing of satisfactions and dissatisfactions reveals that, for a majority of the voters, satisfactions substantially outweigh dissatisfactions, there ought to be a presumption that the electorate will return the incumbent President to office if he is eligible, or return his party to power if he is not eligible. But the practical difficulties of making the calculus are staggering. Recent satisfactions (e.g., a tax cut in election year) may obscure earlier dissatisfactions; the realization of satisfaction or dissatisfaction may depend on subsequent events, coming with a passage of time that finds the President dead before people can evaluate his act; the reports of what the government has done can deceive as well as inform, and an appearance of frankly reporting how a trustee discharged his obligations may cloak a subtle effort to convince the people that they ought to like what they are getting. Probably we face no more difficult job in evaluating our political system than that of defining and estimating the disciplinary power of the electorate in respect to the nation's most powerful single officer.

# 10. CONTROL OF ADMINISTRATION

The payoff of government is in its impact on the citizen. The payoff comes in two forms: declarations of public policy, and acts of administration.

If citizens voluntarily—unguided, unassisted, and unpressured by any further act of government—make their conduct conform to a provision of law, the payoff is in the policy announced in that law. If, however, further action by some arm of government is required to make the policy effective, we may think of those acts of administration as the payoff. Perhaps usually the payoff is dual; the declaration of policy is sufficient to set in motion important changes in behavior, but administrative activity by courts, police, or other agencies of government is required to obtain other changes the lawmakers had in mind. A judicial declaration that Negroes may not be denied accommodations in places serving the public was enough to secure their admission to motels operated by the great chains. However, further court orders were necessary to win their admission to many locally owned hotels, motels, restaurants, and bars in several cities of the South. The payoff that citizens expect when they secure the enactment of a law is often moderated, and sometimes nullified, at the level of administration. Indeed, the expected opposition to the enactment of a law may fail to show up at all because those who were expected to oppose the enactment figure they can protect their interests sufficiently by influencing the acts of administration.

It is obvious that the goals of democratic government are not realized if the acts of administrative officials are not in keeping with the expectations of the people. That is the concern we turn to now: securing compliance in public administration with the expectations and preferences of the people. Our inquiry will be directed toward two principal points of interest: the citizen's personal involvement in administration, and direction and control of administration by elected officials.

## Citizen Participation in Administration

The inquiry is best begun by noting some major differences in the circumstances under which administration occurs. Four main differentiations will suffice for our purpose. First are the activities of government carried on with no perceptible effect on the life of the citizen and often without his knowledge. The effort to maintain peaceful relations with other nations through diplomatic communications and provision of various kinds of aid to the developing states are examples. These activities have no immediate impact on life in the United States, either to disturb or tranquilize it. The citizen wishes only to be assured that he would approve of what is being done if he knew what was being done, that laudable objectives are actually being realized, and that their realization comes at a minimum cost in unwanted consequences including the unpleasantness of having to pay for what is done. Second are the services and benefits that government makes available to the citizen without any obligation on his part to take advantage of them. The postal service and old age assistance are examples. If any citizen does not want to mail a letter or pick up a check that he can have at the cost of filling out an application form, no public official will take him into court to force him to do so. For most parents and their children, opportunities for education in public schools fall in this category. For some, who do not respond as expected and excite a visit by the truant officer, public education falls in the third category. The third category is governmental activity intended to regulate the conduct of citizens (including business firms and other associations) and which presumes that coercion will be applied if voluntary compliance is not forthcoming. Criminal law is the most familiar example. Finally, in the classification of administrative activities useful for our purpose, is the collection of taxes. If taxes are as certain as death, like death they close the accounts on everything. The citizen as taxpayer helps pay for governmental activities that he considers superfluous, luxurious, or reprehensible just as surely as he helps pay for the activities he favors.

It becomes apparent on the most casual contemplation that these varying circumstances have enormous implications for the organization of administration. A permanent working force of public officials and employees must handle all of the class one activities. A publicly employed working force will provide the noncompulsory services and benefits, although individual recipients will do many of the acts necessary for their enjoyment. My father was the truant officer for his children; volunteer help reduces the need for employees in public schools and hospitals; the business firm meters its mail; the trade association informs its members of changes in the law, instructs them as to their rights and obligations, and urges them to cushion the impact of new requirements by good-humored cooperation with public officials. In the area of sanctioned regulations and criminal law cooperation of the general public is essential to realization of the purposes which the law was designed to further. Doctors police the pharmacists; the scheduled airlines patrol their frontiers with the contract carriers; you and I are traffic officers when your snarls discipline the reckless driver and my patient explanation convinces Grandma that she need not pull to the extreme right in order to start a left turn. Finally, contemplate the prospect for additional employees in the federal Internal Revenue Service if citizens refused to report their incomes and employers refused to withhold taxes in making out their pay checks.

This interweaving of two realms, the citizen's pursuit of his personal interests and the achievement of goals announced by government, makes it inevitable that public administration will provide a meeting ground for the two explanations of how the democratic ideal is achieved in our political system—the thesis that the important acts of government are responses to the demands of competing groups and the thesis that the electorate, by selecting and replacing public officials, effectively determines what government will do. If one endorses the second explanation, putting his faith in the populist demand-response system, he must have confidence that the day-to-day administration of public policies is mainly in the hands of officials and employees who are attentive to direction and control by elected officials. But such a person cannot escape the conclusion that, if the people who are governed share in the execution of governmental objectives as I have indicated, the conflicting objectives of these governed and self-governing people will also have a substantial effect on the final impact of public policies. The adherent of the group-competition thesis, contemplating the same scene of practical administration, will have to acknowledge that public officials do not act strictly as neutral referees, carefully measuring the competing demands and finally ratifying the administrative actions that best reflect immediate pressures. If he admits that public officials have some discretion in determining the impact of public policies and acknowledges that they respond to instructions from elected officials who are conscious of a need to please the electorate—in that case the adherent of the group-competition thesis must concede that the populist demand-response system is inextricably interleaved with the pluralist demand-response system.

The argument between the two schools of thought, therefore, is not about which one of the two demand-response systems represents reality, but rather, what is the relative importance of each demand-response system? Where in the political structure does each manifest itself most convincingly? In what sectors of American life does each realize its greatest or most persistent victories? Under what circumstances do the two systems oppose one another or complement one another or combine for a cumulative effect?

I have asserted from time to time that we have made considerable progress in efforts to construct theory applicable to the populist demand-response system, e.g., in respect to behavior of electorates, role of parties, consequences of electoral actions, how representation may be achieved. This branch of study has an ancient lineage. Many items which we read with great interest today were written long before the emergence of a political science discipline in this country. Much less effort has been expended on study that fixes attention primarily on the pluralist system, and most of the writing that offers promise for development of theory is the product of the twentieth century. We have, in this brief period, done much of the necessary pre-theory investigation. We have made descriptive incursions into particular organizations and their activities, grappled with problems of conception, definition, and ordering of phenomena, and speculated about what definitive inquiry will reveal when definitive inquiry has been made. I think it fair to say, however, that the great enterprise of theory-making has scarcely begun. This is the case whether one supposes that the impact of group effort is greatest at the legislative and top executive levels or greatest at the level of administration where the payoff for influence in government is so often realized.

If I am unduly pessimistic and ought to say that construction of theory relating to the pluralist demand-response system is coming along at good pace, I will still attest my lack of enthusiasm by saying that this literature suffers from paucity of neutral analysis and an oversupply of personal convictions and preferences. Certainly much of the writing about the relations of organized groups to the formation and administration of public policy is pervaded by polemical objectives. Three manifestations of bias are most apparent. In some writings there is an acknowledged impatience with, if not disdain for, the common man. The writer, seeing little prospect that the people can control their government through elections, pins his hopes on a resolution of demands and pressures that are heaped upon public officials by spokesmen for competing groups. Having endorsed the group competition process as the best means of securing decisions and acts that will be acceptable to the whole population, these writers tend to inflate the evidence that this process produces the results they ascribe to it. In sharp disagreement with this view of what occurs in the pluralist arena is a line of analysis, argument, and innuendo which claims that the dominant purpose of those who speak for groups, at whatever point in government they appear, is to aggrandize the interests of an identifiable minority, and that the successes of such minorities can ordinarily be entered on the books as a direct cost imposed on an undefined greater number of people called a majority. The bias in this case is in favor of the equalization-of-influence explanation of how the democratic ideal is achieved. The third bias which I discern appears in some of the writing that is concerned primarily with government at the administrative end. It seems to me that some of these critics squeeze the available evidence pretty hard to show that group intervention in government results in serious disturbance of orderly relationships in administration, decrease of efficiency, and departure from equal protection of the law.

Distribution of advantage—who gets what, when, and through what instruments of government—is undoubtedly a most promising starting point for theoretic statements about the pluralist demand-response system. I have, in this essay and elsewhere, declared my confidence that polemical writing and the presentation of normative doctrine can give impetus to analytic study and bring gifts of imagination to theory construction. Indeed, I may properly be charged with considerable boldness in stating my own preferences and personal convictions about how the good life can be achieved through instruments of government. Be that as it may, the likelihood of theoretic statements surviving in a heuristic literature will be greatly increased if those statements stem from an objective scrutiny of reality, untinctured by the wishful thinking that so frequently intrudes when the main objective of the student's enterprise is to advance particular values or ends to which he is attached. Three examples of how interest groups are drawn into administration of public policies will indicate how easy it is to leap, without aid of further evidence, from observed facts about what men have done to conclusions about motives for their actions and judgments about social gains and losses likely to accrue from their acts. The experience we will consider relates to licensing of professions, regulatory commissions, and elected farm committees.

Practitioners of medicine serve on the boards that admit physicians to the profession by issuing licenses and remove physicians from the profession by revoking licenses. It is inevitable, if their decisions are based on evidence and application of judgment, that the acts of the licensing board will partially determine how many men and women will divide the business that goes to doctors. It is probable that if the board consistently refuses licenses to the graduates of a particular medical school, young people will be discouraged from attending that school or, in order to escape that result, changes will be made in the curriculum and faculty of the school.

This brief statement of what occurs invites a conclusion that assigning doctors to license doctors is a fine way to improve the standards of medical practice and medical training. But the facts also invite a conclusion that doctors who are set up in business try to hold down the numbers who will divide up the business, and that doctors who have been out of medical school for some years use their licensing power to discourage innovations in training which they will not go to the trouble to understand. No doubt we are sufficiently skilled in empirical inquiry to find out why the doctors decide as they do, and what effect their decisions have on the total supply of doctors. Possibly we might measure the impact of their decisions on the development of medical training. But we are not now in a position to design the research that would answer these questions: what price does the society pay, in terms of its mental and physical well being, for the existing rather than another relationship of number of doctors to quality of medical service? What provision for selection, instruction, and discipline of medical examiners can be counted on to produce any reallocation of social gains and losses that may be thought preferable to the present distribution? If a sure method of reallocating social gains and losses is found, how can we tell whether the people who prefer the new regime outnumber those who would rather have kept things as they were? These questions are surely pertinent to the design and improvement of democratic institutions and procedures. If they are answered to common satisfaction, it will be done by inquiry that is guided by theory.

Regulatory commissions—e.g., the Interstate Commerce Commission, the Federal Communications Commission, or a state Public Utilities Board—are sometimes referred to as captive bodies, thought to have been captured by men of power in business firms that the commissioners are supposed to regulate. One sometimes reads that agents of the regulated industries police the governmental organizations that were established to do the regulating, protecting the regulators from attack by those who would change the regulatory policies, or even that men who are supposed to be regulated worm their way into seats on the regulatory tribunal and help fashion the policies which they must comply with in their business activities. Let us presume that the charges are warranted. Behavior that college professors have viewed as evidence of an intent by vested interests to preserve a benign authority may have had the less sinister purpose of maintaining in the government a spot where the regulated firm can find a person who at the same time has enough knowledge to understand a complicated problem and enough authority to say finally what government will do about that problem. The efforts of a congressman to support a business firm before the regulatory authority or to protect the regulatory authority from invasion by the President and his administrative entourage may indeed be a response to pressures put upon the congressman by a particular business firm or by spokesmen for an imposing sector of industrial interest. It may also be motivated by the congressman's fear that if he does not intervene in behalf of the firm he will have given an opponent the club he needed to beat him down in the next campaign for re-election.

Let us suppose that the worst suspicions of the critics of regulation by quasi-independent commission are justified. My guess is that a very high percentage of veteran congressmen are even better informed than most of the critics as to how agents of the regulated enterprises join hands with public officials to provide a regime of partial self-regulation. My further guess is that they believe this is the way it ought to be. Congressmen had a choice as to whether regulation should be imposed in the first place, and they wrote the policies they thought needed to guide that regulation. It is not hard to believe that they thought leaders in the regulated industries ought to have a hand, but not an exclusive hand, in making the extensions and modifications of policy that necessarily take place when the requirements of a statute are put into effect. If one were certain that this is the way most congressmen felt about it when they instituted regulation or when they rejected proposals to change it, he could hardly ask for a more convincing confirmation of my contention that the populist and the pluralist systems are inextricably mixed at the administrative level of government.

In the case of our elected farm committees, intent and result are clear and in full accord. The controlling statute specifies that committees chosen by farmers shall be utilized in administering the federal crop control program. Congress wrote this requirement into the law after five years of experience with price support for farm products, during which period elected committees authorized by the Secretary of Agriculture had actively participated in administration. Evidence which need not be cited strongly supports a conclusion that the use of elected committees has continued to enjoy the favor of most congressmen who display a live interest in agricultural legislation.

In an earlier reference to these committees, I said that their authority to fit national policy to local needs is limited but still significant. One illustration of the discretion they exercise will suffice. Disposition of acreage allotments is a constantly recurring problem that calls for investigation and exercise of judgment by the local committee. Allotments (the right to plant a certain number of acres with a particular crop) are made to farms, not to individuals who own or operate farms. When one half of a farm is sold, the buyer does not automatically acquire one half of the allotment, and the buyer and seller cannot determine in the sales agreement how the right to grow the allotted number of acres will be divided between them. The elected farm committee will distribute the right to grow the specified number of acres fixed for every crop cited in the allotments made to the farm. In so doing it will take into account several factors, including the comparative fertility or productivity of the land that is sold and the land retained, the particular fields where each crop was grown in recent years, and what crops the purchaser intends to grow on the part he bought. The business can be quite complicated when a practitioner of diversified farming retires and rents parts of his farm to different farmers or when he dies and the farm must be distributed among several heirs.

The dependence on farm committees that I have briefly described has been the subject of some apprehension by political scientists. It is supposed that the advantages accruing to farmers from the federal program represent costs that must be borne by people who consume farm products, and therefore that a provision for farmers to administer the program is an invitation for farmers to shift costs from themselves to other parts of the population. Fears that arise on this score may be unwarranted. It is my own judgment, informed by a limited study of the price support program, that the significant decisions determining the magnitude of social costs or materially affecting their distribution among the population were made by Congress or by the top officials of the Department of Agriculture. The elected committees and the state committees appointed by the Secretary of Agriculture do make decisions that distribute benefits and costs among the farmers of the area. It must be supposed that their authority to do this is a gateway to favoritism, since farmers often put on quite a campaign to recompose a committee when election time approaches. The alternative administrative arrangement that comes to mind would charge professional administrators with the authority now lodged in the committees. Between the prospect of locally seated favoritism and the discomforts and disappointments inherent in doing business with a bureaucracy directed from Washington, many farmers apparently prefer to take their chance with favoritism.

I·brought these three cases up for special attention to remove several things from any possibility of doubt. It should not be doubted that citizens secure response to their expectations and preferences by resort to two demand-response systems: one set of relationships connecting voters, elected officials, and administrative personnel in a chain of demands and responses that pays high tribute to the ideal of equality; and another mix of relationships connecting citizens and firms, elected officials, and administrative personnel in a network of demands and responses that pays tribute to displays of power rather than the ideals of equality. These two systems are in operation at the same moment and at the same points of decision, and are addressed to the same complex of interests. It ought not be doubted, finally, that the phenomena (manifestations, acts) of one system will be hard to distinguish from phenomena of the other system, if indeed the same act may not in many instances be regarded as integral to both systems.

If one sees these things as I do, he will conclude that hope of understanding one of the two systems depends on a comparable understanding of the other, and therefore that the development of theory to guide study of one system cannot progress very far until theory-making gets underway on the other front also. One of the many shortcomings of my own effort lies in the fact that I have not systematically examined the phenomena of the pluralist demand-response system. Granting this, I proceed from this point on the presumption that something may be gained from a presentation of my views about the expected consequences of direction and control of administration by elected officials and the prospect that such direction and control can be attained and preserved. This is a subject on which I have written at length. I shall not summarize my book *Bureaucracy in a Democracy,* but rather shall record here some convictions and some puzzlements that were heavy on my mind at a time when I was a participant observer of administration and which are prominent in my thinking today. The pages that follow are drawn largely from an essay I wrote during World War II when the President was exercising extraordinary authority and when excessive concentrations of power in Europe and Asia were a cause of genuine alarm for all champions of democratic government. That essay was boldly polemical in character, and while I have taken some of the edge off contentious statements the pages immediately following retain an argumentative tone. I think there may be some profit for the reader in this display of my personal position, even if it stands in sharp contrast to the mood of neutral inquiry I have tried to maintain heretofore.

## Direction and Control by Elected Officials

The basic design of American government creates a formidable obstacle to effective political control of public administration. The high administrative official finds himself answering to two bosses. He is instructed, criticized, and sometimes thwarted by Congress. And he is expected to please the President, with a prospect of losing his job if he fails to do so. This unhappy circumstance invites a constitutional change which would strip Congress of its power to supervise and discipline, and make the President supreme in control of the administrative branch. There is great risk in this solution, however, for the ability of the people to control the President would be endangered.

Political control of administration—i.e., the subjection of the appointed officials to the elected officials—is inextricably bound up with the enactment of legislation and the appropriation of money. And the basic design of our government makes Congress and President near-equal participants in lawmaking and appropriations. If Congress alone answered directly to the people and the President answered only to Congress, then it might be feasible to make the appointed officials answerable only to the President. But our constitutional plan does not feature such a chain of command. The people elect Congress to make public policy and fund the operations of government, but they elect the President to share in these acts. The congressmen may boast that they are closer to the people, but the President may retort that he is the only officer chosen by the entire nation. When Congress and President are at loggerheads on an important issue of policy, the President may conceive that he rather than Congress correctly reads the wishes of the people.

A desire for orderliness prompts us to demand that the chief administrative officials report to a single authority, and the design of our government makes the President alone a suitable candidate for that responsibility. But if we give the President full command of administration, we combine in one office a persuasive influence in making public policy and a commanding influence in its execution. The President thus becomes co-determiner of how the ends of government shall finally be realized. The joinder of power to make public policy with the power to execute it is the first requisite for despotism. And the joinder of these powers in a single official has long been recognized as an invitation to dictatorship. Yet this is a condition toward which the American people have been marching for a full century, and a condition that many political scientists urge us to bring to full realization without further delay.

This is the dilemma. If the chief executive, having the great mass of administrative power (the bureaucracy) under him, does not conform to the policies made by the elected policy making authority, dictatorship is incipient. But the chief executive who commands that mass of bureaucratic power is himself the acknowledged leader of the policy makers and has the greatest prestige of all of them. How are we to resolve this dilemma? How can we free the President to lead, to insist, to coerce perhaps in getting established the policies to which he pledged himself in order to win election to his high office, yet make it impossible for him to use the power he commands in defiance of the wishes of the people?

Writing on this problem falls generally into three schools of thought. First are those writers who propose that the President be made responsible to Congress, giving up his office when Congress no longer has confidence in him or is no longer willing to follow his leadership. These writers would have the United States imitate the British cabinet system. The President and Congress would be elected on the same day (whether to continue the overlapping six year terms of senators would be a

problem); the President would be the acknowledged standard
bearer of the victorious party and the acknowledged leader of
Congress; he would have responsibility for driving Congress to
enact the policies to which he and his party are pledged and
for driving the bureaucracy to put those policies into effect. But
if he turned out to be a weakling, proved incapable of keeping
faith with his pledges, or proved to be a would-be dictator, the
Congress would forthwith turn him out of power and send him
back to the people to try to sell his theories all over again.

This system, when it works as planned, presents many very
admirable advantages. If the top party leader and official (Prime
Minister, President) has proper devices to discipline the legislature when it fails to keep faith with the party's pledges, more
unity of leadership and followship can be achieved than we
frequently have under our system. If the top man proves too
greedily bound for power, the legislature, being many men chosen
from many and diverse constituencies, can be counted on to resist
him. And the cabinet system does provide a way of getting issues
before the people when it seems desirable, without waiting for
the lapse of a four-year term as we do.

Assuming that the British system worked perfectly in Britain,
it would not be easy to decree as successful a form of parliamentary
responsibility for us. The British political machinery has many
gadgets which were developed through generations of experience.
They are geared into the political ways of the British people, and
are essential to the functioning of their system. They have a king,
they have in a showdown only one house of Parliament to deal with,
they elect no official on a nationwide ticket as we do the President.
We could hardly throw out our system lock, stock and barrel in
favor of what the British have developed over the centuries. If
we try to graft their flower on our stalk, we may get a fruit we do
not want. In any event we would have to start all over again
on the task that requires generations in any democracy, that of
bringing the people up to the point where they understand their
system of government and have confidence in their ability to
control it.

The second school of thought on how to reconcile the President's
power with the nation's safety may be called the "power and
faith" school. The doctrine of this school is: give the President
plenty of power, and have faith that he will not abuse it. Its
argument runs something like this: people do not overthrow their
institutions while they are prospering under them; the power of
government can be used to assure that the nation will be pros-

perous; governmental action to that end must be planned, courageous and forceful; planned, courageous and forceful government
can be obtained only under integrated leadership free from
obstruction; such leadership can be found only in the President;
and he must have sufficient power in his own right to thrust the
government forward on social programs that assure prosperity
for the people.

Thus is the case established for power. The argument in support
of faith is not so well developed. The people elect the President;
he represents them; indeed he is the only true representative for
the whole people since members of the House represent their
respective districts and senators their respective states; the people
would not elect as their representatives in the top place of power
a man who would turn against them; and if they did, they would
turn him out before he could do any great damage.

Some writings that have appeared since I first wrote on this
problem at the close of World War II support the endorsement
of a powerful Presidency with proposals for reform of the party
system, the writer believing that the proposed changes would
engender a quicker and more certain compliance, by both President and congressmen, with the promises made in the campaigns
that brought them to office. This later analysis and argument
has not removed the doubts that I expressed twenty years ago.
Now as then, I am neither confident that the proposed changes
in the party system can be accomplished nor convinced that if
made they would secure the certainty and fullness of response to
public expectations that I think requisite for democratic government.

There is a third school of thought on the resolution of the
dilemma presented by the need for vigorous Presidential leadership and the necessity of restraining the President from using
his power contrary to the wishes of the people. This school
accepts as permanent our present system of Congress and President
with the authority given them in the Constitution, but seeks
to achieve a better balance in the interplay of their powers. This
school would arm the President for more effective leadership in
the formulation of policy, but would also increase the power of
Congress to force an accounting as to how the executive power
is used. I see much that is attractive in the changes they would
bring about.

The apprehensions that stirred me to write about political
control of administration two decades ago were aggravated by
the readiness of Congress to permit the President to do by decree

what is customarily done by statute. A similar though less extensive enlargement of the President's authority occurred in the first World War. There is a patent necessity to vest extraordinary power in the chief executive in times of great national danger. There are risks in doing this, however, and the question of how much power to delegate is debatable. My own bias favors a marked conservatism on this point. In my opinion experience has proved that the values of democratic government are best secured if fundamental policy is made and changed only with the concurrence of a representative assembly. When decisions are made by or concurred in by an assembly consisting of a considerable number of individuals chosen by the people from a broad base of independent constituencies and in a position to give their principal attention to the public business, the best protection of the public interest is achieved. When power to make public policy by his sole action is vested in the chief executive too much invitation is given for the *coup d'état*, too much opportunity to move by *fait accompli*.

Perhaps no more need be said on that point. But it should be noted that the President's use of broad powers to make policy, in my opinion, has had a secondary effect of great seriousness. As I see it, the functioning of government by Presidential decree has engendered in the bureaucracy widespread and deplorable disrespect for Congress and other democratic controls. The fact that the President has been permitted to decree so much of the policy continuously since the advent of the New Deal and the fact that Presidents showed so much audacity in exercising that authority on occasions, have caused heads of agencies, bureau chiefs, and more lowly civil servants to believe that Congress is not competent to pass on policies of crucial importance. The fact that the President and his self-appointed advisers did so much of the country's thinking for it has caused many people in the bureaucracy to think that the chief executive and the administrative branch constitute an elite more fit than either the people or their elected representatives to say what is good for the people.

My remarks up to this point have been concerned mainly with the possibility that Congress has receded from its proper place in our governmental system, and that the President has acquired a primacy in fixing public policy and executing it that makes his office a menace to the democratic way in government. If the executive power, inflated in recent decades in its public leadership and legislative aspects, is augmented by a firm control over the vast numbers of people who compose the administrative arms of government, the visage of the President as a menace to government by the people is sharpened. It is important to ascertain, if we can, how the great administrative organizations are subjected to central direction and control. Can a President, benign in purpose, compel the administrative organizations to pursue faithfully the courses of action laid out for them by the elected branches of government? Can a President, bent on further aggrandizement of his personal pre-eminence, be thwarted if he undertakes to use the administrative organizations to that end? Clearly the President has the power to point the administrative departments toward one goal or another and to inspire bureaucracy for good or for evil. But just how much power does he have? How much influence can he exert on the policies and purposes of departments? What can he actually do, for instance, to force efficiency into an organization where efficiency is notoriously lacking?

The writings of political scientists during the first half of this century were overwhelmingly in agreement that the President can exert a complete, dominating, and conclusive control over the bureaucracy if the administrative branch is properly organized and if the President is given proper staff assistance. This is the assumption on which that most influential document, the *Report of the President's Committee on Administrative Management,* was based. This document, submitted to the President and to Congress in 1937, proposed a tightening up of the hierarchical structure which establishes a chain of control from top to bottom through the power of superiors to appoint and remove subordinates. It recommended a great expansion of the staff that reports directly to the President and urged action by Congress which would enable it to check more effectively the activities of the President and the administrative branch. A decade later the first Hoover Commission (The Commission on Organization of the Executive Branch of the Government, 1949) took essentially the same position. These presumptions and convictions about the pervasiveness of Presidential power have been roughly shaken by recent writings which stress the social costs involved in changing the pace and direction of great administrative organizations. They suggest that only a sense of desperate need would justify an intrusion into any of the major federal departments with a view to significant alteration of its ways.

In my opinion, the thesis that has predominated in the American literature of public administration rests on questionable suppositions about the realities of management. It seems to me doubtful that any President, no matter how determined he may be to do so, can maintain an intimate personal knowledge of what is going on in the empire over which he presides. Can the President, in view of the demands on his time, ever know the main features of the policies on which the government is engaged? Can he give enough time to even the top persons in his administration to hear them point out the choices that must be made on the pressing issues of policy? Can he ever do more in the coordination of departments than say "Get together!"? When public clamor or the intense heat of intra-administration warfare forces him to act, can he act with more precision than to smash with an axe?

Surely he can on some issues. The President is for spending federal money on housing or he is against it. If no houses are being built, he can find out why if he wants to, and he can take time to find out why at least once. If it is because his housing program has fallen afoul of the policies of the federal loan agencies, he can demand that the several departments get together and he may even find time to hear the main arguments and contribute his own judgment to a solution.

I do not think the President can do much of this, however. There are not enough hours in a day or enough days in a four year term for a human being to do the other things that the President cannot escape doing, and also give much attention to the direction of administrative departments.

It seems to me that the supervision and coordination of the administrative branch is much more an institutional operation than an act of the President. It is a matter of the way the Bureau of the Budget acts on the plans of departments—both the announced policies of the Director of the Bureau and the undisclosed standards of judgment which the budget examiners adhere to. It is a matter of intelligent action—and unfeeling bureaucratic resistance to action—in the Civil Service Commission. It is a matter of General Accounting Office attitudes toward departmental expenditures which hell and high water could not change.

The Bureau of the Budget, the Civil Service Commission, the General Accounting Office and a host of other offices integrate and coordinate the activities of the administrative branch. The President, nevertheless, can personally exert an enormous influence upon the pace and quality of administration. He can encourage this, reverse that, and make decisions which enliven the whole tone of administration, and he can also take the heart out of everyone who likes to see order, confidence and mutual good will among officials.

The time-honored way of keeping the chief executive and the

administrative branch in hand is to set up a representative assembly to control them. Without exception, every nation that makes any pretense at having popular government depends on an elected assembly to restrain and guide if not to control the chief executive and the bureaucracy. The downfall of absolute monarchies was accomplished by the establishment of parliaments, and one of the very first moves of any dictator is to destroy the legislative body.

The explanation of the power of the representative assembly is as simple as it seems at first glance. Barring an act of God, there is nothing to control the action of men except the action of other men. The representative assembly, in our case Congress, is chosen by separate constituencies scattered from one end of the country to the other. The voters in these constituencies can be just as independent as their interests and their courage incline them to be, and the representatives they send to Congress can and do defy the President when conscience or local interest dictates. It is a great honor to serve in Congress and men of ambition go out for it. Most of the constituencies are populous (entire states in the case of senators) and generally it takes tough men to win the seats and hold them.

Congressmen are pretty stout politicians, and there are a lot of them accumulated in the two chambers. No President has ever succeeded in lining them all up, even in time of war. Rarely if ever does a President have a firm hold even on the loyalty of all members of his own party. An assembly like this is a fatal obstruction to the ambitions of a would-be dictator. Concepts of public interest, loyalty to established institutions and practices, considerations of local, special or personal advantage—all of these things combine to block the autocrat's path to power.

The effectiveness of the representative assembly depends on the quality of the men who are elected to it and the power they have over the making and enforcement of the nation's policies. The quality of the men will be determined by the health and vigor of the entire political system of the country. If the people are concerned about public affairs, if the people are reasonably in control of the local elements of party organization, if the national organization of parties is firmly based on the local party organizations—then it may be taken for granted that as high a quality of men will be sent to the national assembly as the prestige and authority of that body invites.

The methods by which the legislature holds the chief executive and the administrative departments in check are pretty well standardized throughout the world. Save where constitutional provision interferes, acts of the legislature create administrative departments, and determine much of their internal organization and procedures. In enacting the laws which determine what the government is to do for the people, the legislature specifies in varying amounts of detail how the departments shall accomplish these purposes. The legislature appropriates money for the maintenance of administrative departments and for their use in achieving the objectives prescribed by law. Ordinarily such grants are hedged about by precautions as to what the money is to be used for and how it is to be paid out. The legislature constantly shouts its dissatisfaction with administration, questions and criticizes, and may carry investigation to the point of thorough exploration and exposure. Finally, it may have the power to remove the chief executive, department heads, and lesser officials from office—in this country by the seldom used impeachment method and in many other countries by forcing resignation on a vote refusing support to the government of the day.

A legislative assembly composed of independent, courageous and intelligent men may still fail to control the executive-administrative branch because it is not organized to exercise effectively the powers which it has. This is generally admitted to be the case with Congress today. Senators and representatives are as competent and as public spirited a group as any nation is likely to get together in such numbers by any device that might be tried. The powers of Congress under the Constitution give it ample authority for any purpose it could reasonably want to accomplish. But many of the strongest champions of a vigorous legislative power are convinced that Congress is not adequately organized to accomplish its purposes. Congress allows itself to be tied up with matters of local or special concern that divert its attention from matters of greater national importance; it does not maintain a staff adequate to do the investigation and give it the advice which it requires; it destroys any chance of a systematic and coordinated attack on questions of public policy by the way in which it splits up its business and parcels it out to committees; it does not have good working relations with the President; and it has not provided itself with adequate facilities for the continuous review of administrative action.

The relation of Congress to the administrative branch has been the subject of several careful studies since World War II. I doubt, however, that there is more agreement now than there was before the war as to what should be regarded as ideal. There appears to be no dissent from the proposition that Congress should maintain a firm hand on the allocation of money to administrative departments by enacting appropriation laws, but there is a widespread conviction that Congress frequently defeats its own purposes by the limitations it imposes on the way appropriations may be spent. No one will deny that Congress should have the power to bring important new departments into existence, but there will be plenty of argument as to how fully the lawmakers should control the internal structure of the departments and the allocation of activities among departments. Political scientists who would give the President a considerable authority over the structure of departments and the allocation of activities among them will disagree as to whether the President should be able to act finally or should send his reorganization proposals to Congress for approval, modification, or rejection.

No doubt everybody who has thought seriously about how popular control of government can be achieved will insist that all new ventures into the regulation of private affairs and substantial alterations of the services to be provided by government should be decided by enactment of statutes. Opinions will differ sharply, however, as to how much detail should be written into the statutes and how much authority to render broad policies into working programs should be delegated to administrative departments. While everyone readily acknowledges that Congress should have sufficient power to determine whether its policies are being carried out, political scientists will take many different positions when asked how much inquiry, suggestion, and sharp reprimand Congress may subject the administrative official to when it inquires into what he has been doing.

I said earlier that I think that the central control to which the bureaucracy responds comes more from an institutional apparatus around the President than from the President himself. I am by no means certain that the men who constitute this institutional apparatus in turn respond either to the will of the President or the will of Congress with the readiness that I think desirable. If I were convinced that the President could supply the personal direction that some writers attribute to him, I would want Congress to maintain a close watch on what he does and what the administrative departments do under his direction.

It is commonly asserted that whatever Congress needs to do in the way of control over the executive-administrative branch can be done by enactment of statutes, appropriation of money, and formal investigation of alleged abuses of power. It must be appreciated, however, that congressmen will not know what legislation to enact, how to appropriate intelligently, or when to investigate unless they maintain close contact with administrative departments. If congressmen are close enough to the bureaucracy to get the information they need for proper legislative action, they are pretty certain to make suggestions as to how the department can do a better job of carrying out the intent of statutes and appropriations. If, as I suspect, the kind of knowledge that will support intelligent legislation can be had only at the cost of some meddling by congressmen in the day-to-day operations of administrative departments, I am willing to let the top officials in those departments and the bureaucrats under them bear that cross.

# IV

*Limited Government*

# 11. GOVERNMENT BY LAW

This essay opened with a statement that the American political system rests on two foundation principles. Government is controlled by and answers to the people, and government's power over the people is restricted in scope and restrained in method. We have completed our examination of the first of these two concepts. We turn now to the second commitment, that government in the United States shall be limited government.

The limitations that are imposed on government cannot be sharply differentiated. Any way you classify them, they shade into one another; one type of limitation supports and reinforces each of the other types. Recognizing this hindrance to orderly presentation, I shall name six standards that have guided American practice. They are imperfectly realized, but nevertheless they help explain what we charge our governments to do and largely account for the safeguards we erect against abuse of authority. (1) The scope of governmental activity ought to be limited. (2) Authority to make decisions and perform the acts of government should be lodged only in offices worthy of the power to be exercised. (3) All citizens should enjoy equal protection of the laws. (4) All acts of government should be addressed to the welfare of the whole population. (5) Specific restrictions should regulate the way public officials proceed in the exercise of their authority. (6) Abuse of power should be discouraged by dispersing the authority of government.

The last standard in the foregoing list will not be further considered. It is made effective in two principal ways: by dividing the business of governing among many governments; and within each government, by providing for separation of powers and checks and balances. The first method of dispersing power was examined to some extent above in the section titled "Distributed Self-Government." The other style of dispersal, separation of powers and checks and balances, figured prominently in the two chapters preceding this one.

The present chapter deals with the first four standards in the list of six. As rules governing the construction of governments, they pre-date the adoption of written constitutions in this country. Recognizing that I take liberties with a term familiar in Anglo-American law, I shall refer to these four standards as "government by law." The next chapter deals with the restraints on governmental authority which are expressed in the Constitution of the United States. That discussion is extended in two other chapters devoted to certain conflicts of value in public policies that impinge on freedom of speech.

## The Scope of Government Activity

It is logical to start our examination of limited government with the most comprehensive limitations, those that bound the scope of governmental activity. A casual review of the history of public policy in the United States makes it obvious that our governments have persistently refrained from invasion of certain areas of affairs or aspects of life. First to come to mind are the intimate relations of the family, religion, and a vast realm not sharply defined but commonly referred to as free business enterprise. A brief look at the relation of government to each of these sectors will inform us on two matters. One, are there specified boundaries to the political domain? Can one identify areas of human affairs appropriate for regulation by government and differentiate them from other areas of affairs that are out of bounds for government? Two, if there are such boundary lines or frontiers, what are the sources of the prohibitions that keep public officials from crossing them?

Denials of authority to invade an area of affairs or sector of life, regardless of the source, will hereafter be referred to as substantive limitations. The three cases to be examined—family, religion, and business—will reveal that constitutional language and inhibitions rooted in firmly held convictions of the population are inextricably interwoven. They unite to provide substantive limitations on government, but we shall see that uncrossable frontiers are hard to find, if indeed they exist at all.

There is nothing in the United States Constitution or its amendments that refers especially to the relations of husband and wife or of parents and children, neither a denial of power to intervene in such relations nor a regulation as to how a power to intervene shall be exercised. Nor am I aware of anything in a state constitution that comes closer to this subject than a provision that married women may own and dispose of property and share in the property of the husband. There is, however, constitutional language that judges can use to stop government at the threshold of the home if they want to do so. In the national Constitution are two requirements that deprivations of liberty must accord with due process of law, two statements that the privileges and immunities of citizens shall not be breached, and a reference in the ninth amendment to rights retained by the people. If any statutes have been denied enforcement on the ground that these constitutional provisions forbid government to invade the home, they have not figured prominently in the literature I have read.

The family is not completely insulated against the touch of government, to be sure. The marriage contract is regulated by law, divorce is a court proceeding, children are sometimes taken from their parents and put under the care of persons named by a judge. Intervention for these and other reasons is reluctantly made and definitely exceptional, however; the general rule is that lawmakers and public officials are totally indifferent to what goes on in the home.

How shall we account for the fact that government does not intrude into family life, admittedly a realm in which the damage caused by cruelty is lasting and antisocial behavior is often seeded by parental influence? Should we say that our governments are not restrained from a general intervention into the family but, instead, that lawmakers have voluntarily chosen not to invade that realm? Or should we say that our governments operate under severe restraints that are not imposed by constitutional provisions?

I think the generation that produced the United States Constitution would generally have given the second answer. They were devoted to a conception of rights derived from nature and believed that no government could justify violations of those natural rights. They thought it useful to formulate statements of those rights in constitutional documents as best they could. But there was also at the time a considerable doubt that setting limits to power in controlling documents would have much effect on what lawmakers would actually do. Few people appear to have anticipated that constitutions would come to have the great symbolic power that the United States Constitution now has. There was no ground for certainty that judges would refuse to enforce statutes which they thought to overstep the bounds fixed in constitutions. Some persons made clear an apprehension that if some specific limitations were written into a constitution, this would create a presumption that government was free to do anything that had not been specifically prohibited. Listening to an argument in Congress that a Bill of Rights was needed to make sure that the inherent rights of the people would not be infringed, Representative Sedgwick of Massachusetts asked whether that principle did not require a declaration that a man had a right to wear a hat if he pleased, to get up when he pleased, and to go to bed when he thought proper.

It is a matter of some consequence today how one answers the question: Why do our governments not readily intervene in the intimate relationships of the family? If one thinks the abstention from intervention is wholly independent of constitutional language, it may be of no importance whether he concludes that the lawmakers have not wished to intervene, or that they fear disapproval and discipline by their constituents, or that they are restrained by identifiable cultural or societal norms which are the products of past generations and at least tacitly approved by the present generation. But it makes a big difference for one's views about how to achieve democratic ideals in government if he rejects the three alternatives just mentioned and concludes that lawmakers do not try to intervene in family life because they suppose that judges would invoke a constitution to nullify their efforts. If he takes the latter position he attributes a role to judges that makes the organization of the judiciary and the selection of judges a problem of undeniable importance. It also seems likely that his vision of the comparative utilities of the two demand-response systems—populist and pluralist, will differ considerably from that of a man who supposes that the family is immune from political control because the people elect officials who think the home ought to be out of bounds for government.

Religion is the area of affairs that comes closest to complete immunity from government in the United States. The first amendment to the Constitution asserts that "Congress shall make no law respecting an establishment of religion, or prohibiting the free exercise thereof." The reference is to Congress and law, but the inhibition applies to all arms and agents of the national government and to all kinds of acts. In recent years, the Supreme Court has extended the prohibitions of the First Amendment to state and local governments by reading its restraints into the due process of law clause of the Fourteenth Amendment. These denials of power to intrude into the realm of religion are reinforced by

guarantees of religious freedom included in all our state constitutions.

In spite of repeated assertions by one of the present Supreme
Court justices that the prohibitions of the First Amendment are
far-reaching and absolute, it would be incorrect to say that government is wholly removed from intervention in the religious life
of the nation, to say that there is, in Thomas Jefferson's words,
a wall of separation between church and state. Proof for my statement lies in the fact that religious organizations in their external
relations and in some of their internal affairs have the same
relation to government as nonreligious organizations. Churches
must comply with fire regulations and church wardens can be
prosecuted for violating the regulations. Churches own property
and their property rights are fixed and protected by law. Churches
get involved in lawsuits, sometimes in a suit between churches
when a denomination splits and the seceding and residual groups
cannot agree about the distribution of property.

Conceding that I have correctly described an interface of government and religion, can one still contend that there is a realm—
religious belief and practice, creed and ritual—to which government
must be totally indifferent? Perhaps the answer must wait on
future events. We have thought up to this time that the church
needs to be protected against the state; we have not contemplated
the church as aggressor against political authority. We have found
the frontier difficult to patrol where the ways of a sect, rooted in
religious belief and faith, clash with laws relating to education of
children, health standards, and medical assistance. But we have
not yet had to deal with a sect that uses the pulpit and invokes the
help of God in a campaign to overthrow the nation's economic
structure and the political system that supports it. We have not
yet witnessed sustained violence between religious groups. Religious wars in other times and other countries were not simply
contests of economic interest and ambitions for empire. They were
also clashes of passion, Christian against heathen, true believer
against heretic, Christian faith against Christian faith. Finally, as
I noted early in this essay, one can cite brutalities that have been
connected with religious doctrine and defended as inseparable
from the faith. One does not have to strain his imagination in order
to evoke a prospect of conduct rooted in religious doctrine that
any democratic people would find intolerable. Experience of civilized man offers illustrations enough.

The pertinence of these observations lies in the conclusions
they support about the feasibility of efforts to impose substantive

limitations on democratic governments. If the American people have tried to insulate anything from political control, religion is that thing. I have indicated my suspicion that the success we have enjoyed in this effort may be due to the quietude that has characterized religious life in America up to this time. I can imagine a religious renaissance in which the present frontiers cannot be maintained. It is possible, of course, that religion offers a poor test of whether democratic societies can withdraw political authority completely from a sector of life important to a free people. A substantial measure of common mind and common behavior, I have argued, is indispensable for maintenance of government by the people. Rival centers of religious zealotry, unrestrained by a superior force, can shatter the requisite commonalty and make democratic government untenable.

It would be premature to conclude that substantive limitations on democratic governments are not feasible until we have looked at the relationship of government to the economic system. Here one might expect that the American people would have instructed their governments to keep hands off. In the world's view, the United States is the citadel of capitalism. In the view of any American who knows his country's history, private ownership and management of productive enterprises have always been in the top level of the nation's values. The ascendancy of the business man has been threatened sufficiently on repeated occasions to cause him to ponder the utility of a blanket immunity from political intervention. There must have been periods when the popular mood was such that leaders of business could have put into the Constitution any language that they could agree was required for the nation's continued prosperity.

One looks in vain, both in the national Constitution and those of the states, for language that marks a frontier between government and an economic realm. At the time the Union was formed the Americans were rebounding from an excessive paternalism imposed by England in keeping with mercantilist theories of the management of the state. None of the early state constitutions instructed the state government that it should never restore that earlier regime of intensive control of commerce and industry. In none of our constitutions is there a recognition of European doctrines of socialism and a declaration that a socialist state shall not be established in America. Contemporary Americans who abhor the welfare state are denied a constitutional provision that they may thrust in the path of the "creeping socialism" they believe about to engulf the nation and put an end to personal liberty.

It is a reasonable surmise that business leaders did not press for the addition of substantive limitations to the Constitution because they did not need them. Language already in the Constitution stipulating how government should exercise its power, given judicial interpretation liberal or strict as the case might require, afforded enough protection to make campaigns for constitutional amendments unnecessary. The two clauses stating that all deprivations of life, liberty, or property shall be in keeping with due process of law proved to be near-perfect instruments in the hands of judges friendly to private enterprise. Due process of law came to be synonymous with "justifiable in purpose and reasonable in method." For approximately half a century, starting soon after the Civil War, a regulation of business was invalid if a majority of the Supreme Court justices thought it excessively interfered with freedom of choice on the part of owner, manager, or worker, or was unduly burdensome in the means adopted for achieving justifiable ends. Due process of law was thus a barrier that could be lifted to permit enforcement of a regulatory law if the judges thought it was reasonable, or lowered to prevent enforcement if they thought the law unreasonable. The year 1937 is usually cited as the date when the mood of the New Deal came to ascendancy in the Supreme Court and decisions about the appropriateness of economic and social legislation moved effectively from the judicial to the political branches of government.

One occasionally reads that history teaches no lesson except that history teaches no lesson; or that all generalizations are false including this one. The same mood of skepticism makes me reluctant to draw any lessons from American experience with substantive constitutional limitations in the three sectors of life used for illustration—the affairs of the family, religion, and private business enterprise. I shall offer four general observations that may be worth further thought.

First, substantive limitations and procedural limitations are closely related, supporting one another and interrelated in their consequences. Whatever one might hope to accomplish by forbidding government to make intrusions in a specified area of affairs may be satisfactorily accomplished by acknowledging power to enter that field but limiting the way that power may be exercised. This seems almost certain to be so if the procedural limitations are expressed in comprehensive rather than specific language, as is the case with the requirements that legislation and administration accord with due process of law and provide equal protection to all who are affected by the law.

Second, procedural limitations may be preferable in all cases to substantive limitations. My speculation about the possible connection of brutal acts with religious beliefs and rituals reveals my personal doubt that there is any significant area of affairs or aspect of life capable of definition or description in generalized statements that one can be sure ought never be invaded by government for any purpose.

Third, the key to the practical effects of constitutional limitations of any type lies in the office that is permitted to fix the meaning of the Constitution and enforce it on the other offices and arms of the government. If the courts are to interpret and enforce the Constitution, as is the case in the United States, one's views about how precisely constitutional limitations ought to be worded will be greatly affected by his confidence that judges will meet his own tests of good judgment.

Fourth, constitutional limitations and the judges who interpret and enforce them have a regulative effect on politics. Politics is effort to capture offices, make a record, and win return to offices. The promises made at campaign time must allow for constitutional restrictions on what the elected officials can do. And the successful candidates, having come to office, must either devise a set of policies which the judges will let stand or accept judicial rebuff and carry an issue of constitutional change or judicial reform to the people. Ordinarily the elected officials accept the judicial decision and try again with a law they think the judges will accept. But sometimes either constitutional change or judicial reform is made an issue in elections. Students of the process appear generally to believe that the Supreme Court sooner or later comes around to a position that has the support of most people. Little imaginative research has been done on this subject, however, and one can do little better than make guesses as to how far congressmen and Presidents depart from their preferences in order to avoid judicial rebuff and how much influence the acts and statements of the judges have on positions finally taken by the people. We can be sure that the relationship of constitutional limitations to popular control of government would have been even more complicated if the Constitution of the United States had contained a declaration that neither the national government nor any state government may ever replace capitalism with socialism or replace free enterprise with a regime that judges think of as a welfare state.

## The Quality of Office

The rule that every public official ought to be worthy of his
assignment is acknowledged to be a good one, but little has been
written in justification of it. A great deal has been said about the
language that ought to be used in delegating legislative and
judicial power to officials who are neither a legislature nor a court.
But little thought appears to have been devoted to the questions,
what decisions ought a democratic nation insist be made by the
legislative assembly itself and never delegated to any other official
or group of officials; and, what tests ought to be applied in deciding whether an official or group of officials is a worthy repository
of authority that may properly be delegated?

The Constitution states that Congress shall have the power to
declare war. This means, by accepted interpretation, that war can
be declared by vote of a majority of the members present in each
of the two chambers and the approval of the President, or in case
the President vetoes, by action of two-thirds of the congressmen
present in each chamber. But is this the only method we should
ever tolerate for making the momentous decision that the nation
has gone to war? The President, not instructed by a declaration
of war, has committed men and weapons to combat that the nation
thought of as war. The Korean action is an example. In this instance
Congress supported the President with authorizations of particular
actions and with grants of resources. How ought this method of
committing the nation's strength be appraised? Is it appropriate
to the American system for Congress to give the President power
to decide that the time has come for the nation to fight? Or should
the American people insist that making war is too important a
decision to be entrusted to anybody but the elected members of
the national representative assembly themselves?

The power to declare war affords one illustration of a central
issue in theory of democratic government that has too long escaped
careful thought. Elected officials are expected to run the government in a way that is acceptable to the people. To maximize the
prospect that the expectations of the people will be understood
and heeded we create an assembly of many men chosen from all
parts of the country. We give this representative assembly authority to make law, and we allow it to decide when it ought to permit
some of its lawmaking power to be exercised by other officials,
including the President. How much of the critical decision making

can Congress surrender to other officials without dissipating its ability to make certain that government does respond to the expectations of the population?

A study of English and American experience suggests that there may be several kinds of decision that should always be made by a representative legislative assembly, or by a procedure which joins the chief executive with the representative assembly in a lawmaking institution. Possibly to be included in such a list are: the power to define crimes and fix penalties; the power to institute governmental undertakings or thrust the government into affairs in which it was not previously involved; the power to create major organizations for carrying on the activities of government, including the power to say who shall have the authority to make all important decisions not made by the lawmaking body itself; the power to designate sources of revenue and place limits on rates to be imposed; the power to allocate money among the many purposes of expenditure and the many organizations charged with governmental activities; the power to choose and remove the highest administrative officials and judges who are thought not appropriate for election at the polls; and the power to review the work of administrative officials and direct and discipline them.

If one decides that the elected officials need not hold on to the power to decide a certain matter, he encounters the question of how to fashion an office worthy of exercising the authority to be delegated. We have a voluminous literature about administrative organization and practice, much of which is evaluative. The evaluative statements, in my opinion, rest on too narrow a base of theory about what gives an office competence for discharging a particular set of obligations. Most of the writing that expresses approval or disapproval of particular administrative establishments applies one or more of three tests. It asks whether the organization operates efficiently, accomplishing its objectives promptly enough with a reasonable cost in manpower and materials. Or it asks whether the work of the organization is in keeping with the policies of the chief executive. Or it asks whether the work of the organization is well coordinated with the related activities of other organizations.

These undoubtedly are important questions, but they are not the only questions that must be asked if administrative organizations are to satisfy the requirements of democratic government. It is the task of the theory-maker to identify, formulate, and relate to one another the inclusive battery of tests that must be applied in fashioning administrative offices worthy of varying assignments.

Since a theory, convincing in its argument and comprehensive enough to satisfy me, appears not to be in print, I cannot handle this subject by reference to other writings, and a full inquiry would overextend this essay. If one wishes to pursue further my ideas about how to approach the task of theory-making, he may examine two of my previous publications. In a book, *Bureaucracy in a Democracy,* I attempted to relate the administrative organizations of the United States government to the elected branches, Congress and President, and to the conception of democratic government which I develop in the book now in hand. An article which has slept undisturbed for nearly thirty years might also be exhumed. It offers a set of tests I think suitable for consideration when fashioning an office and designing procedures to be utilized for making certain kinds of decisions.*

## Equal Protection of the Laws

The Fourteenth Amendment to the Constitution of the United States forbids the states to deny to any person "the equal protection of the laws." The requirement and the particular wording were expressed in English common law long before their incorporation into our Constitution. The language, "equal protection of the laws," nevertheless inadequately describes the standard. Law does more than protect. The impact of government is not confined to enactment and enforcement of regulative law. And the term "equal," strictly construed, allows for no disparity whatever in relative position. We shall use the term "equal protection" but the reader must bear in mind that the term identifies an ideal better described as like position of all before government and like treatment for all when government acts.

A commitment to equal protection of the laws acknowledges a value position. It is a declaration of purpose to achieve a goal. The concern for equal protection therefore differs substantively from the concern that the official charged with making a decision should be worthy of the responsibilities he has assumed. The theory-maker, at the time of his initial approach to the latter problem, need not be committed to any grand or general thesis about what gives a government its democratic character. He may begin his inquiry by an exploration of expected, probable, and possible consequences

---

* *Bureaucracy in a Democracy* (New York: Harper & Row, 1950); "State Administrative Tribunals and Fair Play," *Iowa Law Review,* vol. 25 (1940), p. 532.

of alternative placements of authority and then issue advice as to how offices might be designed and authority placed to conform to different views about ideal relationships between government and citizens. His ambitions are not blighted when he learns that some who read his work are devoted to equal protection of the laws and that others believe government should treat with favor those who suffer disadvantages in other economic and social realms.

A commitment to equal protection of the laws, however, puts severe constrictions on the theory-maker. He addresses his search to means for achieving a specified end. If his inquiry leads him into alternatives in assigning government functions, defining authority, and creating offices, his examination of those problems will be sensitive to the consequences for equality among persons who appear before government. But the specified end, as we shall see, is not a clearly defined goal or objective. Perhaps the first point of attention for the theory-maker ought to be clarification of the goal itself; certainly this will be a main feature of his final product.

In what senses, under what circumstances, and to what degree should government treat two persons alike or treat two sectors of the population alike? If residents of arid territory press government to augment their water supply, ought the lawmakers refuse to act until they have calculated that no other part of the population will be taxed beyond the value of the derivative benefits expected to accrue to them? If the blind and the crippled cry for aid from government, must the officials turn a deaf ear to both until they have determined how both can be aided in equal measure? If A opposes B in a cause before the government, can any allowance be made for the fact that A has acquired wealth and B is a pauper?

No doubt the American scene has always been agitated by outcries that some people get too much and others much too little at the hands of government. The complaint is that government does not get around soon enough to this or that need and that disparities in treatment run too strongly and too long in favor of certain parts of the population. At no time in our history has there been serious demand that lawmakers refrain from differences in treatment comparable to those mentioned in the foregoing paragraph. The lawmakers in every legislative session divide people into classes and specify that a given law shall apply one way to the people who fall within a class and another way to the people who fall outside that class. So people are divided between those who are blind and those who are not blind, and only the blind receive certain monthly payments, though other people suffering other disabilities may be equally handicapped in making a living. So also men and women who were in military service during a specified period get sent to college at public expense while other veterans who terminated their service only one day before the specified date get no such advantage. Operators of pool rooms may be required to obtain a city license and pay a high fee, but operators of bowling alleys may be free from such requirements; the business firm doing a specified volume of business is subjected to regulations that do not apply to its competitors who do only slightly less business; and the rich man who has arrived at a specified age may receive old age payments which are denied to a man slightly younger who is unable to work and lacks sufficient income to live decently.

All these cases of differential treatment have been defended by legislators, judges, and scholars as wholly compatible with an equal protection standard. It is said that the situations, conditions, circumstances in which people appear before government may be classified for variance in treatment, and that a classification is appropriate if it is reasonably related to the social objectives back of the governmental policy involved in a given case. It is commonly asserted that the social objectives relevant to judicial proceedings and other law enforcement activities are identical for all persons who are involved in the same cause. Justice is said to be blind to evidences of wealth, social position, personal attributes. If practice fully supports this ideal, it must be admitted that the ideal has rough edges. Policemen size up the man before arresting because of an act; juries are attentive to the person in evaluating evidence and arriving at judgments; judges take account of previous records in fixing sentences.

The principle that differences in treatment by government ought to be strictly regulated by the social objectives which the policy is intended to achieve is a useful suggestion for the theory-maker. It answers no hard questions, however, about the limits of an appropriate relevance of social conditions to policy objectives, and it tells him nothing about the calculus of gains and losses that sustains judgments about reasonableness.

These few paragraphs do not circumscribe the range of ideals and experience that will have to be explored and put in order before we can pride ourselves on an illuminating analysis of equal protection of the laws. I hope that my remarks indicate an urgent need to get ahead with this business. Certainly they make undeniable the close connection of a desire for equal protection with the standard we must now examine—the belief that government ought to be devoted to the general well-being rather than the well-being of favored persons and groups. Indeed, the two commitments, to equal protection and the public welfare, may properly be viewed as two ways of looking at the same problems and stating the same concern.

## The Public Welfare

The notion that government ought to serve everybody must be as old as the first popular rebellion against governments that exploited the many for the benefit of the few. It is central to thinking about democratic government, since it is one way of expressing the core proposition that everybody counts. How to determine what is the public welfare and how to advance it have been points of persistent attention in the literature of political science. Writing on this subject can be identified by reference to a number of terms, including public welfare, general welfare, common welfare, the common good, the public weal, the public interest. Some of the most helpful analysis, in my opinion, has been supplied in recent years and favors the term public interest. Students of the subject are trying to develop a particular meaning for the term "public interest," and for that reason I choose another, more inclusive term, "public welfare," to cover my discussion of an ill-defined idea.

Probably the best way to get at what is involved in conceptions of the public welfare is to cite examples. Easiest to handle is the resistance to invasion by foreign military force. On December 7, 1941, Japanese forces bombed Pearl Harbor in the Hawaiian Islands; on December 8, Congress and the President issued a declaration of war. Clearly the declaration of war was an act in the interest of the whole nation. True, the Japanese had not killed anybody in the state of Kentucky or destroyed any property in Kentucky. But the Japanese act was intended to injure the people of Kentucky just as much as it was intended to injure anybody living in Hawaii. In bombing Pearl Harbor the Japanese announced their wish to destroy the strength of the American people as a nation, and Congress and President, in declaring war, acted in the interest of the whole nation.

But what about the War of 1812? England had indulged in a number of acts (e.g., attacking American ships and seizing American seamen) which Congress and the President thought should be resisted by force. But their declaration of war against England was bitterly resented by great numbers of the American people.

Opposition to the war centered mainly in the New England states where great numbers of people were engaged in shipping. These were the people who had suffered most from the offensive acts of England. For a number of reasons they thought that a declaration of war was not the way to deal with England, however, and their resistance to the war was carried to the point of serious proposals to secede from the union.

Were Congress and President acting in the interest of the whole nation when they declared war in the face of opposition by a substantial part of the people? The answer appears indisputably to be yes. The pros and cons of going to war were hotly debated in Congress, in the newspapers, and in the other channels of communication of the time. Supposed advantages and disadvantages likely to be incurred in waging war were weighed in the minds of congressmen and President. They were aware that for a time New England shippers would suffer even greater losses, if we went to war, than they had suffered from England's near-war depredations. But they concluded that the advantages to be gained for the nation as a whole (including long-run gains for New England) outweighed the prospective losses.

Congress and President are up against a similar problem when they decide to improve a harbor. Let us assume (regardless of what the facts may be) that nature has provided a good channel for boats into and out of New Orleans and that people interested in shipping at New Orleans have improved the channel and developed port facilities. Let us assume also that the natural harbor at Mobile is not so good and that people interested in shipping at Mobile did less to improve the port facilities there than other people did in New Orleans. Congress and the President are asked to appropriate money to make the port at Mobile as good as the one at New Orleans. What may they do in view of our insistence that they may act only in keeping with what they consider to be the public welfare?

If the harbor at Mobile is improved it will benefit people scattered over a wide area in the United States since freight rates on goods which they export and import may be expected to go down. But people already living in Mobile will gain even more, for in addition to reduced freight rates they will profit from the increase in business that takes place in Mobile. And finally, the particular individuals who are already engaged in shipping in and out of Mobile, or who own preferred sites and facilities about the harbor, will profit most of all if the harbor is improved.

Are we willing for Congress and President to confer these benefits on certain people by improving the harbor with money that is raised through general taxation and therefore will be contributed in large part by people who will derive little benefit or conceivably no benefit at all from the improvement of the harbor? What about the disadvantages that will be suffered by people living in New Orleans or affected by the prosperity of New Orleans? It is unlikely that shipping through the port of Mobile can be greatly increased without diverting some traffic from the port of New Orleans. Can we allow Congress and President to whittle away the prosperity of the people who are affected by shipping in New Orleans in order to confer benefits on other people as we have described? Or must Congress and the President assess the losses that some people incur because shipping is diverted away from New Orleans (and all other ports that suffer) and require those who benefit from that diversion to make good the losses sustained by other people?

We have a parallel case in the construction of a new state highway or the paving of a city street. Property owners on the new road sell sites for filling stations at fancy prices and a number of filling station operators on other roads go broke because they no longer sell enough gas to keep going. The strongest opponents for any plan to alter the streets and change the flow of traffic in a city are business men and property owners who fear that their own prosperity will be lessened by the new system.

We even up the gains and losses involved in street construction in our cities somewhat by a system of special assessments for street improvements which puts a substantial part (sometimes nearly all) of the cost of the construction on the owners of property adjacent to it. But we do not make any special charge upon business firms some distance away who will profit from the more direct route they are now to enjoy. If property owners along the street which is improved suffer a material loss because we take their property for right of way or obstruct access to it, we pay them for it. But we do not provide any compensation to people operating businesses or owning property on other streets who suffer losses because traffic is diverted from its previous course.

Our national and state constitutions provide that when government takes property away from a man it must pay him a just compensation for what is taken. But indirect losses such as those incurred by diverting traffic from a port or a state highway or a city street are not considered to be a taking of property and there is no constitutional requirement that the loser be recompensed by the public. Many people have urged that we work out some formula for collecting from those who profit and compensating those who suffer indirect losses, but we have as yet adopted no general policies to that end. The idea of excess condemnation is a step in this direction. Some states have enacted laws which permit public authorities to take more land than is actually needed for improvement. The owners are paid what the property is judged to be worth before the improvement; the property can then be sold at its new value and the profit goes into the public treasury. Laws authorizing excess condemnation do not, however, provide that the money which is realized in this way shall be used to pay those people who have suffered indirect losses from the improvement.

The analysis of consequences of governmental action can be extended to virtually every act of government. Somebody enjoys a special gain and somebody suffers an indirect loss every time the national government constructs a dam, grants a patent, or develops an insecticide that increases the yield of a farm crop; every time the state government relocates a hospital for the insane or requires the pasteurization of milk; every time a local government builds a new school house or zones a community for construction of buildings.

Many acts of government are done with full awareness that they benefit one group at the cost of another. A special tax on oleomargarine is intended to divert business from producers of oleo to producers of butter. An import duty that favors a particular industry not only raises the cost of living for buyers of the protected commodity, but diverts business from producers of substitute products and may bankrupt persons who have imported the commodity that is adversely affected by the newly imposed tariff. The federal government breaks up an industrial combination not only to assure favorable market conditions for all purchasers but also to enable smaller firms to survive in a competitive market.

I have sought in the foregoing paragraphs to describe a condition that exists. Is it an unavoidable condition? Must we assume, for an indefinite future, that public officials will usually be uncertain about the distribution of gains and losses resulting from their acts, and that they will continue bestowing benefits on one part of the population in the face of clamor that those gains come at a cost to even greater numbers of people? We are obliged to answer, that uncertainty will continue to loom high in calculating gains and losses and that sometimes if not most of the time one part of the population must pay for the gains realized by another part of the population. Uncertainty will reign because those who formulate and adopt the public policies cannot foresee all the consequences of an innovation. They cannot know that the distribution of gains and losses ensuing immediately will be sustained over the long run, cannot even be sure that what they confidently view as having a beneficial effect will not later prove to have done more harm than good. In the future as in the past, one part of the population will pay for the benefits bestowed by government on another part of the population. This is bound to be the case, for a prime objective of government in democratic societies is to use political power to undo the injuries committed in the economic and social realms, and to reduce those inequalities that excite men to self-help with unduly abrasive consequences.

To the question about prospects for the future we may also say that further development of theory about the public welfare and how to achieve it will both reduce the incidence of uncertainty and minimize injustice in distributing the burden of paying for the benefits that government confers. In their efforts to supply the needed theory, political scientists may find useful models in the writings of economists. The economists have made notable progress in clarifying thought about short-run and long-run costs and benefits, disclosed and hidden costs and benefits, calculation of risk, and how to deal with uncertainty. Their findings on these and other matters involved in public welfare will always be suggestive for the political scientist and often will supply him with analysis readymade for his use.

Still, it must be recognized that economic analysis is based on assumptions about human wants instead of on the direct expression of wants through voting or negotiation. Moreover, people's wants change over time and with learning and persuasion. Thus the condition that governmental action must serve the welfare of the general public requires both political and economic analysis for its fulfillment. Finally, both analyses will always be only provisional because the assumptions about values, interests, and wants that underlie them are necessarily provisional. Like "equal protection of the laws," the "public welfare" is an ideal that calls for continuing, practical examination.

## Some General Observations

An appreciation of the four standards that unite to provide a regime of government by law helps one to understand why the founders of our system, having a vision of self-government for free men, put their faith first in popular control of government and only second in formal limitations on the exercise of governmental power. It emphasizes the importance of a careful placement of decision-making authority in the governmental structure. And it directs attention to some values that are at stake when the nation chooses, deliberately or unwittingly, whether to put its dependence on the populist or on the pluralist demand-response system. A few sentences on each of these points is appropriate.

The men who wrote the early constitutions of the United States firmly believed that governments designed for free men must refrain from intrusion into many areas of human affairs. Yet, with few if any exceptions, they put no language in those constitutions that would bar government from entering particular sectors of life. I offered an explanation of why constitutional limitations of substantive character, forbidding government to legislate on certain subjects, appear not to be a useful restraining device. The best way, it appears, of assuring that government may protect the child from brutal parents yet not generally regulate parent-child relations is to place governmental authority in the hands of officials who have no inclination to force public policy upon the family.

The second standard, that authority to make an important decision must be placed in an office worthy of the responsibilities involved, may be appropriate for specification in a written constitution. It is feasible to list in a written constitution certain areas of critical importance and to stipulate that basic decisions relating to these matters shall never be entrusted to any hands except those of the elected officials. Article I, Section 8 of the Constitution, listing things that the national government may do, suggests a style for listing things that only the lawmaking authority may do. Note also the language used in specifying that money can be drawn from the treasury only in consequence of appropriations made by law. As the Constitution vests certain authority in the President (e.g., the power to make treaties and grant pardons), so a written constitution could describe or characterize some expressions of power that might be delegated by the lawmaking authority to the President but not to a nonelected official.

The two remaining standards, equal protection of the laws and concern for the public welfare, can be cited in a constitution as ends to be approached by government. Indeed, the Constitution of the United States contains two references to the "general welfare" (one in the Preamble and one introducing the list of delegated powers in Article I, Section 8), and one reference to equal protection of the laws (in the Fourteenth Amendment). My comments on these two aspects of government by law should convince one, it seems to me, that tests suitable for deciding whether equal protection is being afforded and whether the welfare of a public is being advanced could never be stated in the succinct form appropriate to a constitution. I tried to make clear that a satisfactory and sufficient battery of tests has not yet been formulated for either requirement. Their development and statement, in my judgment, is not a proper assignment for the judicial branch. Inequalities are often sources of tension and precursors of violence, and the remedy for these grievances, in many instances, is a revision of inequalities at other points in the social system. Legislation that revises the distribution of resources, utilities, and benefits accomplishes that result by a grossly uneven effect on those who have and those who have not. To instruct judges to brand as valid or invalid, i.e., as temperate or excessive, these departures from equal treatment is tantamount, in my opinion, to a license to veto virtually all legislation the judges think not warranted by the exigencies of the moment. I reach the same conclusion about the appropriateness of judicial determination of what furthers the public welfare.

I am convinced that within a decade after the Constitution was adopted most of the nation's political leaders had concluded that the judges of our highest courts ought to refuse to enforce statutes that the judges believed to be in clear violation of a constitution's unequivocal mandate. Their endorsement of judicial review was qualified, however. I am convinced that few if any prominent political leaders of that day thought it appropriate for judges to nullify legislation on the ground that it violated "the spirit of the Constitution" or appeared not to be compatible with an objective stated in the Preamble of the Constitution. It is undeniable that the architects of our system had a keen appreciation of the ideals embraced in a conception of government by law. They expected the officials of a republican government, being elected by the people, to understand and have respect for government by law, and they counted on the people to replace any officials whose conduct failed to measure up to that expectation. To depart from the standards of government by law was to behave as a faction, and language used for some decades after Madison expressed his great concern in *Federalist* No. 10 revealed an apprehension that a majority of the electorate might on occasion act in a factious manner. But it was not expected that the judicial branch would undo the mischief done by faction. If factions were to be avoided or the misdeeds of faction remedied, these results would be attained by the fuller enlightenment of the people and the improvement of the electoral-representative process.

That this was a sound judgment is surely confirmed by my analysis of the conception of public welfare. Conflict within the population arises out of different estimates of personal welfare, group welfare, and national welfare. Elected officials cannot replace the rude judgments of the population with other judgments based on sure knowledge. Judges cannot find in judicial precedents and legal literature answers to the questions that baffle thoughtful politicians.

What then can offer a hope of achieving the common good of the entire nation? The best answer appears to be this: We can construct a decisional apparatus that puts the power to make critical decisions in officials who are chosen by the people and answerable to the people. We can insist that when power to decide is delegated, it must be delegated to an official worthy of the assignment. We can strive to improve the understanding of the voters and we can do what we can to inject health and vigor into the electoral-representative process. It may be efficacious to do something more. We can admonish elected officials to try to understand what different parts of the population hope to achieve, determine whether the different interests are compatible with one another, estimate how many people seem to be aligned on each side when interests conflict, and calculate how important the issue is to each group. We can also exhort our elected officials to proceed thoughtfully and courageously in working out policies that promise to result in a state of affairs they believe most people would approve if the people understood everything that those who are acting for them have found out.

What, finally, does our analysis of the standards inherent in government by law tell us about the values at stake in putting dependence on one or the other of the two demand-response systems? Not what one's first thoughts might lead him to suppose. The requirements of equal protection of the laws and concern for the public welfare fit perfectly with the goals and the rationale of the populist system. They are not, however, incompatible with the pluralist system. They fully support the fundamental proposition that everybody counts; the attempt to distribute influence equally which distinguishes the populist demand-response system is clearly intended to make sure that no one gets counted out. The pluralist system, relying on a resolution of competition among groups, rejects the equalization-of-influence-principle, but that does not necessarily imply rejection of the fundamental proposition that everybody counts. Indeed, the pluralist is likely to argue that his conception of equality is more realistic than that of the populist because it takes into account the intensity with which people desire something and allows for the reflection of these intensities in the process of group organization and competition. Merely counting votes equally may not adequately reflect demands; thus, the adherent of the group competition thesis may insist that he seeks a way of achieving the public will rather than thwarting it. He may contend that everybody profits most in the long run if policy makers are guided by the demands of well-matched competing groups rather than by reading the wishes of voters who have no better way of expressing their wishes than by re-electing or replacing public officials after they have acted.

If this is a fair summation of the position of those who accept the group competition thesis, it follows that they ought to approve the several requirements of government by law as enthusiastically as the populists. Decisions on issues of policy, made by selecting among the demands of groups and fashioning compromises, ought to be guided by a concern that all who are affected by the policy shall be treated as near equally as possible and that the final statement of the policy shall reflect a careful attempt to determine the public welfare. If, however, I am too charitable to supporters of the pluralist system and it is their purpose to exploit the many and distribute the spoils among a few—if that is their game, then the pluralists in practice must reject both the standard of equal protection and the goal of public welfare.

Whatever the avowed and the hidden purposes of the group competition school, they must, like the populists, insist that the authority to make important decisions rest in offices worthy of the assignment. The analysis of the past several pages can leave no doubt that the policy makers will have a vast range of discretion, regardless of how persistently they try to meet tests of equal protection and public welfare. Neither populist nor pluralist can allow so great an opportunity for choice to be given to officials likely not to appreciate what they can do with their power.

# 12. CONSTITUTIONAL GUARANTEES

The limitations on government we discussed in the preceding chapter are general, indefinite, sweeping. They are not specific prohibitions, but are guiding principles from which specific prohibitions may be derived. Further, those limitations are of uncertain origin; they are the accretion of centuries of thought and practice. We shall now fix attention on a class of limitations that, on both counts, differ significantly from those already examined. While they vary in the preciseness of their statement, they tend to be exact and specific rather than general and inclusive. And authoritative statement of each limitation can be found, for they are expressed in the formal language of constitutions and statutes.

It would take several hundred pages simply to print the statements limiting the use of governmental authority that appear in the constitutions and statutes of our national and state governments. Indeed, a typical textbook expounding only the personal guarantees in the United States Constitution is a longer book than the one I am writing. Of necessity, therefore, I must confine my attention to an aspect of constitutional limitations, choosing for study a subject that illuminates the problems we encounter in preventing abuse of power by men who can meet social demands only by a bold resort to power. I think we can illuminate some fundamental problems by an exposure of conflicts in values that occur when the acts of government impinge on freedom of expression. The excursion into this morass of conflicting values must be prefaced by some general remarks about the nature of constitutional and statutory limitations.

## A Regime of Limited Government

Current popular expectations, traditional practices, statutes, and constitutions combine to provide a regime of limited government. They reinforce and support one another, and a particular expression of a safeguard or prohibition can be fully understood only by fitting it to other expressions having a similar purpose. The enmeshing of the several means of expression or sources of restraints on government is well illustrated by penalties for violating the laws of the United States.

The Constitution, in the Eighth Amendment, says that cruel and unusual punishment shall not be inflicted. Judges—on final appeal the judges who make up the United States Supreme Court—will decide whether a penalty specified by law is cruel or unusual. We may be sure that the judges, if confronted with the question, will hold that the Eighth Amendment forbids drawing, quartering, hanging up by the thumbs. They might not hold that flogging is forbidden by the Constitution, since flogging was a common punishment when the Eighth Amendment was adopted. Nevertheless, flogging is outlawed as a penalty for violating federal laws, this result being assured by the absence of any provision for flogging in the statement of approved penalties. On the other hand, there appears not to be any statutory provision or common law rule that forbids the flogging of prisoners for disciplinary purposes. So far as Constitution, statute or common law are concerned, it appears that prison officials may flog prisoners when that seems to the official to be a proper means of discipline. Actually, the practice is exceedingly rare in federal prisons, if indeed it ever takes place. It has been outlawed by prison wardens and officials above them who have imposed restraints on their own exercise of authority. It may be that their refusal to flog is in part due to doubt that flogging is an effective means of discipline. We may be sure that their refusal is in great part response to a widely held public attitude. There is evidence that a substantial part of the population thinks flogging not a proper way for public officials to deal with adult human beings.

Judges have the last word in fixing the meaning of constitutional and statutory language. If the highest court of the land holds that quartering is a cruel and unusual punishment, Congress and the President cannot make quartering an effective penalty unless they induce the judges to change their minds or manage to get the Constitution changed by adoption of a new amendment. If, however, the court holds that flogging of prisoners is illegal only because made so by statute, Congress and President may authorize flogging simply by enactment of a new statute. If flogging is authorized but not required by statute, prison wardens or their superior officials will decide whether to flog at all, and if to do so, under what conditions; they fix their policies, interpret their policies, have authority to change their policies. Public attitudes, of course, are rarely given authoritative interpretation. You read whatever signs you can get, and different people reach different conclusions as to what the public expects. Wrong readings of the public mind are corrected by further expressions of public attitudes. The public itself decides when it will modify attitudes or replace old convictions with new ones; it answers to no one for the persistence with which it clings to a position or the fickleness with which it jumps from one position to another.

Constitutional provisions limiting governmental authority differ in generality of language and in point of impact. Some provisions are stated most precisely; others are phrased in general terms. Some provisions are applicable to a specific stage in governmental action; others are addressed to the governmental process from start to finish. To illustrate: (a) Amendment 7 of the national Constitution applies specifically to the conduct of civil suits in federal courts, and the statement as to how these trials shall be conducted is stated in language that conveys reasonably clear meaning. In contrast, (b) the assertions in the Fifth and Fourteenth Amendments that no person shall be deprived of life, liberty, or property without due process of law restrict government at every stage from enactment of law to enforcement of law. They are so uncertain in meaning that their proper interpretation is still a point of contention among judges and students of law; on occasion they have been given an interpretation sufficiently inclusive to make most of the more specific restrictions superfluous.

The safeguards against abuse of authority that are written into our constitutions may strike the student as incomplete and less than systematic. This results from the circumstances under which the constitutions were written. Our earliest constitutions were intended to condemn and prevent abuses that the American people had suffered at the hands of officials they could not control. Judges fixed the meaning of the earlier provisions in authoritative interpretations, and men who drafted later constitutions repeated the language of earlier documents so as to get the benefit of the judge-made law that had grown up around that language. As a consequence, no constitution in effect in the United States today sets forth a complete and consistent program of limitations on the exercise of authority by government. None of our constitutions, national or state, expressly declares that government shall permit parents to have custody of their children. We must suppose that all our constitution makers acknowledged this to be one of our most essential civil rights; they did not forbid government to separate children from their parents because they did not anticipate that public officials would try to destroy the family.

The men who met in 1787 to draft a new constitution for the new American nation put only a few restrictions on the use of governmental power in that document—mainly in sections 9 and 10 of Article I. Punishment of men and their families by enactment of bills of attainder had been widely and deeply resented in England; therefore the new American Constitution forbade enactment of bills of attainder by either national or state governments. Other abuses of power that must have occurred to the framers were not mentioned for what seemed to them good reason. They thought the new national government would not have much authority over the American people and so would not have much opportunity to trample on people; and they thought state constitutions the proper place to lodge limitations on state governments.

But this view of constitution making was not satisfactory to many influential people, and they demanded that a bill of rights be written into the new document. This was done by the amendment process. The first Congress meeting under the new Constitution adopted twelve proposed amendments and sent them to the states for ratification; ten of the twelve were approved by three-fourths of the states and became the new Bill of Rights for the nation. Although stated as limitations on Congress, they have become limitations upon all officials and employees who hold office in the national government. They do not impose restraints upon our state and local governments by direct application; they are, however, guides to judges in fixing the meaning of some general restrictions on state power that were later added by the Fourteenth Amendment.

A necessary conclusion from the foregoing is that one's conception of civil rights must not be limited to the guarantees that are stated in constitutions. The constitutional provisions that are regarded as fundamental—guaranteeing religious freedom, freedom of expression, right of assembly, equal protection, fair trial, and others—provide a foundation for the status and claims to fair treatment that we have in mind when we speak of civil rights. But the statutes and the administrative and judicial practices that extend and clarify the constitutional requirements are as integral to a regime of individual freedom and personal dignity as are the commands that give the regime its constitutional foundation. Further, it may not be irrelevant to note that conceptions of civil rights vary over time. References to "our liberties" studded political speeches for at least three decades after the Union was formed. The core of this concern appears to have been to make popular government secure and keep it free from domination by any foreign power. Fifty years ago almost all textbooks for political science courses excluded voting and other political activity from the discussion of civil rights, and some textbooks categorically stated that voting is not a right but only a privilege. Today the common, political, and scholarly talk about civil rights is mainly concerned with avoidance of discrimination, freedom of expression, indifference of government to religion, and equitable and considerate treatment by government when one comes into its hands. At the periphery is concern about the obligation of government to equalize opportunity and modify excesses of advantage in a wide expanse of economic and social life, about immunity from public acts which either impound or intrude upon a realm of self-autonomy, and about the need for assurances that political power will not become immune to restraint by countervailing economic and social power. Any of these may be central to thought and action labeled "civil rights" at some future time. If lawmakers and judges display the imagination and boldness that have characterized their behavior to date, they will be able to make language that is now in the Constitution fit every need that public demand induces them to notice.

These remarks about the general character of the restrictions that create a regime of limited government touch only a few of the significant relations that students of the American political system need to understand. Anyone who wishes to pursue my own analysis further can do so by reading my recent exploration of the Supreme Court's utilization of constitutional language.* I trust that what I have said in the past few paragraphs has prepared the reader to grapple with the problems of free speech to which we now turn.

## Free Speech: At What Price?†

It is now thirty years since Mr. Felix Frankfurter, then law teacher, called upon the political scientists for help. I propose to consider in what manner we might respond to his appeal.

In a review of the first book by one of our now distinguished

---

* Charles S. Hyneman, *The Supreme Court on Trial* (New York: Atherton Press, 1963).

† The remainder of this chapter is an address to the American Political Science Association, which I delivered when I was president of that organization. It may show that I think mature political scientists need to be talked to on this subject in as elementary a fashion as beginning students. Reprinted from *The American Political Science Review*, vol. 56 (1962), pp. 847–852.

colleagues, Mr. Frankfurter urged political scientists and economists to quit trying to be lawyers and to act more like specialists in the study of human relationships. "What we have a right to expect from economists and political scientists," he said, "is an analysis of what true governmental problems are, in the light of what actually goes on in the world and wholly apart from the technicalities of American constitutional law. . . . Until the economists and political scientists attend to their special tasks and we lawyers to ours and each has awareness of the other's problems, we shall continue to have . . . cross-sterilization of the social disciplines."[1]

Last week Mr. Frankfurter terminated a quarter century of service on the nation's highest tribunal. From that tribunal come oracular pronouncements of profound significance, fixing bounds to the power of law-making assemblies. I have read many of these pronouncements with considerable care, and I am convinced that the men who utter them need a kind of assistance which the political scientists can supply. I propose, therefore to give you my judgment as to how this profession may render a service which one of the nation's most eminent jurists called for thirty years ago.

I shall speak about the problem of putting meaning into the Constitution's declaration that Congress—and by extension the fifty state legislatures—shall make no law abridging the freedom of speech or of the press. And my objectives will be to identify certain aspects of that problem most likely to be illuminated by the political scientist's kind of attack and, having found the site for our effort, to say enough about what we might do to convince you that we ought to move in with our tools.

The Supreme Court has not yet come to agreement on the basic presumptions which will underlie the decision of nicer issues of legislative authority relating to speech and press. At least two present members of the Court, Justices Black and Douglas, have declared their commitment to a presumption that the prohibitions of the First Amendment are absolute—that the prohibitions of laws which abridge the freedom of speech or press are absolute denials of power to impose restraints on speech and press. It will come out in a moment, however, that they favor a qualified absoluteness.

Opposed to the idea of absolute prohibition is the so-called balancing doctrine—the contention that the nation's interest in freedom of speech and press is in competition with its interests in some other valued things that sometimes are endangered by unrestrained expression, that the competing interests ought to be evaluated and balanced out, and therefore that a test of reasonableness ought to be applied in litigation where abridgment of speech or press is charged.

A third point of view about the fundamental character of the free speech guarantee has been pressed with great persistence by Professor Alexander Meiklejohn of The University of Chicago. The First Amendment, according to him, protects political communication only. It is designed to keep government from restraining what people say in their efforts to instruct, criticize, and control their government. As respects political speech, the prohibition is absolute. As respects all other expression, Professor Meiklejohn argues, government may abridge freedom of speech and press so long as it does not violate any of the constitutional limitations found elsewhere in the Constitution. When a restraint of non-political speech is challenged on due process grounds, for instance, a court should evaluate the gains and losses which can be credited to the act, and determine its validity by application of tests of reasonableness.

No matter which of these three basic presumptions controls judicial thinking about laws that have an impact on self-expression and communication, critical decisions will turn on tests of reasonableness. This is admittedly so, and obviously so, in the case of the balancing doctrine; reason inevitably must rule when choice is made among competing values. Reason, therefore, must rule under the Meiklejohn formula when the restraining act is found to encumber non-political speech.

It has been argued that the concept of absolute prohibition excludes a concept of reasonableness. Justice Douglas has stated emphatically and repeatedly that inquiry into what is reasonable is wholly inappropriate when a court is convinced that speech or press has in fact been restrained. Indeed, I think it likely that Justices Douglas and Black, and Professor Meiklejohn when he contemplates utterances that have political significance, endorse the idea of absolute prohibition because they expect it to remove controversy about what is reasonable from the judical forum.

In my judgment this is a vain hope. The absolute prohibition doctrine runs squarely into issues of reasonableness at three points. When you examine what Justices Black and Douglas have said from the bench and in addresses delivered at other places, you learn that one of them or both of them has asserted: *first,* that the First Amendment does *not* protect *all* kinds of verbal expression: *second,* that expression which the First Amendment does protect sometimes loses protection because it is inextricably mixed up with other action; and *third*, that statements which ordinarily are immune from restraint by government may be forbidden if the words can be said to be the efficient cause of certain punishable actions.

Consider these statements by the two men who have, more than once, said that the prohibitions imposed by the First Amendment are absolute:

Justice Black in a public address, two years ago: "There is a question as to whether the First Amendment was intended to protect speech that courts find 'obscene.' "[2]

Justice Douglas, speaking also for Justice Black and Chief Justice Warren in 1957: "Of course, we have always recognized that picketing has aspects which make it more than speech. . . . I would adhere to the principle . . . that this form of expression can be regulated or prohibited only to the extent that it forms an essential part of a course of conduct which the State can regulate or prohibit."[3]

Justice Douglas, speaking only for himself, in the Dennis case in 1951: "The freedom to speak is not absolute; the teaching of methods of terror and other seditious conduct should be beyond the pale along with obscenity and immorality (341 U.S. 494, at p. 581)."

The bounds of legislative power to abridge speech and press on each of these three frontiers can be fixed only after the judge has decided where a reasonable man would draw the line. I have not time to trace the reasoning which leads to this conclusion. Call to mind the consequences of John Marshall's effort to skirt around the morass of reasonableness inherent in the necessary and proper clause. Find out, he said, whether the act of Congress falls within the commerce power; if the act is an exercise of the commerce power we need not inquire whether it is necessary and proper for the regulation of commerce, for the power to regulate commerce is plenary, whole, complete. By this strategy the judges slipped away from questions of reasonableness at one point, only to walk straight into them at another—when does commerce begin and end?—what is a direct and what is an indirect impact on goods in movement?—and so on. I trust you have not forgotten the *E. C. Knight* case, *Hammer* v. *Dagenhart*, *Carter* v. *Carter Coal Company*.

2. "Bill of Rights," *New York University Law Review*, vol. 35, p. 865, at p. 867.
3. *International Brotherhood of Teamsters* v. *Vogt*, 354 U.S. 284, at 297 (1957).

Believing, as I do, that a rule of reason will control the decisions that mark the front of a developing constitutional law of free speech and press, I can tell the political scientist where he should stake out his claim and assemble his tools. The scholarly study which helps lawmakers and judges decide what government may *reasonably* do to regulate the speech and other expression of the nation—this is what God had in mind for them to do when he created political scientists.

This is a worthy and urgent mission. How shall we go about the job? I shall comment briefly on each of three gateways into this jungle of human relationships.

One. There is need for a fuller and more careful ordering of communication and non-communicative expression, and their relationships to the values, beliefs, expectations, and behavior of men and women.

Two. It is obvious on a reading of judicial opinions and scholarly literature, that our best thought would profit from a few alternative analytic designs—models of analysis designed to identify and relate to one another the components of an issue of unrestrained speech versus restricted speech.

Three. There is need for a fresh look, and a hard look, at the intellectual supports for the grand presumption in favor of understrained verbal expression which underlies virtually every bit of our serious literature.

An equal attention to all three of these points would allow very little time for any of them. I prefer to expand my remarks on the first two. The scrutiny of intellectual foundations, which any of you, or Justice Frankfurter, might think the Number 1 assignment for political scientists will be disposed of right now in the few sentences I can allow.

A hard look at the intellectual foundations might reveal that the case for free speech, as it is made in contemporary American literature, rests mainly on a distrust of government rather than on a high esteem for a free flow of information and a lively combat among the ideas that compete to control action. Note the lack of acknowledgment in this literature that legal regulation of a communication problem, in many instances, may have as its result a freeing rather than a trammeling of communication—this result because enactment of a law on the subject gives the moderates in the community a talking point which restrains the more passionate part of the population from a do-it-ourselves job of policing. The hard look might help us put together more intelligently our supposition that the pen is mightier than the sword and our wish to secure and preserve certain cultural gains. Can anyone doubt that the communication of man to man facilitates the step backward as well as the step forward? Are we so committed to an idea of progress that we must believe that all social change is for the better—therefore that all argument and agitation for change must inevitably result in cultural advance? Comtemplating the history of pogroms and genocide in our own time, I am unable to understand why there is so little support, if indeed there is any support in our literature, for governmental action designed to lessen or prevent the indoctrination of children which produces adults who seek relief in persecution. Do we believe that impregnation with hate ought to be tolerated so that all of us may be enlightened and ennobled by the debate it excites? Or are we simply overpowered by uncertainties, not trusting our elected officials to select for extirpation at the stage of character formation the evil which we will later demand that they destroy on the battlefield?

You will see why I believe we need a speculative attack on the free. speech problem by a mind as disciplined as that of John Stuart Mill, and as free from compulsion by previous writing as Mill appears to have been. You may see, also, why I am reluctant to foreguess what I will be told when one of you writes that book.

I speak with more confidence about the other two enterprises I recommend—the careful ordering of situations in which issues of free speech versus restraint arise, and the development of models for analysis of such issues.

On the first of these assignments, the general survey which reveals where the problems lie, let us start with the forum. Most of our writing is about communication from man to man out in the open. If this be the ordinary situation, then there are special situations that ought to be brought into fuller cognition and recognition.

### CITIZEN TO HIS GOVERNMENT

Possibly this is where speech and press ought to be most unrestrained. But there must be limits as to when and where the citizen can speak to his servant. The judge must be immune from the helpful coaching which interested spectators can supply throughout the trial. And the senators have a point when they say they hear enough if they listen only to one another when they sit in formal session. If we thought more about it, we might conclude that we ought to impose some further conditions on the forum when the individual competes with the great organization in pressing his interests on elected officials or administrative agents. I think this is a hard surface on which we should sharpen our ideas about equality.

## GOVERNMENT TO CITIZEN

When the President was elected, I stood firmly planted in a state of nature, determined to scrutinize the deeds of my servant and help remove him from office if he did not meet my expectations. By the time his first term was up I had been made over. When I voted to give him a second term, and a third term, and a fourth term, did my vote testify to a conviction that a public servant had fulfilled my expectations? Or did my voting merely prove that I had been sweet-talked into accepting anything he chose to give? If you think this is a dilemma only for fuzzy thinkers, ponder the uses of bureaucracy. The congressmen may not enact a law which forbids the individual or a group to conduct a propaganda campaign designed to terminate a social practice or uproot a moral commitment of the population. May the congressmen set a bureaucratic force on a counter propaganda campaign intended to smother the reformers and make ineffective the communication which they are guaranteed a right to advance—and pay for the governmentally based campaign with money exacted from you, me, and the man who got buried?

## COMMUNICATION WITHIN GOVERNMENT

Recently Senator Hubert Humphrey, the majority party's whip in the Senate, introduced me to some of his friends from Minnesota—introduced me as one of his teachers. I told the Senator's friends that there was one thing I had failed to teach the Senator—that is, that a leader of the Democratic party can never be sure who is going to filibuster. I am sorry the Senator is not here tonight, for I would have reminded him that, throughout the decade before he was born, United States Senators who called themselves liberals were chafing at gag rule. Abuses of speech and restrictions of speech within government are not likely to be litigated under the First Amendment. But they lie in that universe of expression and communication to which the nation must bring order, and in respect to which the political scientists must bring counsel.

## COMMUNICATION WITHIN NON-GOVERNMENTAL ORGANIZATIONS

I think Justice Holmes did us a disservice with his reference to yelling "Fire!" in a theatre. Speaking from the floor while the play is in progress on the stage ought not be governed by the rules which govern communication on the street corner. We have supposed that the presiding officer properly determines the order of speakers where all have an invitation to speak. Would anyone argue that the Constitution forbids lawmakers to empower presiding officers, school teachers, and football referees to impose silence on the many while one person makes himself heard?

### THE CARRIERS OF MESSAGES

Does the guarantee of free press deny government the power to impose an obligation to carry messages? Is the right of an editor to print his own crazy ideas a right to keep out of his publication the ideas of all other men he thinks to be crazy—or the ideas he thinks worthy but unsuitable for immature readers? Consider the public need for news in a one-newspaper town; the stranglehold on the flow of information and ideas that lies within the power of the great newsgathering organizations like Associated Press.

Finally, that special forum, the schoolroom. What is the right of government to intervene in the development of character and the equipment of a child for a man's understanding? Does the wish of the constitution-makers and our own confirming determination to have a system of free speech deny us the right to use government to impose educational goals on unwilling parents? Silly questions? Consider this confident statement by a man of considerable distinction in the literature of constitutional law as it relates to civil rights—Professor Milton R. Konvits.

The state may compel parents to send their child to a public or private school where he would acquire the basic means with which to search for the truth *in his own way* . . . it would follow that the state may prescribe only the minimum number of subjects, study of which would be compulsory, such as English, spelling, arithmetic, American history and geography, and hygiene. . . . The state should not make *secondary* education compulsory as against the claims of religious objectors; for I do not see that a free, pluralistic society stands to lose in the long run if some people know their holy books thoroughly but are ignorant of Faulkner and Hemingway or even of Shakespeare, as long as they have acquired the basic tools for the pursuit of secular knowledge and there is a public library in their community to which they can go for books.[4]

I trust I have said enough to make clear what kind of assignment I recommend for political scientists when I urge them to provide an orderly array of the significant relationships between our verbal expression and our other interests and activities. My brief remarks do not disclose the magnitude of that assignment. A scholar's report of the significant relationships will attend to the content of expression and the ear that hears the message, as well as the forum in which the word is delivered. If tests of reasonableness are to determine whether government may impede or inhibit a particular expression, the judge will have to satisfy himself as to the importance of the message to the individual who utters it, to the individual who receives, and to the society which may profit or lose if such messages move freely among the population. When you put the values which support the application of restraint on the scales with the personal and social evaluation of the message, the outcome will vary according to whether the utterance is a groan or a grunt, a foul expletive, a blasphemous assertion of conviction, the idle chatter of a rattle brain, and on through a succession of categories up to the vital message that answers the question: What shall I do to be saved?

Intermixed with the importance of the message—perhaps inseparably blended—is the character of the audience. You would not allow adults to go about the playgrounds advising white children to beat up their Negro playmates; you might be reluctant to forbid the publication of a book which urged the same course of action on adults. The textbook intended for students in medical school may appropriately carry instructions which you would not permit in a book advertised as a do-it-yourself handbook of abortion. (Credit Mr. Malcolm Cowley for the illustration.[5]) The remark which is thought highly appropriate if whispered to an attractive companion may fall before the test of reasonableness if addressed to a group of old ladies.

I am confident that Justice Frankfurter will endorse the surveying job which I have described as eminently suited to the special competence of political scientists. He might insist that lawyers are better equipped than political scientists for the next assignment which I present for your consideration. I referred to it earlier

4. *Fundamental Liberties of a Free People* (Ithaca: Cornell University Press, 1957), p. 122.
5. In *Saturday Review* for July 7, 1962.

as the development of models of analysis which have as their purpose to identify and relate to one another the components of a free speech case. How do you evaluate an act of government— legislative, administrative, or judicial—which imposes a restraint upon speech or press? This is what the judge must do in any litigation where the validity of the restraint stands or falls on tests of reasonableness. I am convinced that none of the judges to date— and this goes for Justice Black, Justice Douglas, Justice Frank- furter, and Judge Learned Hand—I am convinced that none of the judges has so far produced an opinion that stands as proof that his decision rests on a comprehensive, sharply discriminating, and systematic scrutiny of the known and probable social con- sequences of the act under consideration. I think that the interests and the training which mark the thoughtful and competent political scientist make our discipline a prime hope for fulfillment of this need.

We must presume that there is more than one rewarding way of going about the evaluation of a public policy. I would not venture even to guess what alternative approaches and procedures may be turned up in a generation of assiduous scholarly study. In order to make sure that you understand what kind of enterprise I have in mind, I will give you the outlines of my personal attack on this problem.

The structure which I have adopted to guide my own analysis rests on three foundations: value position; suppositions and beliefs about effectiveness of means to ends; and attitudes toward un- certainty.

I can handle value position when I view a thing, a matter, as instrumental; I can do nothing with value viewed as ultimate, self-fulfilling, esthetic. If you tell me that nothing, absolutely nothing, gives you more satisfaction than popping your knuckles, about all I can do to straighten you out is to call your attention to other things you might value more highly if you gave them a trial. But if you say you pop your knuckles because that is the best way you have found to attract attention and cause people to seek your company, I can make a display of evidence glued to- gether by reasoning which may convince you that you had better look for another way of making friends and influencing people. Value, to be a useful concept in analysis, must be instrumental value.

You can fix a value for free speech and press by generalizing the utility of expression—by a conception that free expression is essential to an open society, or to maintenance of democratic gov-

ernment, or to some other end equally sweeping and inclusive.
The generalized approach, in which the instrumental value of expression is seen as diffused rather than identified with particular
goals, is helpful in fixing foundation presumptions concerning
public policy. As I see it, the usefulness of the generalized approach
ends with the fixing of presumption. I regret that the limits you
fix for listening prevent an explanation of why I believe this.

The identification, differentiation, and evaluation of means to an
end is extremely difficult in any social situation that we conceive
to be a significant problem. It is especially so where the problem
is the rightfulness of an act of government which impedes or
inhibits verbal expression. Consider the simple case of courtship
and the hospital. Value 1—Romance. Value 2—Quiet for hospital
patients. Means to romance—the serenade from the sidewalk and
the call to trysting place when the nurse sticks her head out of
the window. Means to quiet for patients—a city ordinance which,
admittedly abridging the freedom of communication, makes it a
penal offense to play a banjo, sing joyfully or plaintively, or call
out in a loud voice on sidewalk or street adjacent to hospital
grounds.

Two central points, then, in the evaluation of means to valued
ends. First courtship. Maybe the nurse will ordinarily or always
not hear the call to romance. If she does hear, the public exposure
of her availability may excite a disposition to mayhem which
thwarts the swain's visions of fond embrace. Countless are the
obstacles which obstruct the path of true love.

This is only one side of the end-means equation. Consider means
for achieving Value 2—the quiet which promises rest for patients
in hospitals. Maybe patients never hear serenades and yelling from
the sidewalk because doctors and nurses make too big a racket.
If heard, maybe the sound is a reassuring connection with the
outside world. Indeed, the behavior which the city fathers sought
to frustrate may have therapeutic effects worthy of an appropriation for periodic serenades.

I choose this simple illustration because it presents the elements
of decision which confront us in all cases of actual or proposed
restraint of speech or press. Always, I am sure, there are differences
of belief about what the particular speech or publication is good
for—what valued end the speech or publication advances and
how surely it advances that end. Always, I am sure, there are
differences of belief about what the proposed restraint is good for.
Will the law which forbids the address actually keep the message
from being broadcast? Will the restraints which are imposed neatly

excise the evil they are intended to combat, or will they spread their effects to consequences we are unwilling to incur? And so on.

This is only the start of analysis. Are there not other means by which the valued end could be achieved? The swain can make a call on the telephone or send a letter—with flowers. The hospital can be insulated against outside noises. We remove the jury temporarily from society so as to allow communication to proceed unconfined. Perhaps we should adopt the same policy for patients who need hospital care.

Beyond all this lies a complex of questions about what might happen if public officials do not attempt to regulate the speech or press that some people find offensive. Individuals or nongovernmental groups may put their own regulations into effect and do greater damage to self-expression and public communication than a thoughtfully drafted legislative act could conceivably do.

Running throughout these imagined events and relationships is a disturbing uncertainty. Not always is the one who evaluates an abridgment of speech or press firmly set in his value position. Rarely, indeed, can he be certain that he estimates accurately the effectiveness of a means to an intended end. Perhaps never can he be wholly confident that he foresees the unintended consequences of an act. Faced with such uncertainties, one man may be loyal to his intellectual processes and do what his analysis recommends; another man, less willing to assume risk, may rush back to the cover of a basic presumption.

It may be that I should have knocked out a few paragraphs of what I have already said, to make room for some comment on the practical use of the analytic scheme I have described. I will say only that it has put in place, for me, some of the formulae which have dominated judicial opinions—clear and present danger, dangerous tendency, gravity of the evil discounted by its improbability. When you spread out in your conception the values which compete for aggrandizement, the complicated pattern of relationships between chosen means and other available means to valued ends, the uncertainties which beset every aspect of your problem—when you spread out all of this in your mind you see better what the familiar judicial formulae are good for and you are alerted to sectors of the social problem which they do not comprehend and put in place. This has been my experience with the particular analytic design which I have inadequately developed for my own use.

You have, in these remarks, one response to Professor Frankfurter's challenge. I have indicated the character of three inquiries which I believe political scientists eminently qualified to undertake. I do not see a more urgent call for our service. A social environment, cordial to self expression and hospitable to sure and easy communication, is essential to the free life we have fixed as our highest goal. But uninhibited self expression and unrestricted communication are not free gifts of nature; they come at a price. I see no more worthy task for this profession than the instruction of lay citizens, judges, and statesmen who must calculate the price and decide how much free speech and free press are worth—when, where, and for whom.

# 13. FREE SPEECH AND SUBVERSION: AN HISTORICAL EPISODE

The Constitution created a government for the United States, specified the affairs that should be within its jurisdiction, and gave it power to make all laws necessary and proper for carrying into execution any and all of the powers vested in this new government or any part of it. One of the expressed obligations of the national government reads: "The United States shall guarantee to every State in this Union a republican form of government . . ." (Article 4, section 4). The First Amendment, added to the Constitution in 1791, asserts that "Congress shall make no law . . . abridging the freedom of speech, or of the press; or the right of the people peaceably to assemble, and to petition the government for a redress of grievances."

In these provisions, obviously, a stage is set for dispute. The people—any part of the population—who wish to participate in the direction and control of their government will expect to do more than vote in elections and say what they want their government to do. They will claim a right to say repeatedly and vigorously that they want their government to quit doing some things and to do differently some other things it continues to do. In listing the means available to the citizen for influencing government, I mentioned his ability to modify a policy by protest and resistance or nullify it completely by refusal to comply. Complaint against policies and acts of government necessitates communication that is embraced in the Constitution's words "speech" and "press." In order to make themselves heard and heeded, citizens will want to speak at the same time and to the same point, and this requires preparatory talk and writing in which they educate one another, agree on the formulation and scheduling of appeals, and instruct one another on plans for action. They may think that being seen together in demonstrations is a good way of emphasizing demands that are stated in words. If they decide to resort to outright resistance, the prospect for success will be advanced if they unite in displays of resistance. Opposed to the claims of the governed that they have a right to speak, write, hold meetings, march, demonstrate, and in other ways force attention to their demands that government alter its course, is the opposing claim of public officials that they have an obligation to make their laws effective in spite of the contrary wishes of a part of the population.

In this controversy the Constitution is on both sides. The declaration in Article I, section 8 that Congress shall have the power "to make all laws" that may be necessary and proper for carrying out the various powers vested in the national government surely must be a declaration that Congress may instruct administrative officials and courts to enforce the laws and endow them with the authority needed for successful enforcement. But the Constitution also says (Amendment 1) that Congress shall not abridge the freedom of speech or press or the right of the people peaceably to assemble and petition their government for a redress of grievances. How do we put these two sets of claims together? How do we give the Constitution's various provisions meanings that keep it from authorizing the citizenry to undo what Congress and its agents have been authorized to do? The invitation to a hiatus is especially clear in the provision that the United States shall guarantee to every state a republican form of government. One of the objectives, clearly avowed, of some of the citizenry is to replace the republican form of government with a different form of government. Where is the boundary between their right to assemble and petition and the authority of Congress to guarantee that their efforts to terminate republican government in one or more of the states will not be successful?

How shall we deal with this invitation to head-on conflict? Shall we, in order to prevent overthrow of government or obstruction of its processes, give the Constitution an interpretation that permits Congress and the state lawmakers to forbid particular speeches and writings so long as they do not impair a set of conditions that is favorable to free and easy communication? Shall we also say that the people are not guaranteed a right to assemble in any way but a peaceable one and that an assembly is not peaceable unless the reasons for coming together are peaceable in character? Should we insist further that when people assemble for political purposes the only thing they are guaranteed a right to do is discuss, agree on, formulate, and send to public officials a protest and request that they act differently in the future?

This is the problem we deal with in this chapter: the right of public officials to carry on government and maintain the present system of government, and the rights of individuals to express their wishes, meet together, formulate and publish demands, unite in behavior intended to obstruct the course of government, and lay the groundwork for future efforts to overthrow the present form of government. No other problem could so clearly reveal and so sharply emphasize the interrelatedness of the two foundation principles underlying the American style of democratic government: the principle of government by the people, and the principle of limited power for government. It is for illumination of this interrelatedness of the two principles that I probe as deeply as I do into this complex of open expression, free communication, assembly, sedition, and subversion. The inquiry takes the form of two case studies: an examination of our first notable effort to deal with sedition (in 1798); then an examination of contemporary policy centered in the Smith Act of 1940.

## The Sedition Act of 1798

In 1798 Congress and the President put three laws on the statute books that excited great controversy at the time and continue to be talked about up to our day. They were designed to curb speech, publication, and other behavior that, in the judgment of those who supported the legislation, brought the government of the United States into disrepute, encouraged rebellion, pushed the nation to the brink of war, and gave aid to nations that would be our enemies if we did go to war. Two of the new laws applied to aliens living within the United States. The other, the Sedition Act of 1798, applied to citizens of the United States as well as aliens. A scrutiny of the provisions of the Sedition Act and experience in enforcing it starkly discloses the tangle of values that disturbed the public tranquility during the first great crisis under the Constitution. We can learn from that experience because a similar clash of values accounts for the bitter controversy that has plagued the American people for two decades since World War II. The Sedition Act should be read with care.

## The Sedition Act of 1798

*U. S. Statutes at Large,* vol. 1, 596.

Sec. 1. *Be it enacted* . . . , That if any persons shall unlawfully combine or conspire together, with intent to oppose any measure or measures of the government of the United States, which are or shall be directed by proper authority, or to impede the operation of any law of the United States, or to intimidate or prevent any person holding a place or office in or under the government of the United States, from undertaking, performing or executing his trust or duty; and if any person or persons, with intent as aforesaid, shall counsel, advise or attempt to procure any insurrection, riot, unlawful assembly, or combination, whether such conspiracy, threatening, counsel, advice, or attempt shall have the proposed effect or not, he or they shall be deemed guilty of a high misdemeanor and on conviction, before any court of the United States having jurisdiction thereof, shall be punished by a fine not exceeding five thousand dollars, and by imprisonment during a term not less than six months nor exceeding five years; and further, at the discretion of the court may be holden to find sureties for his good behavior in such sum, and for such time, as the said court may direct.

Sec. 2. That if any person shall write, print, utter, or publish or shall cause or procure to be written, printed, uttered or published, or shall knowingly and willingly assist or aid in writing, printing, uttering or publishing any false, scandalous and malicious writing or writings against the government of the United States, or either house of the Congress of the United States, or the President of the United States, with intent to defame the said government, or either house of the said Congress, or the said President, or to bring them, or either of them, into contempt or disrepute; or to excite against them, or either or any of them, the hatred of the good people of the United States, or to stir up sedition within the United States, or to excite any unlawful combinations therein, for opposing or resisting any law of the United States, or any act of the President of the United States, done in pursuance of any such law, or of the powers in him vested by the Constitution of the United States, or to resist, oppose, or defeat any such law or act, or to aid, encourage or abet any hostile designs of any foreign nation against the United States, their people or government, then such person, being thereof convicted before any court of the United States having jurisdiction thereof, shall be punished by a fine not exceeding two thousand dollars, and by imprisonment not exceeding two years.

Sec. 3. That if any person shall be prosecuted under this act, for the writing or publishing of any libel aforesaid, it shall be lawful for the defendant, upon the trial of the cause, to give in evidence in his defence, the truth of the matter contained in the publication charged as a libel.

And the jury who shall try the cause, shall have a right to determine the law and the fact, under the direction of the court, as in other cases.

Sec. 4. That this act shall continue to be in force until March 3, 1801, and no longer: *Provided,* That the expiration of the act shall not prevent or defeat a prosecution and punishment of any offence against the law, during the time it shall be in force.

Approved July 14, 1798.

The Sedition Act was a criminal law. It forbade American citizens to do certain things and fixed fines and imprisonment as penalties for those who violated the law. The acts that were forbidden may be summarized as follows.

1. The Sedition Act made it a crime for persons unlawfully to combine or conspire with intent to oppose or prevent the enforcement of measures of the United States government.

2. The Sedition Act made it a crime for anyone to counsel, advise, or attempt to work up an insurrection, riot, or unlawful assembly, having intent to oppose or prevent the enforcement of measures of the United States government.

3. The Sedition Act made it a crime for any persons to write, print, utter, or publish (or cause or assist others to do the same) any false, scandalous, and malicious statements against the United States government or against the President or against either chamber of Congress with intent to (a) bring the government or branch of government or office which is attacked into contempt or disrepute; or (b) excite hatred against the government, branch of government, or office which is attacked; or (c) stir up sedition, or excite unlawful combination for opposing or resisting any law of the United States or lawful act of the President; or (d) resist, oppose, or defeat any law of the United States or lawful act of the President; or (e) aid, encourage, or abet any hostile designs which any foreign nation might have against the United States.

The Act, being a criminal law, required that attorneys for the prosecution bear the burden of proving that any person indicted for committing any of the forbidden acts had indeed committed that act, stated positively that the accused could present evidence showing that his statements were in fact true, and specified that the jury (acting under direction of the judge) should decide both the facts in the case and the application of the law to the case. Finally, the statute asserted that it should be in effect for less than thirty-two months, expiring the day before the next elected Congress and newly elected President would take office.

The Sedition Act of 1798 has been generally condemned by political scientists and historians. A textbook for study of American government says, "If the Sedition Act had been left on the statute books and applied in its full measure, neither the 'loyal opposition' nor free government would have been possible."* A historian writes:

Moreover, the Sedition Act was an implied acknowledgement by the Federalists that force and coercion rather than reason and argument were to be the ultimate arbiters of political controversy in the United States. Differences of opinion were to be erased and the American mind was to be forced into an intellectual strait jacket fashioned by Harrison Gray Otis and company.†

What was wrong with the Sedition Act of 1798? Which of the provisions listed above could be expected to erase differences of opinion from the American mind and make free government impossible? Did the statute cite only evils that government ought to be permitted to forbid? Or did it attempt to outlaw acts and statements that people must feel free to indulge in if they are to be free men who hope to control their government? To answer these questions we must examine the provisions of the statute with a great deal of care.

The Sedition Act forbade men to "unlawfully combine or conspire together" with intent to oppose a measure of the government or to intimidate or prevent an officer of the government from executing his duty. Note that the act did not forbid every assemblage of men who might get together with intent to obstruct government. It only forbade men to get together "unlawfully" for such a purpose. Common law in England and in many if not all the American states at that time forbade certain kinds of get-togethers designed to accomplish illegal purposes, regardless of whether the illegal purposes were actually accomplished. Congress and President sought to make this existing law applicable to get-togethers having as their purpose to obstruct enforcement of the laws of the United States government, and to make that law enforceable in federal courts. There was some doubt in the first years under the new Constitution that Congress was empowered to enact criminal legislation to make the new national government operate

---

* James M. Burns and Jack W. Peltason, *Government by the People* (Englewood Cliffs, N.J.: Prentice-Hall, 1957), 3rd ed., p. 161.

† John C. Miller, *Crisis in Freedom: The Alien and Sedition Acts* (Boston: Little, Brown, 1951), pp. 74–75.

effectively, and the Sedition Act was immediately attacked on that ground.

The need for law having this purpose is not seriously challenged today. If any behavior is sufficiently objectionable for the lawmakers to outlaw and punish it, there is good reason to require the man who commits that behavior to submit to arrest and trial. If a person, suspected of the offense with good reason, resists arrest or breaks jail, we think he ought to suffer a penalty for not cooperating in law enforcement. If we may penalize a man for resisting his own arrest and trial, surely we may punish other persons who aid him in resistance. And so by a series of steps we arrive at the conclusion that all who combine in an effort in which there is proven intent to obstruct law enforcement ought to be punished for making it more difficult for officials to put the laws of the land into effect. Such combinations or conspiracies are punishable under national and state law today.

But the boundary lines that separate a conspiracy or combination with a particular intent from associations of people who do not have such an intent can never be made sharp and clear. Conspiracies do not spring instantaneously into being; they develop out of preliminary talk and association which, if stopped at a certain point, would not be a conspiracy. Not everybody who gets mixed up in the get-together shares in the purpose that makes it a conspiracy and illegal. Admittedly, therefore, we risk doing some innocent persons great injury when we forbid conspiracies. It must be admitted that criminal laws and their enforcement are shot through with many equally difficult problems. It is exceedingly difficult to determine a man's intention when he is unwilling to say what he had in mind. The difference between carrying off something absent-mindedly and stealing it may be wholly a matter of intent, and the decision of a jury that a man committed murder may turn wholly on the jury's conclusion that he fired the gun with intent to injure or kill the man who died.

To forbid a conspiracy is to encroach on freedom of speech. The get-together that is in fact a conspiracy is a group of men who are communicating with one another. Indeed the conspiracy may be wholly developed by speech or writing, for the parties involved may never see one another. The proof in court that there was an associating together and a common intent to accomplish a certain purpose may rest wholly on evidence as to what men said to one another, orally or in writing. It may be that, in legal semantics, the punishment is for the association with conspiratorial intent and not for the speech by which agreement on purpose and action were arrived at. The layman, nevertheless, finds it necessary to fit a prohibition of conspiracies into his thinking about freedom of speech and press.

The relation of the Sedition Act to the constitutional guarantee of free speech and press becomes evident when we turn attention to the provision making it illegal for anyone to "counsel, advise, or attempt to procure" an insurrection, riot, or unlawful assembly. This goes back to events before the illegal get-together takes place. It appears to forbid a man to make a speech or distribute a pamphlet in which he tells other people they might enjoy or profit from a get-together called for the purpose of stopping enforcement of the law. The Sedition Act made such talk or writing illegal only if the speaker or author had as his purpose to cause law enforcement to be obstructed.

This provision of the Act clearly encroached on freedom of speech and press, since counseling and advising necessarily involve communication. How does it square with the constitutional guarantee? We are confronted with a question of timing governmental action. At what stage in a campaign to prevent enforcement of law may government move in to prevent the final act that makes government ineffective? The Sedition Act was clearly addressed to behavior at four stages of a conceivable campaign. Beginning with the imminence of the evil that the lawmakers abhor, stage 1 is the act that accomplishes the evil—actually impedes the operations of government— and stage 2 is the coming together to make plans to bring about the forbidden acts at a later time. Stage 3 is more remote from final accomplishment of the ultimate evil, being the advocacy and stirring up of conspiratorial meetings; and stage 4 is still farther removed, being the creation of states of mind friendly to behavior at any of the other three stages. One can imagine a government reaching even farther back to interrupt a chain of events, and many governments have actually done so. Thus several American states during the period of slavery forbade anyone to teach a slave to read or write, and many governments in Europe and Asia have scattered or exiled a troublesome ethnic group in order to reduce its potential for some later injury to the regime in power.

The question of how far to reach back in an effort to keep willful men from obstructing or overthrowing government faces all regimes, democratic and despotic alike. If it be agreed that the lawmakers may apply preventive measures at stages 1 and 2, why not let them nip the apprehended evil in the bud by punishing men for the preparatory activities which occur at stages 3 and 4?

Two sources of difficulty require lawmakers and enforcement officials to proceed with caution at each of the stages we have identified. They present themselves differently at the several stages, however, and this variance provides the theme for our analysis. The two sources of difficulty are: (a) the need to be certain that an injury to society will take place if preventive measures are not adopted, and (b) the need to be confident that innocent men will not be convicted if charged with an offense.

At stage 1 there is no uncertainty about the injury; law enforcement is actually obstructed and that is the injury the Sedition Act was designed to prevent. Further, the risk of injustice to innocent men is small, for the proof of the offense is in behavior that can be observed by police officers and others who testify in court.

At stage 2 there may be great uncertainty as to whether the anticipated injury will actually occur; the conspiracy may not succeed in interfering with law enforcement. Proof of an offense also presents hazards because intent to interfere with law enforcement must be established and, in the absence of confession of guilt, intent must be inferred from the behavior which took place. We assume big risks at two points, therefore, if we punish at stage 2. In spite of these risks we believe, as shown by the fact that we have many state and national laws to this effect, that as soon as men join forces to obstruct law enforcement it is time to move in on them with punishment; it is not necessary to wait until they have actually obstructed the enforcement of a law.

Both types of risk greatly increase when we propose, stage 3, to punish a man for advising other people to perform an unlawful act. How can we be sure that his urging will cause other people to do what he advises? A crackpot, fanatic, or lone wolf may urge other people to unite in resistance to government without the slightest likelihood that anyone will pay any attention to him. If we punish speechmaking about obstructing government, we may punish many people who cause no injury whatever to society. The risks involved in detecting violators and proving their guilt may be even greater. In many instances, to be sure, a court trial will establish beyond doubt that the speaker did urge people to obstruct justice and did intend to cause his hearers to obstruct justice. Possibly in as many more cases there will be doubt whether the speaker was recommending action or was only indulging in high grade or low grade philosophical discussion. If policemen are invited to arrest, grand juries to indict, prosecutors to prosecute, judges and juries to convict—if these agents of law enforcement are charged to bring to grief everybody who attempts to work up a riot, a jail delivery, a lynching party, must we not assume that they will frequently pick up and even convict a man whose only purpose is to convince people they live under injustice and ought to change their laws? If men and women have reason to fear that their efforts to change the laws, to improve the government, to terminate injustice will be misunderstood and that their innocent and lawful acts will be wrongly construed as counseling others to violate the law and join hands in insurrection—if honest people have such fears, will they play it safe, keep their mouths shut, and let things go on just as they are? Do we have the freedom of speech necessary for democratic government if fear of being misrepresented and wrongly punished puts any notable brake on the willingness of men and women to denounce offensive government and urge drastic reforms?

The two sources of risk we have examined—uncertainty that the intended evils could have been accomplished, and the likelihood that unwanted consequences will accrue from efforts to prevent those evils—loom even larger when we consider the remaining provisions of the Sedition Act. The act made it a crime for anyone to utter, orally or in print, any false, scandalous, and malicious statement against the President, or against either chamber of Congress, or against the government as a whole, with intent to bring about any of several evil consequences spelled out in the act. The act did not decree punishment for every man who told a lie about the government or a public official; it only punished for the lie that was scandalous in character and made with malicious intent. Furthermore, utterances that were at the same time false, scandalous, and malicious were forbidden only if the one who uttered them intended to destroy respect for the whole government or an essential branch of government, or cause hatred of the government, or stir up resistance to the government, or give help to foreign countries that might be planning an attack on the United States. It will readily be observed that the offensive statements that are forbidden by these provisions of the law are even further removed from actual accomplishment of the anticipated evil than are incitements to conspiracy which occur at stage 3 on our scale. The Sedition Act struck also at stage 4—the creation of states of mind that are friendly to obstruction of government.

The congressmen who voted for the Sedition Act and President John Adams who signed it considered three facts about the contemporary scene and from them derived a conclusion that false, scandalous, and malicious statements against the national government or its officials stood a good chance of working great harm to the American people. They took into account (a) the stream of invective that marked public address and political writing and the rioting that then disturbed many American communities; (b) growing evidence that the United States might at any moment be drawn into war with either England or France and strong indications that a good many American citizens (and foreigners as well) were doing what they could to make sure we went to war with the one they disliked most; and (c) the inescapable fact that enough time had not elapsed to make certain that the new national government had won unshakable public confidence.

Historians cite the following remarks as a reliable indicator of the tendency to libel and slander. It is from a charge to a grand jury delivered by Chief Justice McKean of the Pennsylvania Supreme Court six weeks before the Sedition Act was passed.

Every one who has in him the sentiments of either a Christian or gentleman, cannot but be highly offended at the envenomed scurrility that has raged in pamphlets and newspapers, printed in Philadelphia for several years past, insomuch that libelling has become a kind of national crime, and distinguishes us not only from all the states around us, but from the whole civilized world. Our satire has been nothing but ribaldry and Billingsgate: the contest has been, who could call names in the greatest variety of phrases, who could mangle the greatest number of characters, or who could excel in the magnitude and virulence of their lies. Hence the honor of families has been stained; the highest posts rendered cheap and vile in the sight of the people, and the greatest services and virtues blasted.*

Historians agree that the months preceding enactment of the Sedition Act were riotous times up and down the coastline of the United States. President Adams reminisced about the "terrorism" of the day in a letter he wrote to Thomas Jefferson fifteen years later. Allowing for error in recollection and a willingness to exaggerate because his friend Jefferson had scoffed at his efforts to preserve order, President Adams' account sounds probable enough in view of what others have written.

I have no doubt you were fast asleep, in philosophic tranquility, when ten thousand people, and, perhaps, many more, were parading the

* Francis Wharton, ed., *State Trials of the United States During the Administrations of Washington and Adams* (Philadelphia: Carey & Hart, 1849), p. 322.

streets of Philadelphia on the evening of my Fast Day [May 9, 1798];
when even Governor Mifflin himself thought it his duty to order a patrol of horses and foot to preserve the peace; when Market street was
as full as men could stand by one another, and, even before my door;
when some of my domestics, in frenzy, determined to sacrifice their
lives in my defense; when all were ready to make a *desperate* sally
among the multitude, and others were, with difficulty and danger,
dragged back by the rest; when I, myself, judged it prudent and necessary to order chests of arms from the war-office to be brought through
by-lanes and back doors, determined to defend my house at the expense of my life and the lives of the few, very few, domestics and
friends within it. What think you of terrorism, Mr. Jefferson?*

If the only cause for action to preserve order had been defama-
tion of character, incitement to contempt, terrorism and rioting,
one might have thought that the state governments could adequately deal with the situation of 1798. The national government
was especially involved for two reasons. The name calling and the
acts of violence were directed toward the national government;
they arose out of apprehension that Congress might declare war
against the country one admired and out of the wish to force the
nation into war with the country one despised. This alone may
have seemed to President Adams and his supporters reason enough
to impose the repressive measures incorporated in the Sedition Act.
In addition, they could point to uncertainty that the national
government had the support of a deeply rooted national loyalty.
When the Sedition Act was passed, less than twenty years had
elapsed since the last battle of the war for independence from
England. Barely more than ten years before, the first constitution
of the United States had been junked in favor of a new one. Since
then the nation had been almost continuously on the edge of war
and a Whisky Rebellion had been put down. These were the
considerations that led a Federalist President and a Federalist
Congress to conclude that great injury to the nation was impend-
ing and could only be prevented by repressive legislation.

The case for enactment of a criminal law is not complete when
one concludes that proper enforcement of the act will reduce or
avert a great evil. One must calculate the risks involved in enforcement and decide whether he is willing to assume those risks.
It turned out that the risks assumed in enforcing the Sedition Act
of 1798 were considerable. It seems probable that President Adams

---

* Letter of June 30, 1813 to Thomas Jefferson, *The Works of John Adams*,
ed. by Charles Francis Adams (Boston: Little, Brown, 1856), vol. 10, pp.
47–48.

and his Federalist supporters well understood what they were and willingly assumed them.

It seems reasonable to suppose that there were four main points at which enforcement of the Sedition Act could go wrong with adverse consequences for innocent persons. (1) Law enforcement officials and self-appointed guardsmen of the law could harass innocent persons, construing as violations of the law statements that they found offensive but that would never be found punishable in court. (2) Judges might prove to be prejudiced rather than impartial, and work injustice in their interpretations of the law and conduct of trials. (3) Members of grand juries and trial juries might also be prejudiced, indicting and convicting on inadequate grounds. (4) A state of emotionalism and partisanship in the general public not only might abet any of the foregoing offenses, but also might inflict social punishment on persons found innocent in court and add to the penalties imposed by courts on those found guilty.

Historians agree that enforcement of the Sedition Act fell far short of present-day standards for impartial administration of criminal law. Those who view that experience with greatest aversion condemn the program of enforcement on some or all of the following grounds: They find that law enforcement officials and self-appointed guardsmen of the law did harass innocent persons, that judges did stretch the meaning of the statute in order to broaden the range of forbidden statements and acts, and that judges and juries did reveal prejudice rather than impartiality in dealing with persons brought before them. They suspect that fear of wrongful prosecution caused many people to clam up and stop making the kind of criticism that was not only lawful but necessary for the discipline of public officials in a democratic system. These critics also suspect that bitter resentment of the Sedition Act caused many other tough-minded citizens to increase the very kind of abusive talk the law was designed to put an end to. Finally, some historians appear to be convinced that the reason for passing the law was not really to avert a great danger to the well-being of the nation, but rather to cripple the Republican faction of American politics and increase the chances that the Federalists would win the next election.

Writers who most strongly condemn the Sedition Act may overstate their case. The records that historians have so far had to rely on are far from complete, and in the main are reports by men who were deeply entangled in dispute. There is enough difference in the accounts of reputable historians to cause a cautious student to reserve judgment as to what actually took place and as to the consequences of efforts to enforce the act. Even so, we can with confidence state a few conclusions about success and failure in the first effort of the national government to deal with subversion.

## Evaluation of the Sedition Act

We have examined the Sedition Act and its enforcement for the light such an analysis can throw on the conflict of values that comes to the fore when some of the population set themselves up in opposition to government, and for illumination of the entanglement or imbroglio of means from which choice must be made when legislators attempt to resolve the conflict. The same conflict and imbroglio plague us today. Since World War II the American people have been deeply concerned about Communists, and both national and state governments have taken a number of steps to thwart persons who are committed to overthrow of government by force. What to do about Communists, subversion, and overthrow of government by force has been the central point of bitter controversy. Many who have been caught up in the controversy have said that experience under the Sedition Act of 1798 taught us lessons that ought to guide us today. At great risk of having missed the essential lessons, we shall now try to see what they are.

The scurrilous invective that Justice McKean deplored and the rioting that excited John Adams were unquestionably prime characteristics of the months immediately before and after enactment of the Sedition Act. Prosecutions for criminal libel and for rioting were brought in state and federal courts, under provisions of state statute and common law, before the Sedition Act was passed and during the two years it was in effect. Prosecutions continued to be brought in state courts after the Sedition Act expired, and these prosecutions were pushed by supporters of President Jefferson with his active approval. We may conclude that the evils the Sedition Act was intended to correct were real and not imagined.

It is doubtful that any prosecutions under the Sedition Act were for rioting or any other conduct covered in the first two objectives of the act (numbered 1 and 2 on page 218). All prosecutions brought under the Act appear to have been for offenses of the third type—making false, malicious, and scandalous statements about the President, Congress, or the whole government of the United States. This I referred to as stage 4 in a campaign to interfere with the operations of government.

Not many prosecutions were made. During the thirty-two months the Sedition Act was in effect about twenty-five persons were arrested on charges of violating it. Probably fifteen of these persons were indicted by grand juries; of these, it appears that ten were convicted. Most of the penalties fixed after conviction were small; the heaviest penalty fixed was eighteen months in jail plus a fine of $400 plus court costs of about $50.

Most of the trials were in federal circuit courts. In circuit court, a member of the United States Supreme Court presided. One or two other judges sat with him. Justice Samuel Chase of the Supreme Court was involved in a number of cases, issuing instructions to grand juries and presiding over court during trials. Justice Chase was hot tempered, a vigorous supporter of the Federalist position, and a ready expositor of his personal convictions. It is generally supposed that Justice Chase prejudiced jurors against the accused. Charges of this character have not been lodged against other judges who sat in cases arising under the Sedition Act, and some historians have expressed confidence that all except Chase behaved in proper judicial manner.

Some historians have made a great deal of the fact that federal marshalls empaneled jurors who thought the Sedition Act a good law and believed it ought to be vigorously enforced; it has been strongly hinted that the typical jury intended to convict regardless of the force of evidence. It should be borne in mind, however, that then as now a man was counted not proper for appointment to a jury if there was ground for believing him opposed to enforcement of the law under which indictments would be brought. It should be borne in mind also that attorneys for the defense participated in the selection of jurors. It must be pointed out that we do not know what evidence was put before juries and how they reacted to it. One of the historians who appears to have combed the source material thoroughly says there is some reason to suspect a biased jury in one case but no evidence to support such a conclusion in any other case.*

The Sedition Act was enacted and enforced in a period of highest emotionalism and partisanship. This state of turmoil encouraged the kind of statements and acts that the Sedition Act was designed

---

* The historian last referred to is Frank Malloy Anderson, in *The Enforcement of the Alien and Sedition Laws,* Annual Report of the American Historical Association for 1912 (Washington, 1913). Severe charges of bias in enforcement of the Sedition Act are made in John C. Miller, *Crisis in Freedom; The Alien and Sedition Laws* (Boston: Little, Brown and Co., 1951); and Marshall Smelser, "The Jacobin Phrenzy: Federalism and the Menace of Liberty, Equality, and Fraternity," *Review of Politics,* vol. 13 (1951), p. 457.

to punish and, hopefully, to put an end to. If these statements and acts were to be punished at all, the law had to be enforced right when emotionalism and partisanship were at their highest. It may be that a community is in no mood for fairness in enforcing the law against assault and murder at the time when Jack the Ripper is at work. If you want to put an end to Jack the Ripper you have to go after him when he is operating, when the community is most worked up, when people are most likely to demand the arrest of every suspicious looking character and the conviction of any person brought into court. So we can hardly argue that Adams and his Federalist supporters should have waited till calmer times to enact the Sedition Act.

One can never know what effect enactment of a law has on public attitudes and social treatment of persons suspected or convicted of violating the law. We do know that in 1798 parts of the population were dealing cruelly with other parts of the population in communities up and down the east coast. This was the case before the Sedition Act was passed, while it was in effect, and after it expired. It may be that enactment of the Sedition Act stimulated some people to persecute their neighbors more cruelly. It may also be that enactment of the statute led some people to suppose that public authorities had the situation in hand and so resulted in a reduction of cruelties on their part.

We cannot even roughly estimate the effect of the Sedition Act and its enforcement on freedom of speech and criticism of government. One can never know how many people were scared by the Act and refrained from making critical statements that were not false, malicious, and scandalous. Neither can we know how many people were infuriated by the Act and responded by indulging in increased criticism of government. There is a good deal of evidence that many newspaper editors who had been printing virtually anything handed to them began to exercise some editorial judgment after the Sedition Act was passed and effectively limited the distribution, if not the writing, of the kind of statements the statute was designed to terminate. It seems also that a number of new newspapers were established while the Sedition Act was in effect, and that most of these bitterly opposed the Sedition Act and the government that enacted and enforced it. We know also that bitter criticism of the President, of Congress, of the courts, and of the Federalist party did continue throughout the period in which the Sedition Act was enforced. We know that some of the strongest official denunciations of the Federalist position (the Kentucky and the Virginia Resolutions) were adopted while the Sedition Act was in effect. We know also that a vigorous political campaign went on in the summer and fall of 1800 and the Federalist party was effectively broken up by the election of Thomas Jefferson and a Congress dominated by his Republican party.

Finally, the lessons that this experience might afford us in dealing with subversion today are partially obscured by the state of politics during the period of the act's effect. The Sedition Act was companion to other statutes that dealt drastically with aliens who stirred up opposition to the government of the United States. The Sedition Act itself was directed against activities of American citizens as well as foreigners. The acts it made unlawful were not attacks on government in principle. It made unlawful certain kinds of attack on government as it was being carried on by President Adams and his Federalist supporters. The men who were punished under the act were, in the main, supporters of a party out of power; the utterances for which they were punished were, in the main, ammunition designed to help put that party into power. When different interests of the population get drawn into this kind of conflict, it is not clear why men do what they do, and we mistrust their statements about what happened and about the consequences of the events. We do not know whether the men who put the Sedition Act into operation thought this a necessary means for averting a great injury to the nation or a smart trick for assuring their continuance in office. Neither do we know what ends were uppermost in the mind of incoming President Thomas Jefferson when he ordered all pending prosecutions dropped, and pardoned all persons under sentence. "I did this," he wrote to the wife of John Adams, his great political opponent but also his great personal friend, "without asking what the offenders had done, or against whom they had offended, but whether the pains they were suffering were inflicted under the pretended sedition law." Why Jefferson so sternly opposed the Sedition Act is not clear. Judgments on that matter must take into account a paragraph in his second inaugural message (1805), surely a careful statement of his personal position. After congratulating himself and the nation for having proved, during his first term in office, that a government can stand in the face of outrageous attack, he said:

No inference is here intended that the laws provided by the States against false and defamatory publications should not be enforced; he who has time renders a service to public morals and public tranquillity in reforming these abuses by the salutary coercions of the law; but the experiment [i.e., the experience of the preceding four years] is noted to prove that, since truth and reason have maintained their ground against false opinions in league with false facts, the press, confined to truth, needs no other legal restraint; the public judgment will correct false reasonings and opinions on a full hearing of all parties; and no other definite line can be drawn between the inestimable liberty of the press and its demoralizing licentiousness. If there be still improprieties which this rule would not restrain, its supplement must be sought in the censorship of public opinion.*

* James D. Richardson, ed., *Messages and Papers of the Presidents*, vol. 1, p. 369.

# 14. FREE SPEECH AND SUBVERSION: A CONTEMPORARY SOLUTION

The circumstances that led to enactment of the Sedition Act of 1798 have their parallel in our own time. Today, as in the first decade of the Republic, there is apprehension that the political system might be destroyed, determination to thwart those who would obstruct government or overthrow it, and willingness to make significant encroachments on personal choice and freedom of action if that seems to be a necessary price for orderly government and national security. The analysis pursued in connection with the earlier law and the conclusions, tentative or firm, derived from that analysis are fully applicable to the legislation now in effect. In this chapter, therefore, we continue the analysis and evaluation that was begun in the preceding section.

In 1948 Congress revised and codified the criminal laws of the United States. One chapter of this criminal code is entitled, "Treason, Sedition, and Subversive Activities." This chapter fills approximately five pages of the statute book. In these five pages the lawmakers specified the things American citizens were forbidden to do on the ground that to do them would endanger the security of the nation or impair or destroy democratic government in this country. The acts that were forbidden and for which punishments were specified in this chapter of the criminal code can be listed under these heads: (1) treason and misprison of treason (misprison of treason being failure to report treasonable acts of others); (2) rebellion or insurrection; (3) obstructing the operations of military forces of the United States or impairing their morale or loyalty or interfering with their discipline; (4) engaging oneself or inducing others to serve in armed forces hostile to the United States or promoting the success of such hostile forces; (5) seditious conspiracy; and (6) advocating overthrow of government by force or violence.

Of these six categories of criminal law, only the last one—advocating overthrow of government—is a recent addition to the code. The first Congress that met under the present Constitution fixed penalties for treason and misprison of treason, and criminal law relating to all other subjects in this list, except advocating overthrow of government, was added soon thereafter. Seditious conspiracy, as we have seen, was a criminal act for more than two years during 1798-1801; it was made a permanent part of the law three months after the firing on Fort Sumter in 1861. During World War I this law was greatly extended by two acts of 1917 and 1918 that made it a crime to obstruct the prosecution of the war in any of several specified ways and also made it a crime to willfully advocate, teach, defend, or suggest that other persons do any of these forbidden acts. A broad interpretation of this part of the law would make unlawful any widespread appeal for American citizens to overthrow their present government and construct a new kind of government. But the provisions that were added in 1917 and 1918 are applicable only while the nation is actually at war with another country. They differ significantly, therefore, from those introduced into the law of the United States in 1940.

Since 1940 it has been illegal to advocate resort to violence for overthrow of government in the United States at any time, whether in war or peace. The objective of this later legislation is to safeguard our present form of government for its own sake, not solely to free ourselves from trouble at home so that we can effectively fight a war abroad. This new body of law was put into the criminal code by three separate enactments—The Alien Registration Act of 1940 (or Smith Act), the Internal Security Act of 1950 (or McCarran Act), and the Communist Control Act of 1954. The Smith Act defined the specific offenses that collectively are referred to as advocating overthrow of government by force, and it is this particular law that we examine most closely in the present analysis. Those definitions are therefore given here.

## The Smith Act (Alien Registration Act)

Approved June 28, 1940. U. S. Statutes at Large, vol. 54, p. 670.

Sec. 2. (a) It shall be unlawful for any person:

(1) to knowingly or willfully advocate, abet, advise, or teach the duty, necessity, desirability, or propriety of overthrowing or destroying

any government in the United States by force or violence, or by the assassination of any officer of any such government;

(2) with the intent to cause the overthrow or destruction of any government in the United States, to print, publish, edit, issue, circulate, sell, distribute, or publicly display any written or printed matter advocating, advising, or teaching the duty, necessity, desirability, or propriety of overthrowing or destroying any government in the United States by force or violence;

(3) to organize or help to organize any society, group, or assembly of persons who teach, advocate, or encourage the overthrow or destruction of any government in the United States by force or violence; or to be or become a member of, or affiliate with, any such society, group or assembly of persons, knowing the purposes thereof.

A good many American citizens of unimpeachable loyalty and undoubted intelligence have stated clearly and emphatically that they think the Smith Act carries far more promise of injury than of benefit to the nation and therefore ought either to be repealed or declared invalid by the Supreme Court. The Act is justified as appropriate and necessary by other persons equally entitled to be listened to. But nowhere near all of the citizenry are active in the controversy. Many, perhaps the majority, of alert and thoughtful citizens are troubled by doubt as to how laws designed to secure orderly government and national security can be accommodated to the rightful claims of personal liberty. A careful analysis of the legislation and its probable consequences ought to replace doubt with confidence on some aspects of the subject in dispute. This we undertake now, concentrating mainly on the Smith Act but placing it in relation to objectives sought and means adopted in related legislation. Pursuing the analytic design utilized for the Sedition Act of 1798, we shall consider (1) the objectives of the legislation—the evils that the law is designed to prevent; (2) the means adopted for dealing with the evil—the points in a chain of events at which the law strikes; and (3) the risks assumed in pursuing the course adopted by the lawmakers.

Federal legislation relating to sedition and subversion, forbidding six classes of acts, is directed to three great evils. One evil is getting the nation into war, or increasing the duration and hazards of war, or obstructing our efforts to prosecute the war. A second evil is the overthrow or destruction of government within the United States or interference with the operations of government. The third  evil is establishment of a regime that now carries the statutory designation "totalitarian dictatorship."

Surely we may ignore the argument of any person who would

contend that Congress and the President may not seek, by appro- priate means, to prevent individuals from accomplishing the first of these evils. War with even the weakest opponent gets some- body killed, costs money, and may carry in its wake immeasurable adverse consequences. There may be general agreement that the country ought to go to war on certain occasions. But the risks in- volved in war are far too great for us to allow Tom, Dick, and Harry to work one up or stretch one out. Therefore we vest the power to declare war in Congress and the President and give them the entire authority to manage it.

We may expect general agreement also on the second evil. Un- less one is an anarchist, contending that there should be no gov- ernment, he has to concede that lawmakers may, by proper means, protect the existence and operations of government. If a nation wants government badly enough to set it up, it does not want somebody to tear it down. If people want something badly enough to authorize government to do it, they want to see that it actually gets done. To say that the authority and power of government cannot be used to keep government going is, in practical effect, to say that a great part of the population cannot do something that a small part of the population may wish to interrupt or prevent.

The third great evil that recent legislation seeks to avert—estab- lishment of a totalitarian dictatorship—appears to be one special consequence of the evil we just discussed. In 1940 we made it illegal to advocate overthrow of government by force because Congress and the President thought there is ample opportunity to change government in this country by peaceful means and be- cause they thought persons who are satisfied with the government we have ought not be required to defend it against displays of force. In 1950 and again in 1954 Congress and the President took further steps to protect our present form of government, striking this time at efforts to establish a totalitarian dictatorship, especially a dictatorship supported by communist ideology.*

Again we have no difficulty in recognizing as evil the set of conditions that the statutes are designed to prevent. Totalitarian dictatorship, one of the statutes asserts, repudiates the rights and the liberties that are allowed to the individual under democratic governments, and maintains control over the population by fear,

---

* The Internal Security Act of 1950 (or McCarran Act), *U.S. Statutes at Large*, vol. 64, p. 987; Communist Control Act of 1954, *ibid.*, vol. 68, p. 775. These two statutes state at some length the objectives and methods of "a world Communist movement" and "the Communist Party of the United States."

terrorism, and brutality. One may argue whether the label "totalitarian dictatorship" should be restricted to regimes that push people around this way. Certainly there will be argument about appropriate and best means of escaping such a regime. But we can hardly doubt that a regime which does what the statute attributes to dictatorship is indeed an evil that the lawmakers may properly try to avert.

In our analysis of the Sedition Act of 1798 we found it helpful to identify four stages in campaigns to accomplish something that the lawmakers wish to prevent. Stage 1 is the actual attempt to do what the law is designed to avert. Stage 2 is one step removed— the coming together or joining in efforts (conspiring) to bring about the overt acts which occur at stage 1. Stage 3, urging other people to perform those overt acts or enter upon a conspiracy to do them, is still further removed from accomplishment of the evil. And stage 4, even more remote, is the development of states of mind in other people that may some day bear fruit in attempts to accomplish the evil to which the legislation is directed.

We saw also in our analysis of the Sedition Act that there are two types of risk that must be assumed in governmental efforts to thwart such campaigns. Risk 1 lies in the possibility that the acts we forbid would never, if tolerated, result in the injury to society that we wish to prevent. Risk 2 lies in the chance that our preventive efforts, even if they do help to avert the evil, may have consequences we do not anticipate and set up other injuries to society greater than the evil we are attempting to strike down.

We now have a battery of laws that strike at all four stages of effort to incite or aggravate war, overthrow government, or set up a dictatorship. It is unlawful to resist arrest, to show contempt of court, to obstruct the movement of troops, to give various kinds of information to a foreign government, to burn down public buildings, to assassinate public officials. These are overt acts of stage 1. Preventive efforts that strike at this point involve least risk on either of the two counts noted above. Legal provisions of this type are not the subject of noteworthy debate and need concern us no further here.

Law that strikes at stage 2—getting together, combining, conspiring to bring about the forbidden overt act later on—is amply illustrated by the section of the criminal laws (Title 18, chap. 115, sec. 2384 of the U.S. Code, originally enacted in 1861), which subjects each person to fine or imprisonment if two or more persons, within the jurisdiction of the United States, "conspire to overthrow, put down, or to destroy by force the government of the

United States, or to levy war against them, or to oppose by force the authority thereof, or by force to prevent, hinder, or to delay the execution of any law of the United States, or by force to seize, take or possess any property of the United States contrary to the authority thereof." Those Americans who are most fearful that injustice will be done to innocent persons are at least dubious about law that punishes for conspiracy. Assuming that such feeling did exist, it was pushed into the background in 1940 with the adoption of the Smith Act, which made it a crime to advocate or teach overthrow of government by force. This new legislation clearly offered far greater opportunities for injustice than the longstanding prohibition of conspiracy, and opponents of the law were quick to point this out. Critics of the Smith Act, trying to get it repealed or declared invalid, turned to the argument that the earlier laws that punish conspiracy to overthrow government give us all the security we need. In order to create opposition to the legislation they feared most, many who took this line of argument endorsed other legislation that, it may safely be said, they earnestly wished to see removed from the statute books.

Without question the Smith Act strikes forcefully at the third stage in a comprehensive campaign to overthrow government by violence. It declares it to be a crime for anyone (1) knowingly or willingly to advocate, abet, advise, or teach such a doctrine; (2) to contribute to the distribution of literature advancing such a doctrine, doing this with intent to cause government to be overthrown; (3) to create or help create organizations, or be a member of or affiliate with an organization that advances such a doctrine, knowing the purposes of the organization. In dealing with this stage of the campaign, the Smith Act is even more sweeping than the statute of 1798. The earlier law made punishable only the acts of recommending, urging, and helping to bring about cooperative efforts to obstruct law enforcement. The language of the Smith Act, declaring it a crime to teach a doctrine, reaches much farther back into the events that precede the coming together and making of plans that constitute a conspiracy.

It seems necessary to conclude, therefore, that the Smith Act strikes also at stage 4—the development of states of mind in other people that may some day bear fruit in attempts to accomplish the evil to which the law is addressed. The second of the three crimes listed in the preceding paragraph makes punishment dependent on intent to cause the downfall of government; the statute does not mention intent or purpose in defining the other two crimes. We may regard this as a defect of drafting; students of constitutional law understand that advocating destruction of government by force is punishable only if it is done with intent to bring about the acts of violence that are recommended. The presence of intent in the mind of the advocate is, of course, a matter to be determined in court. It is also the business of the courts to decide whether the probability of violent action taking place is great enough to warrant a conviction for purposeful advocacy. Allowing for these and other requirements that will be read into the statute, it still must be acknowledged that the Smith Act forbids certain efforts to prepare minds for future attacks on our system of government.

A society assumes some risk of injuring innocent people in every enactment of criminal law. It happens that one man confesses to a crime for which another man has already been hanged. There is risk in punishing men for the overt acts we cited above, and risk in punishing men for conspiracy to bring those overt acts about. We shall not attempt to examine the risks at these stages of preventive effort. We have enough to do if we examine risk where it is greatest—in legislation that attempts to prevent development of certain states of mind. We shall try to uncover the risks that lurk in legislation of this character by examining the controversy that centers about it.

The protest that has been raised against the Smith Act is not a cry in unison, for those who fear or dislike the statute are not in full agreement as to what is wrong with it. The following seem to be the main lines of argument against the law:

The acts that are forbidden cannot be clearly differentiated from acts that are lawful. The nation must encourage discussion that objectively describes what we have, what we do not have, and what we could have in the way of government; discussion that critically evaluates the alternatives available to us; discussion in which people declare what they like and do not like and appeal to other people to see things as they do; discussion in which people urge retention of what we have or recommend change to something else and argue ways and means of accomplishing the ends they have in view; discussion in which one man denounces another and people get mad and say things they later regret; and discussion running still beyond these things. Talk and writing of this character edges up against discussion that says: "Don't wait for people to find out what is wrong with their government and improve it; tear down this government that I say oppresses you and build a new one that will be run by people on our side; and resort to force if necessary to bring this oppressive regime to an end." If you try to prevent talk and writing of this second (use-force-and-violence) kind, enforcement officers and judges and juries are bound to misjudge intent, and occasionally they will punish people for talk and writing that ought to be tolerated because it is actually of the first (talk-people-into-changing-their-minds) kind.

A conscientious effort to enforce the law requires enforcement officers to probe into personal conduct in ways that people ought not to have to put up with. To detect violations of the law, it is necessary to investigate conduct simply because it looks suspicious. Someone must listen to speeches and read pamphlets in order to see whether the suspected man has made statements that justify indictment and prosecution. This leads to inquisitions that undermine and erode qualities of independence, integrity, and self-confidence. In time such inquisitions will destroy the nation's capacity for self-government. Further, say those who oppose such legislation, laws that penalize one man for advising other men to commit unlawful acts are likely to be misused by those who are charged to enforce them. Responding to public demands for rigorous enforcement, police, prosecutors, judges, and juries will make unnecessary investigations, arrest without proper cause, indict on too little evidence, convict without adequate legal justification. Injustice to individuals will thus abound and the decomposition of the fibre of a democratic people will be hastened.

It is at least possible, the argument continues, that unrestrained advocacy of overthrow of government by force is an important contributor to public understanding in a democratic country. Enemies of democratic government will survive and work toward their ends no matter what we do to thwart their efforts. It is better that they work aboveboard than underground. Great sectors of the population, not just the few who hold public office and serve on juries, should look them in the face, hear their arguments, push their words back in their teeth. It is by grappling with danger that people learn how to deal with danger. It is by hearing their system challenged that people make up their minds what they value most and learn how to defend it.

Finally, the opponents of the law contend, the Smith Act should be repealed even if all the foregoing arguments are rejected. It ought to be repealed, they insist, because it is a response to a false alarm. There are not many people in the United States who wish to overthrow government by force. Such as there may be are known to police and can be picked up whenever they apply the first stroke of violence. Even if there are many of them, they constitute no danger because the nation as a whole will neither heed their teaching nor respond to their call to arms. Even small prices are too much to pay to nip in the bud a movement that has no chance whatever of coming to flower.

The first links in this chain of argument assert that the nation assumes great risks in outlawing speech and writing that advocates overthrow of government by force. The closing point is that these risks need not be incurred because the danger of government being overthrown is not great enough. The argument may be countered on both grounds: that the risks inherent in a vigorous enforcement of the law are not as great as alleged, and that the danger is great enough to justify the risks no matter how stupendous they be.

Those who support the effort to punish persons who advocate and teach the overthrow of government in the United States by force do indeed reply on both of the above grounds. The burden of their argument rests on four main points.

First, the likelihood of injustice to individuals is not as great as portrayed by those who fear this legislation. Certainly there is risk when you make punishment depend on a particular intention and when the prohibited act is not strikingly different from acts we wish to tolerate. It is a risk we know how to handle because we have long been assuming it. We do not refuse to convict for theft because the accused stubbornly insists that he intended to return the object he had taken. We do not refuse to punish for rape because in so many instances it is virtually impossible to determine whether consent was given. Risk has to be assumed wherever danger is encountered. The path of hope is not to ignore the danger but to meet it head-on with laws that clearly specify the acts that are forbidden and procedures designed to differentiate what is forbidden from what is lawful. The legislation now on the statute books is worded in meaningful language. Our law enforcement procedures are adequate to the situation because we have had generations of experience in administering difficult problems of criminal law.

Second, in the view of those who support the law, opponents of the Smith Act exaggerate the evils that are likely to result from unintended restraints of speech and writing. Supporters of the statute are convinced that our democratic condition does not rest on as precarious a base as some critics of the law seem to think. The nation's liberties are not destroyed if we curtail speech at a few points. Parents impose curbs on what their children can say. Despots scattered throughout the population intimidate people into silence today and release them from restraint tomorrow. A newspaper is a channel for vigorous debate in this community; civic leaders or a moneymaking publisher clamp down a censorship somewhere else. Looking at the nation's behavior, it is apparent that there is a lot of leeway in our resources for assembling ideas and information and passing them on to others. It is unlikely that many people who are innocent of criminal intent will be deterred from public communication by the penalties of this act. If some are, the nation will not greatly suffer from their temporary silence.

Third, it is argued, such risks as there are on either count will become less as the law succeeds in its purposes. Action by government is not the only resource a population has for dealing with things it fears. Individuals and organizations move in on other individuals and groups that are viewed as a threat. Here is the real danger of injustice to individuals, curbing of free speech, and destruction of moral fibre. Nothing dissolves this unofficial rushing to the ramparts like a public notice that appropriate laws have been passed and firsthand evidence that law enforcing officers are moving in on the danger.

Finally, the argument comes to this point. Suppose one concludes that the critics of the Smith Act are right about the risks involved in enforcing a law that penalizes men for advising other men to commit unlawful acts. Grant that those who are charged with enforcement will be overzealous in their efforts to fulfill their obligations. Does this force a conclusion that the risks ought not to be assumed and the statute ought to be repealed? The conclusion does not follow, in the opinion of those who most staunchly support the contemporary effort to root out subversion. Threats to the American way of life, in their opinion, are real enough and the prospects for their success are imminent enough to justify assumption of every risk that has been pointed out. Granted that right now not many Americans are allied in the apparatus of revolution, it does not take many to do enormous damage. If the apparatus cannot take over the country, it nevertheless can force us to great costs in anxiety and counter effort, and we may properly object to paying these costs. We must not measure the strength of the organization by the number who serve its cause in this country. Organized efforts to overthrow government in the United States is only one section of a worldwide revolutionary movement. If the nations that direct that movement should ever make war on the United States, the apparatus they maintain in this country might determine the outcome of that war.

In presenting two sides of a great debate, I have tried to bring critical issues to attention rather than to reproduce the argument that actually goes on. There are not just two sides to the debate, but many sides. Opponents of the law are not in full agreement as to what is wrong with it, and supporters of the law give different arguments in its defense. Emotion rather than reason accounts for many of the statements both in attack and defense. If my own reasoning is sound, the differences in apprehension and belief that ought to be pondered are as I have presented them.

It must have been noticed that my analysis of efforts to deal with sedition and subversion, both in this chapter and the preceding one, makes few references to decisions of the Supreme Court. The deference to that tribunal that marks nearly all writing about constitutional guarantees makes it necessary to explain why I depart from custom. My objective was not to determine what the law is, or even to reason out what the law ought to be. Rather, I tried to disclose the considerations that legislators and judges ought to take into account in deciding how to deal with a conflict between highly cherished values. Stated more precisely, my purpose was to provide the reader with a method of analysis that he can use in making up his own mind where to draw the lines between permissible action that makes government effective and preserves its democratic character and action that ought to be condemned because it hems in or encroaches upon a domain of personal freedom. The clashes of values and of evaluations that have been brought before judges and the reasoning of judges in resolving those conflicts help you and me in establishing personal positions. But there is no more reason for letting the judges fix our conclusions, thereby removing alternative conclusions from further consideration, than there is for saying that Thomas Jefferson settled the question as to whether the "demoralizing licentiousness" of the press ought to be corrected "by the salutary coercions of the law," or that the prohibitions of the Smith Act are proved appropriate and well chosen because a majority in two houses of Congress voted in favor of them. Having this opinion about the inconclusiveness of such fountains of thought as Supreme Court judges, congressmen, and Thomas Jefferson, I cannot feel guilty because I have deprived the reader of such conclusions as I have arrived at myself.

# V

*Democracy on Trial*

# 15. THE NEGROES' CHALLENGE

American democracy has lately been placed on trial by the civil rights movement. Its wholeness, vigor, and durability are now being tested, and the nation is required to prove the democratic character of its political, economic, and social institutions and ways. The challenges are voiced by the Negro leadership, but all elements of the population, Negroes as well as whites and other nonwhites, must answer to the challenges.

Let us say tentatively that the goal of the Negroes is their full incorporation into the American society. The proof of their incorporation, when it is realized, will be seen mainly in the economic and social realms. The payoffs of the good life in the United States are principally in economic welfare and social status. One strives for political influence in order to improve and make secure one's position in the economic and social realms. It cannot have been supposed, at the close of the Civil War, that the black men so recently freed from slavery would immediately be rewarded with prosperity and easy interaction with the population that had previously owned their bodies. The promises of equal protection of the laws and the right to vote, supplied by the Fourteenth and Fifteenth Amendments, were viewed as assurances that the Negro could enlist the authority of government in his behalf as he made an arduous climb to economic well-being and a social status that a free man could regard with pride. The promises of post-emancipation days were not fulfilled, and today the Negro strikes for improved status on three fronts: the economic, the social, and the political. It is appropriate in this essay for us to focus our attention on his determination to be justly regarded by government and to be accorded a rightful share in control of government.

Statements about the condition, aspirations, and determinations of Negroes that are true for the Negro population as a whole cannot be precisely true for particular Negroes or for Negroes in every part of the country. We shall speak here as if all Negroes have the same status in the society, have the same needs, are caught up enthusiastically in one movement for release from their present condition. I bear the responsibility for making my statements generally true; the reader must fit the generalizations to the varying realities with which he is acquainted and which attract his interest.

## Demand for Justice

The Negro's condition and his current campaign impeach the American claims to a democratic political system, challenging the validity of those claims profoundly and from start to finish. Consider first the three states of mind and behavior which I proposed as requisites for democratic government: personal and group autonomy, equality, and commonalty. The Negro, denied recognition as an equal of the white man, was restricted in his ability to choose his place in the societal labyrinth and mark out for himself a personal domain which he could rule according to his own judgments and defend from intruders. He was hemmed in or fenced out in the world of business and industry, the professions, labor organizations, recreation and sports, and the maze of community organizations. He was not totally denied opportunities to make the decisions and bear the responsibilities that are proof of personal autonomy, but his opportunities were grossly restricted. Denied a chance to develop the understanding and capabilities that accrue from experience in being a man of affairs, the Negro was deprived of leverage that would have given him a chance to win the treatment that is proof of equality. Generally apart from the busy life of the nation and denied recognition as an equal when he was in contact with the dominant whites, he could not unrestrainedly absorb and attach himself to the beliefs, convictions, creeds, and myths which are the stuff of a national mind and behavior fit for self-government. The Negro came to exhibit in most respects the mind-stuff and the ways that constitute the American character as exemplified by the white population, but he also developed and expressed himself in a subculture of his own.

To the extent that the Negro's attitudes and ways differ significantly from those of the white population, the commonalty requisite for democratic government is breached. How seriously it is breached we have yet to find out. It remains to be learned whether

the Negro will make the adaptations necessary to incorporate himself wholly into American society, modifying the present culture
but not significantly setting his race apart from the rest of the population. If the conduct of the Negro in the indefinite future follows
the course recommended by those who urge a Negro state within
the American state, then we shall learn either that the commonalty
necessary for a democratic society is critically deficient in America
or that the commonalty I described earlier is in fact not a requisite
for democratic government.

The Negro's campaign also exposes the mutually supportive
character of the two foundation principles of the American political
system: popular control of government and limited power to govern. Regardless of the date fixed for initiation of the current drive
for improved status, 1954 or earlier, it started with a marked emphasis on constitutional rights. The first dramatic victories were
won in courts. The Negro learned that the judiciary would back
up his claims that governments were violating constitutional man-
dates, and not only would nullify unconstitutional acts when
committed but would also aggressively institute nondiscriminatory
regimes in education and possibly in other areas of communal life.
These victories in forcing compliance with constitutional guarantees supplied the tip-off that the Negro could force a recognition
of his right to participate fully in the institutions and proceedings
by which the American people direct and control their governments. Within a year after the orders were issued in the segregation cases Negroes had boycotted the public transportation system
of a Southern city. Within another five years sit-ins and other
physical demonstrations gave proof that the Negro had come alive
politically in the South. By the end of the decade inaugurated by
the segregation decisions Congress had passed and the President
had signed a Civil Rights Act that put the force of the national
government back of the Negro's assertion that he would no longer
be denied access to the polls and other forums of political decision.
As he enters more fully into the political activity by which officials
are selected and platforms are written, we can be certain that the
Negro will utilize his resources to force a fuller compliance with
the constitutional guarantees and other legal and traditional restrictions on governmental power that promise him equal status
with the white man.

Finally, the strategy and tactics of the Negro remove any linger-
ing doubt that the populist and the pluralist demand-response
systems interlock in any all-out effort to achieve goals of great
importance. To the reluctant or resisting white, the strategy of

the Negro must appear remarkably shrewd and his tactics richly variable. He reaches directly for what he wants (by drinking at the fountain marked only for whites and entering the polling place in a community that formerly excluded him); he inconveniences and intimidates the persons who withhold what he claims (by picketing or boycotting their businesses); he enlists the sympathy and support of those who think of themselves as third parties (by engaging in nonhostile behavior that excites his opponents to hostility); he invokes the aid of the nation's institutions where they can serve his ends (by suits in courts and pressing claims on public officials and philanthropic organizations); and he strives to assure a friendly response to the claims he presses on government (by participating in elections and other political activity).

His current tactics appear to be linked to longer-range strategies. Demands for change in the initial stages of the campaign may have been concentrated in the South because that was a sure way to win support from whites in the North and offered promise of eroding opposition that would be encountered when the campaign should later be carried to all parts of the nation. Present strategies directed to the long run and enjoying support among present leaders may quickly give way to new strategies if masses of Negroes turn from their initial leaders to new ones. It seems unlikely that the Negro's campaign has yet reached its peak of involvement and activity. There are signs that its future course will be less pacific than its course to date. There are prophets and demagogs on the scene who espouse goals that do not include the incorporation of the black man into an American society. It is possible that some of the prophets are not false prophets and that some who appear to be demagogs will later be revered as statesmen. If Negroes do turn to goals not yet announced, it must be supposed that they will adopt strategies not now foreseen.

This meager description of the Negro's strategies and tactics is none the less sufficient to show how he resorts to both the populist and the pluralist demand-response systems. He votes where he is permitted to cast a ballot, and when he enters the polling place he participates equally, man for man, with all other voters. He institutes actions in courts where, while the ideal is not fully realized, one man's claim to justice is on a par with the claim of his adversary. But the Negro also takes his claims into forums and arenas where equalization of influence is not a rule of the game, and heads are not counted to determine the will of a majority. Predominance in numbers may be an asset of great importance in these arenas, but deficiency in numbers may be overcome by amplitude of resources. The decision goes to those who put together the best combination of whatever it takes to win over the particular adversary on the particular issue at the particular time—resources of intellect and will and stamina among leaders and followers, resources of sympathy and encouragement and tangible aid from allies, resources of wealth and ability to reward and deprive others, and so on. Unable to generalize as to what have proved to be critical resources in contests on issues of paramount importance, we say that victory goes to those who make the superior display of power.

The Negro's demand for incorporation into the society forced the American white to face a moral, social, and political problem. The strategy and tactics with which the Negro presses his demands, and some of the responses that his campaign has elicited, present the whole nation, Negro as well as white, with a second problem: What are the bounds of permissible political action? What limits on efforts to coerce ought to be established by a nation that adheres to democratic ideals? What kinds of activity supported by what displays of power can be tolerated in the pluralist arena by a nation that vests authority to govern in public officials chosen by an inclusive electorate?

A comprehensive and painstaking evaluation of the Negro's efforts to achieve improved status would be a book in itself. I shall direct my attention here, not to particular strategies and tactics, but to the aggregate of activities that may appropriately be labeled organized protest and resistance. And the consideration of this ill-defined problem area will be limited to one concern: What are the bounds within which organized protest and resistance must be confined in a democratic political system? This excludes inquiry into the validity of claims that precipitate protest and resistance, search for effective means of achieving goals, and innumerable other interests that might serve as starting points for an elaborate inquiry.

The Negroes have no monopoly on organized protest and resistance. Attitudes and practices of the whites excite action by the Negroes, some of which is in the form of organized effort. The response of the Negroes provokes further defensive and retaliatory action and new aggressions by whites. The Negroes, reconsidering the effectiveness of their campaign, adopt new strategies and tactics. Controversy feeds upon itself. Organized protest and resistance, under the most skillful leadership of men devoted to pacific measures, nevertheless skirts upon violence and excites violence.

The particular acts that combine to produce the seething social disturbance can be plotted at successive points on several continua; for example, one ranging from the wholly peaceable to the most violent, one ranging from the admittedly lawful to the admittedly unlawful, one that starts with acts attracting no attention and ends with acts that excite other people to fury. It may be helpful, in pursuing the reasoning that follows, to fix in mind certain kinds of behavior, which we shall term "activity-types." At the least, three activity-types should be borne in mind. One is activity that is lawful, peaceable, and neither creates notable inconvenience for others nor arouses their apprehensions. A second activity-type, farthest removed from the first, is savagely violent action, admittedly unlawful and calculated either to crush opponents or excite them to counterwarfare. A third activity-type, lying between the first and second, is nonviolent action that is *per se* lawful but destined, and perhaps intended, to provoke violent and illegal behavior by others. Such action, lawful in its first instance, may become illegal by virtue of causing excessive inconvenience to others or provoking others to unlawful action.

I see no reason to think that the central question—what are the bounds of tolerable organized protest and resistance?—can be answered to general satisfaction in our day. The most we can hope to do here is illuminate the problem by some ground-clearing analysis. We shall proceed to that end by attending to three questions: (1) Does American experience, expressed in approved patterns of behavior or philosophic statements, provide sufficient justification of the organized protest and resistance we witness today? (2) What considerations deserve prime attention in any careful effort to fix the bounds of tolerable protest and resistance? (3) Does the Negro's marginal political status justify the strategy and tactics of his current campaign? The first question will occupy our attention for the remainder of this chapter; the other two questions will be explored in the next chapter.

American history provides five patterns of thought and action worth consideration in a search for experience that might justify the organized protest and resistance of today: Loyalty to personal conscience; Religious opposition and withdrawal; Popular enforcement of the Constitution; Lawlessness; Revolution.

### PERSONAL CONSCIENCE

"The only obligation which I have a right to assume, is to do at any time what I think is right." These are the words of Henry

David Thoreau in his famous essay *On the Duty of Civil Disobedience.* This sentence asserts an obligation to be ruled by personal conscience and denies obligation to obey an order of the state that commands one to violate the dictates of his conscience. This is only one tenet in Thoreau's doctrine of civil disobedience. He announced also that, because the state was so deeply involved in injustice, "I simply wish to refuse allegiance to the State, to withdraw and stand aloof from it effectually." But to withdraw and stand aloof appears to have meant only renunciation of personal obligation, not rejection of opportunities for personal advantage. "In fact," he wrote, "I quietly declare war with the State, after my fashion, though I will still make what use and get what advantage of her I can, as is usual in such cases."*

American history is dotted with declarations and conduct that have borne the label "civil disobedience." The manifestoes have been alike in putting conscience above law and asserting obligation to disobey the law that requires one to do a thing his conscience condemns. The conduct of the dissenters has differed, however, in the extent of the breach with civil authority. Few, I believe, have stated as unabashedly as Thoreau that they would choose as they pleased among the advantages offered by the state without acknowledging an obligation to submit to any of the state's commands.

In searching for experience that may have inspired and guided the protest and resistance of our own days, I think it best to differentiate refusal to perform an immoral act on the state's command from the more inclusive denials of civil obligation. We shall first consider the response to personal conscience and then consider withdrawal from civil authority as exemplified by certain religious groups.

The doctrine that personal conscience is superior to civil authority provides only a partial justification of the pro-Negro and anti-Negro campaigns now in progress. The conscientious objector does not attempt to line up other persons to act in unison with him. His defiance of government is intimately connected

---

* The essay *On the Duty of Civil Disobedience* is included in Henry David Thoreau, *Walden* (New York: New American Library, Signet Classic, 1960). The quoted sentences are on pp. 223 and 236 of this printing. A good collection of statements by Americans who have resisted civil authority for various reasons is: Staughton Lynd, ed., *Nonviolence in America: A Documentary History* (Indianapolis: Bobbs-Merrill Co., 1966). Two careful discussions of civil disobedience are: David Spitz, "Democracy and the Problem of Civil Disobedience," *American Political Science Review*, vol. 48 (1954), p. 386; and Sidney Hook, *The Paradoxes of Freedom* (Berkeley: University of California Press, 1964), chapter 3.

with the principle that governs his personal conduct. He does not refuse compliance with law A in order to secure repeal of law B or to cause other men of conscience to demand the enactment of law C. Surely there is a great deal of conscience wrapped up in the Negro's campaign, but it seems to me his tactics result from shrewd calculations of political effectiveness rather than determination to live righteously. I think it must be recognized that the overriding objective pervading all aspects of the Negro's drive for equality is to make sure that the white man will accede to his demands rather than to avoid personal involvement in acts of government that offend the conscience.

If the reasoning I have pursued is convincing, one need not rebel against the conclusion. It is important that we carefully observe what is going on, try to understand why people do what they do, and frankly acknowledge what we find out and conclude. Only if we do this can we decide whether the current phenomena accord with our previously fixed standards for democratic behavior, and in case they do not, set upon a re-examination of those standards to see whether they are too confining.

### RELIGIOUS OPPOSITION AND WITHDRAWAL

Opposition to government that stems from religious conviction is principled, organized, and directed by leaders. In these respects it is like the drive for improvement of the Negro's status and its countermovements. Here the resemblance ends. The cause of the religious group is rooted in a principle that none of the protagonists in the present struggle can accept. The religious objector responds to a command that he regards as higher than civil authority—the command of God as clarified in religious teaching. In the case of general withdrawal, the sectarian seeks to remove himself from governmental authority, justifying his action by a claim that civil government has invaded a realm that has been withheld from civil authority for administration by God through His church. This controlling principle is antithetic to the encompassing purpose of the Negro's present crusade. The Negro seeks the support of government (as do his opponents). Indeed he seeks to force the officials of government to fulfill their acknowledged obligations and enlarge their conceptions of obligation.

Instances of religious objection that do not involve general withdrawal from civil authority, directed to particular policies or commands of government, are expressed by refusal to comply with the particular policy or order. I do not believe that religious protesters try to block one governmental program as a strategy for obtaining the repeal of another and different governmental program. If they are opposed to the use of force, they refuse to serve in military or police assignments; they do not interrupt traffic on the highways or boycott the business interests of public officials as a stratagem to force abandonment of the policy they oppose. If they refuse to pay taxes that support military activities, they make it clear that they stand ready to pay taxes for support of other governmental activities. This is in marked contrast to the Negro's effort to improve his status. Viewed as particular ends, his objectives are many; put together, they call for action on a broad front. Striking for many things in one campaign, it would defeat his purposes to direct particular actions to single and differentiated objectives. What he needs to do is resist discriminatory policies and practices, discourage objectionable uses of authority and encourage favorable uses of authority, and win the support of all parts of the population that can be brought to view his cause sympathetically. For a campaign engaged on so broad a front, the experiences of religious protest and withdrawal can supply few instructions.

### POPULAR ENFORCEMENT OF THE CONSTITUTION

James Madison soothed apprehensions that the new central government might abuse its power by assuring the people of New York that unwarranted acts would be overcome by opposition. "The disquietude of the people; their repugnance and, perhaps, refusal to cooperate with the officers of the Union," coupled with impediments erected by the state governments, he asserted, "would present obstructions which the federal government would hardly be willing to encounter." (*Federalist*, No. 46). The proposition that the people may and ought to refuse to obey any law believed to be in violation of the Constitution dates at least from 1798. This doctrine was pressed upon Congress by Representative Edward Livingston of New York in debate on the proposed alien and sedition laws.

After declaring that the proposed legislation was an open, wanton, and undisguised violation of the Constitution, Livingston asked whether the people and the states would submit to the proposed laws if they were enacted. "Sir, [he said] they ought not to submit; they would deserve the chains which these measures are forging for them if they did not resist. . . . My opinions, sir, on this subject are explicit, and I wish they may be known; they are, that whenever our laws manifestly infringe the Constitution under which they were made, the people ought not to hesitate which they should obey. If we exceed our powers, we become tyrants and our acts have no effect." A few days later, in the same debate, Albert Gallatin of Pennsylvania, later to become Jefferson's great Secretary of the Treasury, affirmed Livingston's declaration of principle. Unlike Livingston's speech, Gallatin's remarks were reported in third person. Gallatin said he understood Livingston to have asserted "a general position that they [the people] had a right to resist and would resist unconstitutional and oppressive laws. He [Gallatin] believed that doctrine to be strictly correct, and neither seditious nor treasonable. The opposite doctrines of passive obedience and nonresistance had long been exploded. America had never received them."

If the sentiments of Livingston and Gallatin struck any of their colleagues as sound doctrine, each of them must have turned in his mind the question: How many of the people must be agreed that a violation of the Constitution has occurred in order to give legitimacy to a popular movement to nullify a law? Representative John Allen of Connecticut asked that question and answered it for himself: "The people, I venerate; they are truly sovereign; but a section, a part of the citizens, a town, a city, or a mob, I know them not; if they oppose the laws, they are insurgents and rebels; they are not the people."*

The doctrine of popular enforcement of the Constitution by resisting laws thought contrary to it has had a hardy career in American political life. It was asserted by men in high places immediately before and during the War of 1812. Undoubtedly it reinforced efforts to achieve nullification of national laws by state governments off and on from 1798 to 1858. No doubt it also provided a salve for conscience when secession and civil war took the front in the American political drama.

Here, undeniably, is a true progenitor of present-day organized protest and resistance. White people in the South announced their adherence to Livingston's doctrine promptly after the Supreme Court issued its orders for desegregation of the public schools in 1955. Less than a year after the Supreme Court spoke, ninety-six

---

* Interesting parts of the debate are printed in Charles S. Hyneman and George W. Carey, eds., *A Second Federalist* (New York: Appleton-Century-Crofts, 1967), pp. 72–76. For the original report see *Annals of Congress*, 5th Congress, 2nd session, pp. 2005–2015, 2093–2101, 2107–2111. Livingston spoke on a bill relating to enemy aliens; Allen and Gallatin spoke on the bill that became the Sedition Act.

congressmen from Southern states signed a "Southern Manifesto" declaring that the Supreme Court had acted "contrary to established law, and to the Constitution." During the period of initial shock eight of the eleven states that once seceded from the Union officially announced their rejection of the Supreme Court's interpretation of the Constitution. The most extreme of the documents declared the Supreme Court's orders null and void within the state; the Mississippi legislature put it: "in violation of the Constitutions of the United States and the State of Mississippi, and therefore . . . unconstitutional, invalid and of no lawful effect within the confines of the State of Mississippi." The people of Arkansas, by popular vote and by overwhelming majority of those voting, approved an amendment to the state constitution instructing the state's officials to employ the full power of the state for nullification of the Supreme Court's "unconstitutional desegregation decisions."

White resistance to desegregation in the South has been verbally justified, persistently, by the assertion that orders to desegregate that stem from a view of Constitutional obligation, stem from an erroneous interpretation of the Constitution. I see no reason to doubt that resistance to judicial orders for desegregation are "legitimized" for the resisters by conviction that the Constitution of the United States is on their side. Without question the official declarations of judicial error and "true" constitutional interpretation by state legislatures greatly bolstered the popular rebellion against the Supreme Court's decrees. White people in states that did not officially oppose the judicial orders did, here and there, resist the call to terminate segregation in the schools, and cited wrongful interpretation of the Constitution as justification for continuing segregation. This and other evidences give every reason to believe that, in the absence of official interposition, substantial numbers of people scattered throughout the South would have announced their competence to judge the "true" meaning of the Constitution and would have made their readings of the Constitution ground for standing fast against the Supreme Court's reading.

As I see it, the Negro is no less devoted than the white man to a thesis of personal interpretation and enforcement of the Constitution. The Negro and his supporters have refused to comply with state and local statutes, ordinances, and administrative orders that sustained discrimination against the Negro. Let us suppose that in every case those who violated the local law were advised by lawyers that if resort were made to judicial action, the ultimate decision would approve the violation. This would appear to be good reason for resorting to judicial proceeding, and equally good reason for complying with the local law until an appropriate judicial voice had confirmed the personal judgment that the offensive law is indeed discriminatory and unconstitutional. It seems to me that declarations of personal competence to overrule the established public authorities on a question of what is a "true" statement of the law are essentially the same phenomena regardless of whether the authority one relies on is words in the Constitution or words of the Supreme Court that were not addressed immediately to the issue in dispute. At the least it ought to be agreed that where the stakes are high, personal statements of the "true" law will differ, and if action in defiance of public authorities proceeds on the basis of one interpretation, a counteraction from those who stand on a different interpretation ought to be anticipated.

The doctrine of popular interpretation and enforcement of the Constitution is hard to down in cold analysis. It rests on the supposition that WE THE PEOPLE did indeed ordain and establish the Constitution. The nation rejected the claim of states to secede from the Union on the ground that the people of the United States had, by creating and affirming the Constitution, put the Constitution above any part of the people and the subordinate governments of the people. Can you assert this and not also assert that the Constitution stands above all parts of the national government, including the judicial organs? And if you assert that the Constitution stands above the courts, what are you to do when you believe that judges violate the Constitution? When a Breckinridge asks the question (in 1802), "Who checks the Courts when they violate the Constitution?" is it enough to answer that the highest judges of the land cannot violate the Constitution because the Constitution requires just what those judges say it requires?—which is exactly how I understand the Supreme Court did answer the Kentucky Senator (and all others who have asked that question) 150 years later in the case of *Cooper* v. *Aaron*. "It follows [from long acceptance of the doctrine of judicial review]," said the Court, every judge signing the statement, "that the interpretation of the Fourteenth Amendment enunciated by this Court in the *Brown* case is the supreme law of the land, and Art. VI of the Constitution makes it of binding effect on the States 'any Thing in the Constitution or Laws of any State to the Contrary notwithstanding'" (358 U.S. 1, at p. 18, 1958).

## LAWLESSNESS

Closely akin to popular enforcement of the Constitution is the unabashed violating of the law that has been practiced by Americans continuously since they became a nation. It is unnecessary to describe the phenomenon or try to calculate its incidence; mountaineers taking pot shots at revenue officers, respected citizens lightheartedly violating gambling laws and traffic regulations, millions of Americans defiantly evading the national prohibition law and perhaps hoping that by so doing they were nullifying a provision of the Constitution—this is the kind of behavior I refer to as lawlessness.

A first superficial judgment is likely to be that past violations of law can provide no justification for new violations of law; that the behavior I call lawlessness has no philosophic foundations and therefore can afford no moral support for the organized protest and resistance characterizing both the Negro's drive for equality and the opposing efforts to restrain the Negro. The contemptuous attitude toward law that has been apparent throughout our history has not been a response to principle; the objective has been neither to enthrone the commands of conscience nor to prove to tyrants that they must submit to constitutional requirements. What we find on a first casual inspection are simply cases of people refusing for a wide variety of personal reasons to comply with legal requirements they acknowledge to have been prescribed by authorities who had a right to decide as they did and who may rightfully enforce those requirements if they can catch the violators.

The plausibility of this superficial judgment is challenged when one contemplates the possibility that lawlessness is a consequence of selective enforcement of the law as well as personal dislike for law. We enact laws with the expectation that public officials will exercise a wide discretion in enforcing them. It is a way of rewarding good behavior and forgiving weakness. An arrest or indictment or bringing to trial of a "respected" citizen will punish him, even if found not guilty, by detracting from his store of respect. Furthermore, he is "the kind of man" who probably will try to live up to his word if he promises not to offend again. If he can do it without paying too high a price in public complaint, the officer does not arrest, the prosecutor does not seek indictment or press for trial, the jury goes easy, the judge suspends sentence. The same impulses to leniency apply when the offender is a flustered old lady or carrier of some other built-in appeal to pity or forbearance. To one element of the population this is a way of doing justice by mitigating the harshness of the law. In the view of those who are not the beneficiaries of such leniency and to all who identify with those who take the rap, there is one law for the rich and another law for the poor, the law is an instrument of social tyranny, the equal protection guarantee of the Constitution is a farce.

There are two other reasons for enacting a law with expectation that it will not be enforced with regularity: it may be intended only for the flagrant offense; or it may be designed for use only when the community is bent on a crusade. There may be no expectation that automobile drivers will habitually stay within the 60-mile speed limit on open highways, but the offense of speeding is a sure ground for conviction when a man is picked up for reckless driving, and few tears are shed if he gets two penalties, one for endangering lives and one for speeding. The practice of easing up and cracking down in local law enforcement must be familiar to every reader. Police, prosecutors, judges, and juries engage in it and lawmakers anticipate it. The boundaries of offenses can be pushed outward and penalties can be made more severe if the lawmakers are confident that the penalties will be invoked only on those rare occasions when the community has "had enough" and is determined to clean up for a change.

Whatever the reasons for selective compliance and selective enforcement of the law, it must be admitted that this practice flourishes and extends its own boundaries. Expectation that law will be violated invites violation. Professor Sidney Hook, who might get my vote as the leading American political theorist of our day, writes that: "The consequences of the widespread violation of the Prohibition Amendment, by making crime a way of life and encouraging a cynical attitude towards law enforcement, were far more harmful to the community than the arbitrary and unjust restrictions which this ill-considered amendment placed upon the sumptuary habits of American citizens."* I do not know how one could find proof that this is so, but I would rather undertake to prove that it is so than to take on the job of proving that it cannot be so. I do not see how people could grow up in a regime of low regard for law and laxity in efforts to enforce the law without being confirmed in a disposition to count on continued looseness in the fit of law to social conduct.

By such reasoning I conclude that readiness to take to the

* *The Parodoxes of Freedom* (Berkeley: University of California Press, 1964), p. 115.

streets in the present controversy about the Negro's status must have been quickened by the nation's history of selective compliance and selective enforcement of the law. Especially in the case of the Negroes, the contemplation of our system of selective justice may have given an aura of legitimacy to any trespass on the rights of others that might appear expedient. The Negro, at least in the South, has long been accorded special treatment in the administration of the white society's justice. His thefts and assaults, though widely publicized, often went unpunished in the white man's courts when white men were going to jail for like offenses. But they went unpunished only if their immediate consequences were confined to the Negro community. Here was selective justice indeed, and I find most imposing the hypothesis that a long period of tutelage in the white man's views of law removed a moral question from their minds when Negro leaders saw advantage in organized resistance of the white man's laws.

I will not venture an opinion about the consequences of selective justice for the moral position of Southern whites who have resisted the Negro's demands for incorporation into the society. I am not reluctant, however, to express a judgment about the relation of differential application of the law to the readiness of Southern whites to resort to violence in their efforts to confine the Negro to his previous status. The long-standing practice of applying to the Negro, in and out of court, tests of obligation and penalties that were not applied generally to the white community undoubtedly rendered unnecessary any extended argument that once more the time had come for white men to fashion particular remedies for the particular challenges the Negro placed before him.

REVOLUTION

A right of revolution figures prominently in the literature of political thought. For that reason I mention it here. I see no reason to believe that it has an important place in the attitudes of either whites or Negroes in this country. Granted an awareness that the nation came into existence by revolution, there must also be a high awareness that a revolution was put down by the Civil War. Their current rebellion is not conceived of as revolution by Negroes —certainly not at the moment, and surely not destined to become so. Rebellions that begin and end with a dominating purpose to change a political system rather than terminate it and create a new political system are not revolutions in the vocabulary of political thought. For many of the American colonials, the first hostile acts of 1775 and 1776 were designed to force the King and Parliament to concede to North Americans a treatment that would make them content to stay within the British empire; only later did a goal of separation from England come to dominate the American effort. A rebellion grew to be a revolution. There are Negroes who talk today about a separate Negro state; possibly some of them contemplate a change so drastic that, after its accomplishment, the old United States would have come to an end and a new United States or successor system would have come into being. If so, their goals do not dominate the Negro's present campaign. The white man's countercampaigns, of course, are even further removed from revolutionary implications; they are wholly directed to preservation of the present system.

If one has a broad enough view of the political process he may contend that everything that happened in the past has some consequence for everything that happens later on. Guided by that kind of presumption, one must suppose that past experience with revolutions and contemporary awareness of the nature of revolutions has made some impact on the goals, the resolution, and the methods of the protagonists now engaged in racial conflict. My contention is that this element of our heritage is of minimal importance in accounting for the near-warfare of today. It does not deserve attention at a time when we are baffled as to how we may trace out and appraise the most significant precursors of the organized protest and resistance that now disturbs the nation.

# 16. ORGANIZED PROTEST AND RESISTANCE

The state cannot keep the individual from resisting its authority short of putting him in shackles and taping his mouth. Laws are instructions for the behavior of people. Full compliance is voluntary compliance. The agents of the state cannot hover over every citizen at every moment. If a man is courageous and stubborn enough in his determination to resist government, the prospect of penalties will not keep him from doing so. In jail, he may pride himself that he is not obeying the law that accounts for his being there. He may even be able to make his prison cell a sounding board that enlarges the audible range of his protest.

It is different with organized protest and resistance. If public authorities are unable to silence a multitude of voices or induce compliance with law where non-compliance is a test of group loyalty, they nevertheless may hamper or destroy the organization that gives the multitude a plan for common action and hope for triumph. Without organization, purposeful coordinated action gives way to the frenzied acts of mobs. Mobs can be destructive but they do not win drawn-out contests with agents of the state when most of the population is loyal to the state. I shall not inquire into the means available for nipping dissent in the bud, disconcerting incipient rebellion, or putting down mature insurrections. My concern will be only with considerations that ought to be weighed in deciding whether to tolerate organized protest and resistance and what bounds to put upon it when tolerated. My discussion will be cast in a mold fixed for me by the social environment that envelops the present conflict in race relations and the goals, strategies, and tactics of the protagonists.

## *Protest and Resistance Evaluated*

Two presumptions control my thought about the bounds of permissible protest and resistance. These presumptions I make personally, though I believe they are widely shared in our society. The first: Anybody and any number of persons, singly or in groups, spontaneously or in response to leadership, may utter verbal protests against any policies, laws, and acts of government. Verbal protest means oral statements, written statements, showing of pictures; it does not include throwing stones, firing rifles, burning buildings. This is a presumption; it is not a declaration of unrestricted right. A presumption can be overcome by the introduction of relevant considerations that were unknown or overlooked when the presumption was formed. The burden of producing the evidence and reasoning, the duty of making the argument, that overcomes a presumption or limits its application is on the man who opposes the presumption.

My second presumption is that no one, and therefore no groups, may refuse to comply with any policies, laws, or acts of the government at any time or under any circumstances. Since this is a presumption, it also may be overcome or its application may be restricted by a convincing display of evidence and argument.

The gain that comes from clear understanding about the presumptions lies here. I am not required to say why it is desirable that people be free to declare their dislike for what their government is doing, and why it is desirable that people comply with the laws and other acts of their government. I am permitted to proceed at once to the conflict among the values represented by the two presumptions. There is value in a right to dissent, in ability to communicate that dissent to others, and in freedom to assemble with a view to fixing goals and considering ways and means of achieving goals. There is, equally, value in realizing the fruits of government, and that value is lost if laws are not obeyed and the authorized acts of public officials are obstructed.

It may be that one can, to his own satisfaction, so define each of the two sets of rights that they abut upon one another without overlap or conflict, so define them that any display of words and force is either wholly justifiable as an expression of dissent or totally reprehensible as a defiance of government. I do not find such an enterprise attractive. I prefer to say that right and obligation do overlap and do come in conflict. Viewing the relationship of right and obligation in this way, I have to acknowledge that when conflict occurs decisions must be made as to how far one of them ought to give way to the other. The decision in any case ideally will be dictated by the circumstances of the case; I say ideally, meaning that if those who make the decision honestly endeavor to balance the competing values of right to withhold consent and obligation to comply with law, the outcome of their deliberation will be determined by the way those values are presented in the conflict situation confronting them.

My task then is to illuminate, if I can, the problems encountered in resolving such conflicts. More specifically, I hope to identify the considerations that ought to be taken into account in resolving the conflict of values presented by the campaigns of protest and resistance now disturbing the public tranquility. The pertinent considerations may be arrayed in relation to four questions: (1) Who is protesting? (2) What are the objectives of the campaign? (3) What strategies and tactics are utilized? (4) What consequences of the action-program can be anticipated and what allowance should be made for unforeseen consequences? These questions are not neatly separated. We shall see at once that an exploration of the first question inevitably leads into the second.

## WHO IS PROTESTING?

Differences in color and ethnic origins are irrelevant in fixing the limits of permissible political action, but the following may be relevant: Consciousness of being a group differentiated in the society; the social distance of the group's removal from the society's norms; the size of the group; the depth of its convictions; and especially whether it is or is not accorded full participation in the means available for sharing in control of government.

## WHAT ARE THE OBJECTIVES OF THE CAMPAIGN?

Any group that is outside the populist demand-response system will be handicapped in its effort to lay claims before the society and obtain satisfaction. How may it proceed for rectification of its situation and satisfaction of its critical needs? In order to gain access to the electoral-representative process, should the group be limited to formal petition and the arts of verbal persuasion, or may it resort to coercion? Pending its admission to full participation in the political system, must it hold its other demands in abeyance or may it simultaneously press by coercive means for both admission to the system and redress of other wrongs? Once

admitted to equal participation in the political system, should a
conscious minority thenceforth be limited to the instruments of
persuasion and influence thought appropriate for those regarded
as predominant in the society? Or does desperateness of condition
—social distance from what is viewed as the society's norm—entitle
a deprived element of the population to utilize instruments of
power denied to the rest of the population? These considerations
are at the heart of thoughtful debate about the social crisis shaking
America today.

## WHAT STRATEGIES AND TACTICS ARE UTILIZED?

I announced a presumption and asserted that I need not defend
the claim that individuals and groups have a right to dissent, to
express dissent verbally, and to assemble for consideration of goals
and means of achieving them. In my judgment this presumption
of right ought to include a right to demonstrate—to make any
display of words and actions—in any manner thought appropriate
by the group so long as it entails no inconvenience or disturbance
to others. This far I go by presumption; call it assertion of right
by fiat if you wish. Beyond this point, when the demonstration
is abrasive to other people, a call for inquiry must be sounded.
Minor and transient irritations to others may be dismissed sum-
marily if a cause is thought just; irritations that promise to excite
others to counter-irritations clearly cannot be so easily dismissed
from consideration. Marches and sit-downs that inconvenience no
one may have a payoff for the demonstrators in increasing public
awareness of demands, recognition of wrongs, appreciation of the
determination of those who protest. Awareness, recognition, and
appreciation may be sharpened if the demonstration carries a
stinger in inconvenience and irritation for many elements of the
population. Demonstrations that are per se nonviolent can carry
the sting that excites violent reactions. Ought one conclude that
there should be no limits to expression of protest by concerted
action so long as that action is itself not an imposition of force
on other people?—i.e., that no limits should be placed on nonviolent, nonforceful demonstrations no matter what degree of inconvenience, irritation, and challenge to self-respect they impose
on other people?

The limits one fixes for permissible action that is nonviolent but
abrasive on other elements in the population may vary according
to how that action squares with the law. One may think it wholly
permissible for Negroes to obstruct traffic by extended marching

on public highways, even on streets in the busiest part of town; be doubtful whether they ought to invade privately owned hotels and keep the elevators filled with passengers who want to go nowhere except up and down; be certain that the loading of elevators should stop at once when a judge issues an injunction declaring it an unlawful trespass. One may think it appropriate for Negroes to violate any laws which by a reasonable showing support racial differentiations (e.g., invade swimming pools and golf courses of private clubs that will not admit Negroes); be doubtful whether acts of reprisal should be permitted (e.g., despoil the golf course and cut power lines into the club house); and wholly condemn unlawful acts that injure third parties (e.g., wrecking the trucks of business firms that deliver supplies to the club house).

## WHAT CONSEQUENCES OF THE ACTION-PROGRAM CAN BE ANTICIPATED AND WHAT UNFORESEEN CONSEQUENCES OUGHT TO BE ALLOWED FOR?

Organized protest and resistance of the proportions we are considering in these pages does not occur unless the stakes are high. Those who institute the protest would not incur the discomforts of demonstrations and risk penalties for violating law if they did not expect success to bring them substantial rewards. They would not need to mount a campaign if their demands met no opposition, and opposition emerges only if some element of the population thinks it will suffer if those demands are satisfied. The clash of wills is a contest to control the future, and all in the society, not just the contending groups, will be inheritors of the future. The future can never be accurately predicted, but sometimes it is possible to say: These things are bound to lead to something we do not want or (if we cannot be that sure) there is too big a chance that these things will lead to something we do not want. Where ought the power to control the future lie?

If the long-run consequences of the struggle appear to be unimportant for the population at large, one might say that the future can be entrusted to a resolution of the forces exerted by the contending groups. If, however, the anticipated consequences are of great importance to the population as a whole and the range of unpredictable but possible consequences is of disturbing proportions—in that case one may think it imperative that official agents of the entire society move into the arena, not just to enact laws relating to the issues in conflict but to regulate the struggle.

Thus, in the first years of the Negro's present crusade one might have favored unlimited right to demonstrate so long as trusted leaders promised that the demonstrators would strictly refrain from violence. Today a fear that further demonstrations will inevitably lead to rioting and deaths might cause that same person to recommend restraints on the same kinds of demonstrations.

I introduced the four questions that have now been discussed with the statements that a conflict of values—a right to dissent and an obligation to comply with law—is inherent in organized protest and resistance, and that decisions about how this conflict shall be resolved must turn on the circumstances of the particular case in which the conflict is presented. If my analysis is convincing, the decisions will take into account considerations of the kinds I have indicated in the preceding paragraphs. It will be clear on most casual thought that I cannot in this essay undertake an evaluation of the interlinked campaigns and countercampaigns that rage about the status of the Negro today. It may be useful, however, to carry further the evidences that the relevant considerations are bafflingly intertwined. This I shall try to do by examining what appears to be a simple proposition: that the strategy and tactics of the Negro, in his present campaign, are justified by the fact that the Negro is excluded from the political system.

## The Negro's Marginal Political Status

It has been said frequently and earnestly by many people that the strategy and tactics adopted by the Negro are wholly justified by the fact that he stands outside the political system and is trying to get in. A correlative statement is that the measures adopted by whites who oppose the Negro's cause cannot be justified because of the fact that those whites are within the political system and possess sufficient means for presenting their case to the whole society. What may the assertions mean? Is the central thesis valid —that exclusion from the political system justifies extraordinary behavior? If valid, how much of the present situation is it good for? To what aspects of the present phenomena does it apply?

How do you know whether a man has or has not been admitted to the political system? More precisely, what are the proofs that a man is or is not permitted to participate in the processes that give government in the United States its democratic character? If you define democratic government as a system in which the critical decisions are made by officials chosen by an inclusive electorate (as some writers do), the conclusion must be that relatively few adult Negroes living in the deep South could participate in the political process when they began their campaign of protest and resistance. Negroes living in other parts of the country, however, were free to vote if they wanted to, and in many places they were a part of the critical electorate I discussed earlier (pp. 118–23). The reasoning that concludes that Negroes could march in the South *because* they were disfranchised does not cover the marching rights of Negroes in other parts of the country where the polls were open to them.

It may be argued, however, that the Negro population should be viewed as a unit, as a conscious minority or a sub-system in the inclusive political system. In this case, the argument would continue, Negroes everywhere, no matter what their access to the polls locally, have a right to join in the organized protest and resistance that is intended to bring into the electoral process those Negroes who have not been allowed to vote. This poses some difficult questions about what ought to be recognized as a conscious minority or sub-system. It appears to me, after some thought, that this formulation of the Negro's right to demonstrate would not give his white sympathizers a right to come to his aid by resort to the same tactics. From the Negro's point of view this formulation does have one great attraction, however; it provides no support whatever for countercampaigns on the part of whites who oppose the Negro's cause.

Move now to the opposite extreme in conception of what gives government in the United States its democratic character. This is the position of a man who maintains that elections and arrangements for representation in legislative bodies are of minimal importance and that response to the expectations and preferences of the people is achieved by a balancing of demands made by competing groups. In this conception, the balancing will be done by elected officials, but the extreme proponent of this thesis will contend that it does not make much difference who is chosen to sit in the office and do the balancing. In this view of how political power is manifested, the question we are considering answers itself; of course the Negro's campaign of protest and resistance is justified by the fact that he is outside the political system and trying to get in. In the view of the extreme pluralist, one does not knock on the door and seek admission to the political process; one just kicks the door down and enters the arena. No group is ever admitted to political participation; it simply surveys its re-

sources, resolves to share in the benefits to be gained, and an-
nounces its presence in the arena by a display of force and
influence. The Negro was a full-fledged participant in the political
process the day that he launched his campaign of protest and
resistance; his admission to the political process (if you insist
on that term) was confirmed the minute his principal competitors
recognized that he was a force to contend with.

Aside from this first objection—that it is irrelevant to the proposition we are discussing—the extreme pluralist position has another unpalatable consequence from the Negro's standpoint. It
legitimizes the white man's opposition to the Negro's cause as
fully as it legitimizes the Negro's efforts. I do not say and do not
mean to imply that the most extreme pluralist condones violence
or approves the violation of law. My point is that whatever he
approves, he approves equally for all groups in the society. Since
his dependence for government by the people is on matching of
strengths, his test of right to enter the contest must be possession
of strength. If there be a set of rules specifying the instruments
of pressure that may be used and fixing limits for the permissible
use of those instruments, they must, in order to comply with the
least exacting tests of democratic character, apply alike to all
groups, to the white man as well as the Negro. If rules for operating in the pluralist arena exist, I have not seen them. Reasoning
as best I can from the fundamental thesis of the pluralist school
of thought, I see no reason to think that exclusion of the Negro
from the election of public officials is ground for restricting the
right of his opponents to contend in the forums where those
officials make their decisions.

We have still to consider conceptions of the democratic way in
government that fall between the two extremes already presented.
My classification of the channels available for participating in
control of government will be helpful at this point. I cited six
means of exerting influence and attached special significance to
three of them. I asserted that election of public officials by an
inclusive electorate is the bottom level instrument of democratic
government, and said that appeals and pressures and public reaction to acts of government are also important. I see these several
means for participation as components of a system; they complement and support one another rather than standing independent
of one another. Being of this mind, I conclude that ineffectiveness
in the use of one instrument justifies increased resort to other
instruments. Denial of opportunity to participate in selection of

officials justifies increased effort to persuade and threaten officials when they make their decisions.

Exclusion of Negroes from the polls in the South invites the disfranchised Negroes to organize for protest and resistance. This much I derive from my initial proposition that the six channels of participation combine to form a system. But the initial proposition does not answer the question whether the disfranchisement of Negroes in some states is sufficient cause for resort to organized protest and resistance by Negroes and whites who live in other states and have free access to the polls. I shall not inquire further into this question of common cause, not because the subject is uninteresting but because it is too big. A thorough consideration of the problem would require some thought about what constitutes a minority, about tests for deciding whether dissenting groups have enough in common or are sufficiently interrelated to be called one identifiable protesting group rather than two or more separate but allied protesting groups. If organized protest and resistance is to be a recurring phenomenon of political life, it may be helpful to bring to that phenomenon one's thinking about sympathetic strikes in industrial relations and his views about the conditions under which a general strike is justifiable.

My initial proposition that voting is only one instrument of influence in a system made up of several instruments makes it logically wrong for me to say that admission to the voting place determines whether or not a man has been admitted to the political system. A man is a full partner in democratic control of government when, taking all proper means of expression into account, his opportunities for political influence meet a test of sufficiency. Tests of sufficiency have not been proposed and agreed on, and for that reason I think such phrases as admission to the political system and full partnership in the democratic process are not helpful in precise analysis. We exhaust their usefulness when we use them to lead up to the margins of precise analysis or to present conclusions and evaluations in general terms.

I am not so pessimistic, however, as to believe we can make no advance toward tests of sufficiency. One of the basic propositions in this book is that the democratic character of a political system is determined by finding answers to a three-part question: How much of the population shares, in how much of the critical decision making, with how much impact or influence? At that point I frankly acknowledged the improbability that scholars will soon develop measuring devices capable of providing answers to these three questions of "how much"; but also at that point I pressed the necessity of searching for measures and noted that it is the function of theory to guide that search (pp. 9–11).

We are now at a point in this essay where the need for theory has become painfully obvious. Thoughtful Americans, facing a prospect of recurring violence, wrangle about the rightfulness of opposing claims for toleration. They angrily argue the obligation of the whole society to tolerate the action programs of Negroes and its obligation to tolerate the countermeasures that some whites have adopted to withstand the Negroes' claims. They wrangle because systematic, persuasive thought has not provided that array of prime values and that illumination of probable relationships among ends and means that permits orderly debate to supplant disorderly dispute. It is with hope of clearing ground for later construction of theory that I probe, for a few more paragraphs, into the significance of the Negro's marginal political status for judgments about the rightfulness of his present campaign.

Believing, though I cannot measure it, that the Negro's impact on public policy has long been generally low, I think he should be allowed a resort to organized protest and resistance that may appropriately be denied to white men who wish to keep the Negro in restraint. I think that the Negro's political power is presently attenuated, in spite of the strategic importance of the Negro vote in many American cities, because he lacks resources to influence the votes of other people, and because he does not win an attentive hearing when he addresses public officials with appeals and pressures. Since I cannot put a measure on his loss of political influence due to low estate in the society, I cannot say how much tolerance should be extended to him when he bids for attention by marching, violating laws that appear to hem him in, and doing other things he thinks likely to speed the process of raising the black man to the status of the white. I can, however, identify some considerations that ought to be taken into account in forming judgments on this issue.

First, the objectives of his campaign. Reasoning from the premises so far announced, it would be logically unsound to restrict the Negro's demonstrations to what may be thought appropriate for gaining the enfranchisement of Negroes in places that now deny them a right to vote. At the least, Negroes may rightfully strike for a more favorable position in the command of political influence, all means of making an impress on public policy and acts of government being taken into account. But command of political influence seems to be a function of economic and social status. Therefore, if he would move intelligently with a view to long-run results, the Negro's present campaign must be directed toward betterment of his position in all aspects of life.

Adhering strictly to this reasoning, one can contend that any element of the society identified as having common status and notably disadvantaged must be allowed a resort to organized protest and resistance as a strategy for correcting its disadvantaged condition. If one finds this prospect attractive, or concludes that it is inescapable and must be endured, he will need to move his inquiry over to other questions. How great must be the deprivation? What is a reasonable time schedule for showing proof of change? What means for winning attention and forcing concessions may be utilized? What limits ought to be imposed on any campaign because of the prospect of unwanted consequences?

Some earlier remarks (pp. 264–65) presented the main things I have to say on a second point, the evaluation of the strategies and tactics that are invoked in organized protest and resistance. The reasoning in the several paragraphs immediately preceding this one commits me to a judgment that it is appropriate for a severely deprived group to attach to its demonstrations a considerable sting in the form of inconvenience and irritation for the elements of the population that can, if stirred to do so, alleviate the conditions that inspired the demonstrations. But to approve the imposition of inconvenience and irritation is not to approve violation of law or even that nonviolent action which irresistibly provokes other people to violent countermeasures. Lawmakers and judges have not yet reached agreement about where to draw the line that differentiates the right of one man to proffer an evaluation of his neighbor's character and the right of his neighbor to redress an insult. It will be infinitely more difficult to reconcile judgments about where lines ought to be drawn in regulating exchange of insults among groups that are playing for high stakes. So will it be difficult to establish any widespread agreement about violating the law and overlooking violations of the law. I may withhold my censure if I understand that the Negro unlawfully bedded himself down in the club house because he hoped that his arrest would alert the whole nation to the fact that he cannot play golf on the club's estate. In that case, neither will I censure the local peace officers if they refuse to make the arrest, refraining in hope of defeating the Negro's plan to bring third parties to his aid. But condoning minor infractions of law and departures from rigid law enforcement is not to condone major infractions by citizens and indiscriminate toleration of infractions by officials. There may be no specific boundary line between the minor offense and the major offense, but this does not justify a statement that one little step invariably leads to another big step. Each of the steps between the known first and the conceivable last is a point at which it may be possible to stop the march toward total breakdown of law.

Finally, a few sentences about unwanted consequences, foreseen and unforeseeable. Anticipated consequences are the cause for mounting a campaign of protest and resistance, and alternative sets of consequences, clearly or dimly foreseen, are the stakes in a contest between contending groups. I have argued that where a group is notably deprived it may rightly press its claims by measures that go beyond verbal appeals and electoral effort. This acknowledges the right of the protesting group to define and announce the social changes that will be the consequences of its efforts if those efforts succeed. The intended consequences must be carefully studied by critical minds in all sectors of the society, however. The intended consequences of any act almost invariably are accompanied by an array of unintended consequences. Salient and profound social changes always come at a price to someone, and it may be that always those who gain most from the change pay high prices for their gains.

The protagonists in a campaign of protest and resistance are not likely to be clear sighted in their estimation of probable consequences. The leaders are emotionally aroused, and their vision of an unfolding future becomes more and more confused as compromises are made among factions in order to confront the rest of society with a solid front. Thus the Negro, even if clear enough about what he wants and wholly satisfied with the strategy that guides his present crusade, cannot be sure of its reception by the white man. The most respected students of prejudice do not know enough about how it is expanded, intensified, and passed on to others. The most perceptive and thoughtful white men may make better guesses than the most perceptive and thoughtful Negroes as to the prospect that particular strategies and tactics will perpetuate, intensify, and diffuse more widely the prejudice that mainly accounts for the Negro's lowly estate.

The scheduling of social changes also illustrates the necessity for scrutiny of plans by critical minds that approach objectivity as nearly as may be possible in a time of tension. The Negro's demand for "freedom now" may be a useful, even the best conceivable, slogan for enlisting adherents to his cause and convincing opponents that he is going to press hard terms in a settlement.

But freedom that can be won "now" is likely to be more significant for symbolic value than for alteration of behavior. The social change that lifts a depressed element of the population to an estate formerly thought beyond hope of achievement is never accomplished in a year and probably never in a decade. The Negro may be the greatest gainer if thoughtful people who are scorned as moderates and gradualists develop an alternative schedule for realization of the goals the Negro is determined to attain.

## Lessons from Disorder

The Negro is not the only part of the population that stands to gain from the turmoil that convulses the United States today. All of the nation, future generations as well as present, have an opportunity to profit. I do not refer to the prospective increased productivity of a part of the population previously underproductive. I refer to the instruction in politics that can be found in the experience of this decade.

Three salient facts that press upon our attention as we survey the current scene will introduce us to several lessons waiting for the nation's contemplation. I call them facts, but each is a bundle of realities, a nucleus in a seething mass of social relationships. They are: (1) the deepened antagonisms between the white and black populations; (2) the sharpened disaffection of the Negro; (3) the vitiation of a sense of political obligation. If any reader think any of these not to be a fact of life in this decade he may treat my descriptive statement as a premise and find it no less provocative of thought.

One acknowledges sharpened antagonisms between the races when he speaks of a "crisis" in race relations. The increased incidence of rioting in which Negroes and whites are commonly identified as adversaries is a sufficient evidence of antagonisms brought to the surface of the social system. My own reading of the signs causes me to believe that displays of violence have not yet reached their peak. If, happily, I am wrong and the contest rapidly moves from the streets to conference rooms, legislative chambers, and other places of orderly debate and decision making, still I shall insist that we have had too much violence already.

The lasting consequences of the conflict cannot be known as yet, of course. One can conceive that the struggle will prove to have been a catharsis of the social ill-humors, that settling the racial issue by restrained warfare may have solved a lot of other social problems. Grant that this is conceivable, a society ought not to take a chance on such unplanned benefits. A study of past experience indicates a far greater probability that conflict of the kind and magnitude we have witnessed so far inflicts wounds that cripple social relations and are long in healing.

Companion to the deepened racial antagonisms, if not a special aspect of them, is the sharpened disaffection of the Negro. It is not now certain that Negroes are generally committed to a goal of full incorporation into a society of all Americans, white and black undifferentiated. It was generally supposed heretofore that the aspiration of the ambitious, resourceful Negro boy and girl was to live the life exemplified by white men and women who live well. Now they have been exhorted to seek a life apart from the white population, to maintain integrity as Negroes, to be a society within a society. That goal may be viewed as an honorable one by persons who consider it ill-advised; the reasons offered for rejecting integration and the language in which they are presented too often can only be deplored by any man devoted to a tranquil society. Negroes are told that the black man must reject the white man's society because the white man is degenerate, his society is corrupt, his culture is effete, and his day is past. It may turn out that those who speak this language of excoriation will not increase and that their appeals will not be heeded. But it cannot be doubted that ideas are being planted that are capable of a long life and a sturdy growth. It does not mitigate one's apprehensions of future harms to acknowledge that the Negro has not yet verbally assigned the white man to an estate more despicable than white men have long ascribed to the Negro and tried to make real by disciplinary measures. It does not improve the promise of social tranquility in the future to contemplate the prospect that the Negro will work as diligently as the white to push the other race below a level of respectability.

The third salient fact to be pondered is the evident deterioration of a sense of political obligation. Devotion to a public order and recognition that government is authorized to police the public order are conditions of stable societies. Let us call this devotion and recognition political obligation.

The state of political obligation in any society defies measurement at this stage of learning. Granting this, we can say with assurance that political obligation has been and is being challenged and shaken in the United States today. Reason tells us that if men, in great numbers and elated by the spirit of a crusade, willingly violate laws and repeatedly assert that no apologies are required for having done so, then lasting effects in low regard for law must be expected. This is true even if the purpose back of the concerted violation of law is to force an improvement of the whole body of law. Evidence confirms the testimony of reason. The evidence of a deteriorating political obligation is not found only, and perhaps is not found mainly, in the front line combatants of today's conflict. Rejection of the state or repudiation of government, *in toto* or in respect to particular matters, is boldly announced by persons who have not been publicly identified with the more aggressive aspects of the racial struggle. This rejection is announced and justified in words that do not closely connect it with the issue of racial equality. Thus a frequent contributor to a prominent literary magazine sees the current protest and resistance of the Negroes as a model for all enlightened Americans who aspire to a richer life. The restrained insurgency of the Negroes, he writes, "gives me hope for the vast underprivileged majority to which I myself belong, the affluent poor-whites, those helots, servants, and sutlers of the modern state. With the example of the Negro before them, there is hope that they too will read the Declaration and the Constitution, take heart of grace, and determine on organizing their public business in a manner more nearly manlike."* College professors and others who command public attention publicize their intention to pay no taxes that replenish or augment the resources available for waging a war. Organizations are created and campaigns mounted for the declared purpose of hindering recruitment for military service of young men who, were it not for the appeals and pressures of these campaigns, would have responded to the call to service. Three conclusions that are unprovable but nevertheless beyond reasonable doubt emerge from the evidences that crowd upon us. The deterioration of political obligation is contagious, it was triggered by the conflict over the Negro's status, and its effects on the polity will not quickly be rectified.

At numerous points in this essay where it would have been pertinent to do so, I have rejected opportunities to comment on organized efforts to overthrow the present government of the United States as a necessary step for instituting a radically different regime. Anything I could have said on that subject, and more, is said again and again in the voluminous literature on the threat to democratic government that inheres in communist ideolo-

* Emile Capuya, in *Saturday Review*, May 16, 1964, p. 43.

gies and their implementation by overthrow of popular governments. Nevertheless, I must call attention here to the preparation
of the social terrain as a seedbed for sedition and subversion that
inevitably results from the conditions just described—bitter antagonisms between major elements of the population, contemplation
of a severing of ties with the main part of the population by
leaders of a numerous and powerful minority, and an erosion of
political obligation to an extent and depth as yet unknown. In
such a cauldron of ferment and tumult, it is easy for an agent to
conceal his cause. The conspirator committed to destruction of a
system can pass himself off as one of the many who are agitating
for deep cutting reforms in the system. Detected, the conspirator
may escape exposure; exposed, he may escape arrest and removal
from the scene. Impatience with those who plead for restoration
of order and quiet negotiation, distrust of government and those
who transmit its commands, and an emotional over-quickness to
come to the aid of allies—these are realities of the present decade
that enable the forerunners of an authoritarian and oppressive
regime to advertise themselves as combatants in a common cause
and gain admission to the counsels where other men make plans
for a more perfect democracy.

Meager as it is, my recital of salient facts about our present condition and the conclusions derived from them exposes lessons that
the American people must ponder. A democratic government is
inextricably enmeshed in a democratic way of living. Egregious
departures from democratic ideals in the status of any sizable
sector of the population entails hazards for the maintenance of
government that is directed and controlled by the people and
responds to the expectations and preferences of the people. For
generations the Negro was denied equality and cramped in autonomy. The result was a dangerous breach of commonalty. Aside
from the demands imposed by sentiments of humanity, hindsight
tells us that we allowed the depression to sink too deep and last
too long for the security of the political system.

# 17. CONCLUSION: ON THE PRESERVATION OF DEMOCRATIC FOUNDATIONS

In the two preceding chapters I made the contemporary controversy about the Negro's status a vantage point for testing the
foundations of popular government in the United States. I could
have used, for the same purpose and with the same results, any of
several other issues that currently excite many Americans, first to
question the right of government to pursue certain policies and
then to withhold compliance if a policy fails to meet the individual's tests of justice. Indeed, I could easily have found suitable
examples of obstreperous behavior in times past, for Americans
have always been quick to resist intrusions upon conscience and
invasions of privacy.

Granting all this, it is surely a fact that today's public scene
issues a special challenge to scrutinize the foundations of our
democratic system. For the raucous and violent behavior of our
time appears to be rooted in social conditions that can hardly have
run their course. The almost precipitate movement of population
to urban centers, lifting people out of familiar environments,
severs tenacious bonds that made the experience of the past a
restraint on current behavior; feelings of insecurity in a new environment that bears little resemblance to the old stir people to
self-help and excite reprisals for actions that are only misunderstood. Insecurity that stems from these sources is augmented by
current lack of income, uncertainty about future employment, or
a stark prospect of continued unemployability for oneself and one's
children. The most radical leaders of thought and action speak
directly to the masses, and appeals that in a former day would
have been filtered out or toned down by trusted men of the community now penetrate and ferment in the minds of men whose

limited experience provides few checks for the passions that are aroused. Between the intellectuals, the men of high achievement, men busy making a living, and men submerged in ghettos of public or personal creation—between any of these groups there are disabling obstacles to communication, understanding, sympathy, and confidence.

The contemporary discord and the deep-seated social disturbances from which it springs are doubly related to the conditions I believe to be requisites for democratic government. They stem in large part from failure to maintain a sufficient amount and an appropriate balance of autonomy, equality, and commonalty; and they further erode each of those requisites and aggravate the imbalance among them. Any person who shares my conviction that popular self-government can flourish only if due measures of autonomy, equality, and commonalty persist will surely agree that political scientists have no more urgent task than a full description of the interrelations of those requisite conditions and the institutions and operations of popular government. It seems appropriate, therefore, to close this book with some personal judgments about priorities in extending the exploratory inquiry that must precede rigorous research.

I observed, when I introduced them as requisites for democratic government, that autonomy, equality, and commonalty are mutually supporting, and difficult to differentiate in their practical manifestations. They are conditions of a society's organization and behavior that, if mixed in proper proportions, create a milieu in which popular government can be realized. I did not trace out the relations that tie them together or express a judgment about what amount or measure of each makes the combination a firm foundation for self-government. I cannot describe their actual interrelations now for my efforts to trace them have not produced satisfying results. My judgments about what constitutes a proper balance among them are rudimentary and tentative.

Some notions about how they get out of balance, and the consequences of too great an imbalance of autonomy and equality appear in my discussion of the relations of these requisites to the pluralist or group competition model of democratic government (pp. 49–52). Autonomy of groups is a *sine qua non* for a pluralist society. Autonomous groups contend with one another in the forum where important decisions are made. Men who are contending with one another profit from the weaknesses of their adversaries and, while leaders of groups may favor some measure of equality among their respective followings, they do not form a coalition insistent upon equality of status for all men irrespective of group allegiances. Excess of autonomy for groups can thus entail intolerable departures from equality among the population as a whole. Efforts to correct such an imbalance, in turn, may elevate equality at too great a cost to the autonomy of groups and individuals. Fear of such a consequence is expressed in recurring cries that laws designed to protect small business keep inefficient firms alive by restricting the efficient, that the freedom of choice which "right to work" laws secure for individual workers hinders efforts to secure greater freedom for all workers by collective bargaining, that each step toward "the welfare state" marks the further retreat of self-reliance, individual enterprise, and personal choice in styles of living.

Commonalty is my term for the likeness of mind and behavior that characterizes a population. A high measure of commonalty is compatible with varying degrees of autonomy and equality. This is proven by the experience of societies marked by sharp differences in concentration of political and economic power and in the distribution of privilege and advantage among classes and among individuals within classes. In many societies, great masses of people tolerated a submerged status for long periods of time; there was general acceptance of the established regime, rebellion was not in evidence, force was not a principal means of keeping men in their places. Common values, common expectations, common ways of behaving in recurring situations—these components of commonalty make possible the continuation of whatever has become fixed and familiar. Granting that there may be limits to what men will tolerate, it remains a fact that commonalty is a substitute for force in maintaining nondemocratic and democratic systems alike.

It seems probable, however, that commonalty is enhanced as a society moves in the direction of greater equality. The reduction and elimination of differences in social condition is accompanied by the abandonment of beliefs and behavior that supported the earlier discriminatory regime, and the new beliefs and behavior, supporting a new regime of more nearly equal status, win a wider and firmer acceptance among the population at large. Equality and commonalty thus appear not to be opposed to one another. Autonomy and commonalty are less congenial. To be autonomous is to be able to fix goals and chart courses of action for achieving goals. The values of autonomy are realized as the individual or group departs from what is customary and expected. A vigorous, wholesome autonomy keeps commonalty from becoming slavish conformity; excessive autonomy reduces commonalty to ineffectiveness.

If this abbreviated account of their interrelations is accepted, it will be acknowledged that the distribution of emphasis among autonomy, equality, and commonalty is of highest importance to a democratic nation and presents a severe challenge to its political theorists. In my own tentative exploration of this problem I have found autonomy the best point from which to start inquiry. The United States beyond any other great nation is committed to private ownership and competitive business enterprise. Personal liberty, individual initiative, and self-reliance are extolled as special virtues of the American people. Personal and group autonomy are therefore entrenched. Demands for equality appear as proposals to even up advantage, and the justification of each additional step in the direction of equality is found in the abuses of autonomy. A problem continually facing theorists and statesmen in this country up to now has been: How do we chart and schedule a retreat from the excesses of autonomy without resort to an overdose of equality and with confidence that the American people will understand and support the intended changes of policy? I say that this has been a problem up to now because our history has been marked by a persistent curtailment of autonomy and a persistent movement toward equality. Events of our day show that this tendency has not yet run its course. But persuasive voices—men who must be heeded before one makes up his mind—now tell us that we have unduly restricted the freedom of individuals and groups, that we have already surrendered too much of personal initiative, that nervousness about equality stifles boldness in enterprise, and that the commitments, faiths, and common understanding that once united the nation steadily give way to distrust and division.

I see little reason to fear that the American people will lose their democratic government primarily through the erosion of personal and group autonomy. Civilizations have gone down, and catastrophe could coincidently shatter all foundations of popular government in this country. But a gradual drift or choppy transition from self-government to anarchy or to despotism is not likely to make its first great inroads in the sector I call autonomy. The safeguards against seizure and abuse of power that lie in the pluralist structure of our society appear to be as firm now as they ever were. I recognize some formidable threats to personal autonomy, but I suspect that before this population is rendered incapable of self-government by loss of capacity to exercise choice and make critical decisions, the equality and commonalty that are essential to democratic government will long since have disappeared.

It is possible that I exaggerate the security of personal and group autonomy in the United States, because I may have been unduly impressed by the social distance Western man has traveled during the past few centuries. Nothing remotely resembling the American style of self-government could have been possible for the people of England five hundred years ago. Too few of the island's population had sufficient control of their own daily actions to provide a prudential basis for regulating the behavior of their neighbors, not to mention persons unmet and unheard of. If messengers had brought news of problems to be dealt with, few of the population could have found in their personal experience guides to general standards or specific rules that offered promise of solving those problems. I shall not review the evidence that causes me to believe this. If one has not read about the state of man at a time when today's social life would have seemed a utopian fantasy, he can hardly expect to appreciate the state of man in his present time and place. If I enjoy an enlightened view of the social conditions that made possible a transition from imposed government to self-government and give self-government a measure of security today, it has been gained by reading about man's existence in earlier periods. For one who has not started such exploration, I recommend two items that especially influenced my own thinking: G. G. Coulton, *Medieval Village, Manor, and Monastery* and J. J. Jusserand, *English Wayfaring Life in the Middle Ages.**

My optimism about the continuance of a sufficient autonomy is not shared by others as reliable in prophecy as I am. Many critics of the social order are alarmed especially by four conditions that now characterize American life and appear to be increasing in prevalence and portent. They are: extension of the period of preparation for adult employment and social activity; growing uncertainty of employment for most people and a prospect of permanent unemployment for many; bureaucratization of life for both the employed and the unemployed; and public invasions of individual privacy. The first two conditions—delay of adult status and temporary or permanent removal from productive employment —tend to deprive people of challenges to exercise choice and make decisions, limit their resources for realization of choices that they

---

* Both are in paper covers. Coulton's book is in the Harper Torchbook series of Harper and Row (New York); Jusserand is in University Paperbacks of Barnes and Noble (New York).

may be ready to make, and remove them from situations that force choice upon them. The third condition—bureaucratic intrusions into American life—takes the edge off personal enterprise not only for the economically deprived but also for great numbers of other people who enjoy opportunities for choice and have resources for effectuating the decisions they make. Persistently, new bureaucratic structures appear and familiar structures wax in power—in government, in business, in the associational life of trades and professions, in organizations that address themselves to community affairs, and even in the undefined realms of entertainment, recreation, and loafing. In ever increasing degree, organizers and managers set goals for sectors of the population or all of the population, fix bounds to the range of undirected social drift, structure the alternatives available to those persons who are of a disposition and have the resources for making personal choices, and scatter about rewards and punishments which induce people to make choices that the society's managers prefer. These effects are exacerbated and extended by the fourth condition, increasing readiness of government and nongovernmental organizations to scrutinize the individual, record his behavior, and catalog his personal characteristics and the contents of his mind. While they acknowledge that great social payoffs may be realized by systematic collection and analysis of accurate information about the wants, the doings, and the potentialities of the population, many critics of the social order fear that continuing subjection to public scrutiny will cause individual conduct to adhere more closely to social norms, take the edge off independence, and dry up important sources of innovation and invention.

In the view of the critics, these four conditions combine to create a deadly hazard for the autonomy that is essential to the democratic way in government. I have indicated that I think the critics are unduly pessimistic. I cannot deny that the individual is constrained and beset as they allege. But I am not convinced that the consequences are as debilitating as the critics think them to be. At the very time when autonomy is endangered it is stimulated and reinvigorated. The innovations in industry that remove some persons from employment are proof that other men respond boldly to opportunities for choice. The expansion of bureaucracy that represses initiative among any part of the population issues new challenges to the imaginations of those who constitute that bureaucracy, enlarges the responsibilities of those who direct its operations, and draws additional men into the network of its decision making. Furthermore, the American people are thoroughly aware that autonomy is threatened and the history of recent legislation reveals a persistent concern to counter every threat I have mentioned.

I have recorded at considerable length my suppositions about the relation of equality to democratic government (esp. on pp. 22–26 and 185–88). I stated why I think some measure of equality is essential for the enjoyment of popular control over government, and announced my conviction that prolonged denial of a due measure of equality to the Negro largely accounts for the intemperance displayed in his present effort to achieve a closer approach to equality. I characterized the constitutional requirement of equal protection of the laws as a challenge to achieve an ideal, but argued that the mix of value considerations prohibits a common conception of that ideal. I did not attempt to draw a line to differentiate a sufficiently close approach to equality from a too distant removal from equality, a sufficient likeness in status from too great unlikeness in status, an appropriate selectivity from an intolerable favoritism in the impact of government on individuals and groups. The failure to propose a line or delimit a zone that differentiates enough from not enough was for good reason. I think it impossible to formulate a general statement that will hold good for all conditions, and for my speculations on particular conditions to be convincing they would have to be developed at a length inappropriate for this book.

I do think it appropriate to press a bit further my recommendation of caution in fixing one's notions about the ideal of equality. We may have been unfortunate in adopting the word "equality" for the social condition we have generally in mind. Equality suggests identity. I can be sure that A is equal to B only if they are alike in every respect; if they are different in any respect, then the difference may accrue to the advantage of one and the disadvantage of the other. Being, in all controverted matters, uncertain where advantage is rooted and aware that small advantages can swell into great ones, we are tempted to avoid a charge of violating the mandate by imposing identical status on all participants in any social situation. "Equity" might have been a better word than "equality" for the norm we have generally in mind. It invites contemplation of fairness, of reasonableness, of balancing the preferred with the feasible. It encourages persuasion and bargaining. The connotations of "equality," in contrast, invite men to state their claims as absolute rights and to justify them by dogmatic assertions.

We ask for trouble when we encourage people to make demands

that cannot be satisfied. Recognizing this, one may still contend that ideals ought always to outrun performance and that aspirations of absolute equality provide essential motivation for reducing the spread of practical inequalities. In any case, whether one welcome or deplore a wide gap between expectation and realization, the problem for statesmen is to determine what is equitable, and to provide for equity. In this business they will need all the help they can get from other thoughtful persons, including the academic students of politics.

The unsatisfactory state of thought about the relation of equality to other goals and values becomes apparent when one contemplates current discussion of the estate of the Negro. The dispute about how to bring a new order into existence trips over uncertainties as to what that new order ought to be. Debate about what the Negro may justly demand and what the white man has obligation to give is marred by the fact that too few of the debaters see clearly and see alike the fundamental conditions of a good society, either biracial or raceless. Persons who are agreed that white and black children must be mixed in school and on playgrounds differ sharply as to whether this is an essential means of socializing children of both races or rather an arrangement for improving the quality of education for Negroes. Adult whites who, in Peter Carmichael's* phrase, would make the white school child a facility for elevating the intellectual and cultural levels of Negro children will not entertain a companion proposal that Negro families of lowest cultural attainment be relocated in bluestocking communities so that adult whites may do for adult Negroes what the children of one race do for the children of the other. Assertions that segregation in schools "generates a feeling of inferiority" and tends to "retard the educational and mental development of Negro children" (Chief Justice Warren in The Segregation Cases, 347 U.S. 497) are not matched by inquiry as to whether greater damage to personality and greater retardation of learning may result from injecting the Negro child into a school predominantly white, where he is constantly reminded that he is of a minority, sees reasons for believing that the few are not wanted by the many, and finds that those who dominate his daytime environment are contemptuous of the environment to which he returns at the close of the day. Persons who firmly believe that individuals and groups of refined taste ought to be regarded as models and be emulated by the rest

* Peter A. Carmichael, The South and Segregation (Washington: Public Affairs Press, 1965), p. 3.

285

of the population have not boldly faced the possibility that good taste flourishes and is best exhibited when people of refinement live in communities that resist invasion by the rude and unrefined. We skirt the edge of dispute as to whether certain aspects of life should be withdrawn from government and returned to the private sector, so that individual and group decisions may introduce and secure differentiations that are incompatible with the equal protection that government must provide.

The commonalty of belief and behavior that is requisite for popular government appears to be in greater jeopardy than either autonomy or equality. Two circumstances account for its precarious condition. For decades the denigration of conformity has been a persistent theme in appeals to the American public. This is true of oral communication in the form of speeches and conversation, and of printed statements that are fed directly to the general public or get there by the roundabout route of scholarly publications. These appeals are not confined to a representation that diversity in personal beliefs and modes of behavior contributes to the realization of other desirable ends such as innovations in management of the economy, proliferation of art, or reinforcement of the autonomy that is necessary for self-government. People are constantly bombarded by assertions that conforming is bad per se; that it is good to be different for the sake of being different. They are told not only that "Life will be richer if you explore more widely," but also that "Life is stultifying if you are concerned about the good opinion of your neighbors." Statements that Americans are sheeplike in their acceptance of prepackaged beliefs are not qualified by reassurances that a substantial amount of common belief is necessary for a society to cooperate voluntarily rather than under compulsion.

The bias in the public's education that I have described assures a hospitable reception for a second threat to commonalty in our day. A cumulation of social ills, some of which I mentioned at the start of this chapter, have lately erupted in dissension, taking sides, and violent conflict. Awareness of disadvantage and identification of specific injustices spur men to unite in groups opposed to other groups. The contending groups formulate grievances, propose settlements, and fashion arguments. Conflict removes ambiguity from statements of grievances, replaces tentative proposals with uncompromising demands, and converts arguments into dogma. Claims that ought to have won ready settlement become bones of contention in which determination to win, humiliation ensuing from defeat, and face saving take precedence over giving and obtaining justice. Resolutions that ought to have crumbled when confronted by reason persist as hard lumps in the mix of social relationships and indefinitely complicate the negotiation and bargaining that produce self-government instead of imposed rule.

The price that must be paid for an insufficient commonalty is indeed a high one. As the realm or universe of common values and conventional behavior diminishes, the impulse to respond to a central leadership decreases and ability to fall into accord on public policies is lessened. Government either steps up its coercive measures or it withdraws from problem areas which are centers of controversy. If coercion is greatly increased, a benign regime is displaced by harshness and severity. If coercion is avoided by withdrawal of government, either the social problem is not attended to and grows worse, or other instrumentalities of correction and control move in to deal with what government shuns. The first prospect is a gloomy one, for it is unlikely that many social ills are cured by allowing sores to fester. The second prospect is less forbidding. No doubt many things that government tries to do would be better done if left to nongovernmental organizations. But there is small chance that the problem which is too hot for government to handle will be given an equitable settlement by the instrumentalities that take it over. The claims for a fair gesture to equality are not likely to be honored, and there is a risk that both the processes of deciding and the terms of settlement will further breach the needed commonalty.

I expressed my confidence that we have the degree of autonomy necessary for continued enjoyment of popular government in the United States. We have less adequately provided for the requisite equality, but the response of the white population to the Negroes' demands assures us that most of the nation is aware that the deficiency must be repaired. If the prospect for an enduring regime of vigorous self-government is precarious, it is because the essential degree of commonalty is threatened. It may well be in under-supply right now, and tendencies of our time promise to diminish it still further. These convictions cause me to conclude this essay with some speculation as to how further deterioration of commonalty may be stayed and perhaps some of the lost ground recaptured.

The specific proposals that I shall make for securing a wholesome commonalty have as a common result the modification of conflict by encouraging and cultivating a spirit of toleration. A population that is aggressive in its effort to wring comfort out of nature is bound to proliferate conflict. It is not to be expected that men who constitute such a society will agree on a set of goals and will refrain from pushing forward additional goals not included in the set that has previously been agreed on. When goals have been stamped with common approval we must assume that members of an aggressive society will differ as to the best means of achieving those goals. If the population is indeed determined to advance physical comfort and other features of the good life, differences in convictions as to means and ends will abound, alternative proposals will be expressed with vigor, and competing demands will be pressed forward with stubborn tenacity. This is conflict.

But the grandest objectives of a population can be achieved only if there is some measure of order in the society—some adherence to rules of behavior that enable one man to circumscribe an area within which another man's future actions will be confined. Rules that limit the behavior of an aggressive society cannot be made effective by display of governmental authority alone; there must be voluntary adherence to the rules. Voluntary adherence to rules that restrict one's own conduct is the fruit of a tolerating state of mind. It follows that a spirit of toleration must have a high priority in the goals of a democratic society. Those who hold authority in a democratic government must constantly strive for policies and procedures that invite men to reduce their pressure for personal advantage in order that other men may share in the general allocation of advantages. And men outside of government who are influential in the making of minds must constantly advance a conception of public interest and general welfare and must evangelize a gospel that nobility of personal character is proven when one forgoes a sure personal advantage in order to secure an idealized public welfare.

But toleration does not come easily. It is not easy to extend charity to the particular act if one distrusts the whole man who performs the act. We find it easiest to be tolerant toward those people who do not ask us to tolerate very much. Need for toleration recedes as agreement increases. The homogeneous society can have more of common, national, policy—arrived at by a democratic process and vigorously enforced—than the heterogeneous society can win for itself, for in the homogeneous society there is greater harmony in value holdings, greater concurrence on social goals, greater agreement as to means by which goals may be attained. The democratic government must, therefore, be dedicated to the enlargement of agreement among the population, for the enlargement of agreement narrows the area in which conflict abounds, takes the edge off bitterness and so creates a climate favorable to toleration, and increases the possibility and the likelihood that the policies and acts of government will, in fact, represent a choosing from among and an amalgamation of the many demands that emerge from the people who are the nation.

I am impressed that opportunities to encourage and cultivate toleration, and so fill out and invigorate a requisite commonalty, confront us on three fronts.

First, we can work more diligently for the improvement of our electoral-representative institutions and practices. In my evaluation of two demand-response systems, the populist and the pluralist, I commented on the educative effect of the arguments and appeals of candidates for office, the activities of party leaders and party workers, and the reporting, explication, and harangue emanating from newspapers, radio, and all other instruments of communication that become involved in political campaigns (see pp. 48–51). Passions are roused and divisions created, but the net consequence of all the business of choosing, instructing, and evaluating public officials contributes positively to the generality and typicality of mind and behavior that I call commonalty; the likeness of organization, practices, and programs of the two great political parties proves this. There is great unhappiness with the American party system and it can hardly be doubted that it exacts some prices, notably a restriction of the alternatives that receive consideration when solutions are sought for social problems. I do not advise a stubborn retention of every feature of the system we have developed, but I do offer an earnest caution to those who contemplate reform. They must not confine their concern to the quality of public policy and the efficiency of administration. It is essential that the new that supplants the old contribute positively to the commonalty that stands as a foundation to the nation's democracy.

Second, by a thoughtful management of distributed self-government we may be able to escape certain tensions that impose excessive demands on commonalty. A prime reason for dividing authority among national, state, and local governments, I noted earlier, is to permit adaptation of public policy to the differing needs and demands of the population. Regulation of the manufacture and sale of alcoholic beverages took different forms in the several states prior to 1918, as it did again after 1933. I suppose that state liquor legislation is being sabotaged in more than one state today, but at least there is not a nationwide effort to nullify a national prohibition policy.

We began only a few decades ago to enact national legislation asserting minimum standards with which state laws must comply. Careful use of this device may provide, for many of our bitterest issues, a satisfactory adjustment of the national conscience and the special expectations and demands that exist in any of the fifty states. But it must not be supposed that this stratagem, fixing limits within which the states must stay in fashioning their laws, guarantees universal acquiescence in the national policy. Recent resistance to national legislation and judicial orders designed to terminate segregation and reduce discrimination ought to settle one's mind on that point.

I ought also to acknowledge that many thoughtful observers of our experience and our present environment have concluded that the federal arrangement has outlived its day—that, henceforth, such governmental control as may be required over any significant area of life must be concentrated in one government with nationwide jurisdiction. I consider this conclusion to be premature. Surely the American people will insist that the President and congressmen give personal attention to the most troublesome social problems and exercise their own judgments in fashioning policies to deal with those problems. Surely they will also insist that these elected officials exercise effective control over the national administrative organizations that put public policy into effect. Can these expectations be realized in view of the volume of public business that is entrusted to the national government today? Can the elected officials possibly cast their minds over all they are required to answer for? If it turns out that some sweeping delegations of authority must be made, is it a necessary conclusion that the movement will be wholly in the direction of more power for the national administrative organizations? Is it not likely that we will scrutinize the vast range of power vested in the national government, identify some affairs suitable for regulation by state or local governments, and charge these officials with making decisions we do not wish to entrust to national bureaucracies that are already too numerous and too powerful to be contemplated with comfort?

A third hope of restoring and enlarging commonalty lies in a conscious effort to combat intolerance and widen the scope of agreement among the American people. I do not propose a happy chorus singing "togetherness," but I shall cite some things I think we ought to quit doing. The persons I admonish to change their ways are the men and women who specialize in having ideas and throwing them out for consideration by other people; the writers and the performers who speak to the nation in print, on TV and film, and by microphone; the academic men, the college professors, including especially my own little group—the professors of political science. I shall call all these people the communicating elite. I do not suggest that there is no individuality in this group, but I do declare my belief that, generally, they speak with too much assurance, from too little evidence, and with too little charity. Their offenses of which I complain are quickly stated.

They show too great a disdain for the common man. They glorify the common man when the nation is at war, and they respectfully salute the voice of the people on election day. But in between these times of crisis and moments of tribute they picture the common man in his collective manifestations as a horde of non-responsive automatons who resist all calls to higher social responsibilities, or as a plastic if not a volatile mass, quick to respond to the zealot who preaches a doctrine of conformity and of distrust for the man of intellect. Of course, not all of the communicating elite display this scorn for the common man, nor perhaps does any of them condemn him all of the time. But collectively, it seems to me, they see that distant part of the population called "the people" to be a brake on the wheels of progress. It is as if men who were lifted up to opportunities for leadership impugn the role of leadership because they think all people should be as enlightened as they are.

It seems to me that this rejection of the empathy that a leader should share with his followers is rendered socially abrasive by displays of partisanship when thoughtful analysis and sympathetic counsel are critically needed. I do not deny the need for, and I think I do not downgrade the value of, partisanship among the communicating elite. Men of intelligence must formulate programs of public policy and present those programs to the public for consideration. The case for each of the competing programs must be carried to the public by men who have committed themselves to that program. It may be that some of them render greatest service if they have blinded themselves to weaknesses in their own offerings and to strengths in what their opponents propose. But partisanship must not monopolize the talents of all in this communicating group. There must always be many to whom others can turn for counsel that is the product of honest, probing, tenacious thought, as free as one can make it of encumbering commitments and personal preferences. Of course, some of us are implacably committed to realization of this model. I contend only that men of this mood are too few. I think, for instance, of many teachers of political science who are devoted to the two-party system on Sunday, but who spend their Mondays and Tuesdays ridiculing the program of the party they personally oppose and defaming the character of political leaders who espouse that party's program.

The spirit of partisanship is not confined to issues that must be settled today or the day after; it is apparent in discourse dealing with issues that are never solved. I have said in other writings that we are trapped in one-value analysis. A cramped perception of values cripples our literature relating to freedom of speech, press, and other forms of expression. We say that the pen is mightier than the sword, but we seem unwilling to acknowledge the damage that can be done by the man who wields the pen. High on the agenda a few years ago was excoriation of the loyalty oath. The impressive argument against the need for giving and taking oaths was rarely balanced by a reference to the service oath-taking has rendered by causing men to ponder political obligation in critical times. As I write, men who acknowledge that they have no solution for a critical public problem do not hesitate to obstruct the address in which another man tries to justify the policy he espouses for solving that problem.

The bias, distortion, and partisanship that mark so much of our literature are dangerous to commonalty. The common man is perceptive enough to observe the low regard in which he is held and sensitive enough to resent it. He is enough of a partisan himself to recognize special pleading even when it is panned off as finding arrived at by scholarly study. He, or another man to whom he listens, is adept enough in analysis to find flaws in reasoning that wholly condemns a widely held belief, and the lore and tradition that give continuity to social experience may tell him exactly what is missing from the analysis he distrusts. Aware that he is viewed with disdain if not held in contempt, the common man is prepared to put an uncharitable interpretation on every act of the communicating class that strikes him as questionable. Given reason to believe that he is not being dealt with honestly, his initial mistrust grows into positive distrust and eventual hostility. In his eyes a severe criticism of the industrial structure that made the nation rich becomes the impractical dream of a soft-headed academic; a thoughtful proposal for mitigating the cold war becomes a scheme to turn the American government over to Communists. If he realizes that many of the communicating elite are wise and honest men, still he applies an equivalent of Gresham's Law. As bad money drives out good money, so the most distrusted of the communicators drive out of public acceptance those who are most worthy of being trusted.

I would offend if I permitted my words to imply that all persons we call the man in the street abhor all persons I include in the communicating elite. My point is that one numerous population has far too little confidence in what it is told by another numerous population. This judgment is shared by all who complain that a climate of anti-intellectualism has settled over the land.

The social cost of the anti-intellectualism I have described is not measured by the discomfiture of the intellectuals or the withholding of financial support they would like to enjoy. Intellectuals and other communicators do very well in this country, no matter how hostile the climate. The damage to the society lies principally in the fact that the common man does not receive—if offered, he does not accept—an intellectual service he badly needs. Included in this part of the population are millions of men and women who not only are amenable to but actively seek the cautious counsel of men of thought and knowledge. They seek the counsel of men who reveal in their expressions a genuine esteem for less favored people and a sincere concern to help them arrive at prudent judgments about the complex world that hems them in and pins them down. Not finding in sufficient measure the patient and sympathetic counsel they hoped to get from scholars and interpreters of scholarship, they turn to another leadership. It is a leadership that specializes in plain talk, dogmatic assertions, and sympathy for its audience. This is the leadership of the extremes in public policy, right and left. This leadership, which attracts because a more trustworthy intellectual leadership is not trusted, capitalizes on distrust and cultivates distrust. It divides the nation when the nation most needs to be united. Its most enduring handiwork is the construction of barriers to commonalty. Its most pervasive effect is a general deterioration of the foundations on which democratic government rests.

# OTHER WRITINGS OF
# CHARLES S. HYNEMAN

*A Brief Bibliography Compiled by Charles E. Gilbert*

As noted in the Introduction, parts of this volume are based on some of Charles S. Hyneman's previously published papers.

"Bureaucracy and the Democratic System," *Louisiana Law Review*, vol. 6 (December 1945), pp. 309-49.

"What is the Best Form of Government for the Happiness of Man?" The Daniel Lecture, University of Oklahoma (Norman: University of Oklahoma Press, 1955).

"Conflict, Toleration, and Agreement: Persisting Challenge for a Democratic Government," The Edmund J. James Lecture, University of Illinois, 1962. University of Illinois Bulletin, No. 75, 1962.

"The American Lesson in Democratic Government," address at the University of Tennessee, 1962. In *Government and World Crisis* (Knoxville: The University of Tennessee, 1962).

"Free Speech: At What Price?" *American Political Science Review*, Vol. 56 (December 1962), pp. 847-52.

"Current Challenges to Democratic Procedure," and "Legislative Representation and Judicial Policy," in Clyde J. Wingfield (ed.), *Political Science: Some New Perspectives* (El Paso: Texas Western Press, 1966), pp. 33-59.

The progress of Hyneman's thinking can be traced in his publications prior to this book. The most important of these publications are listed, in addition to the foregoing, below.

## Books

*The First American Neutrality* (Urbana: University of Illinois Press, 1935).

*A Collection of Materials on Government Regulation of Business* (2 vols., mimeographed; Urbana: University of Illinois, 1935).

*The Constitution and the Judicial Process* (Mimeographed; Urbana: University of Illinois, 1936).

*Bureaucracy in a Democracy* (New York: Harper & Row, 1950).

*The Study of Politics* (Urbana: University of Illinois Press, 1959).

*The Supreme Court on Trial* (New York: Atherton Press, 1963).

*A Second Federalist; Congress Creates a Government*, edited with George W. Carey (New York: Appleton-Century-Crofts, 1967).

## Articles

"Judicial Interpretation of the Eleventh Amendment," *Indiana Law Journal*, vol. 2 (February 1927), pp. 371-89.

"The Problem of Providing Incentive for Prison Labor," *Journal of Criminal Law and Criminology*, vol. 17 (February 1927), pp. 603-21.

"Preliminary Work in the Codification of American International Law," *Indiana Law Journal*, vol. 3 (March 1928), pp. 464-73.

"Public Encouragement of Monopoly in the Utility Industries," *Annals of the American Academy of Political and Social Science*, vol. 147 (January 1930), pp. 160-70.

"The American Understanding of the Obligations of Neutrality during the European Wars of 1792-1815," *American Journal of International Law*, vol. 24 (April 1930), pp. 279-309.

"The Case Law of the New York Public Service Commission," *Columbia Law Review*, vol. 34 (January 1934), pp. 67-106.

"Legislative Experience of Illinois Lawmakers," *University of Chicago Law Review*, vol. 3 (December 1935), pp. 104-18.

"Administrative Adjudication: An Analysis," *Political Science Quarterly*, vol. 51 (September, December 1936), pp. 383-417, 516-37.

"Cumulative Voting in Illinois" (in collaboration with Julian D. Morgan), *Illinois Law Review*, vol. 32 (May 1937), pp. 12-31.

"Tenure and Turnover of Legislative Personnel," *Annals of the American Academy of Political and Social Sciences*, vol. 195 (January 1938), pp. 21-31.

"Executive Centralization in Administration," *Proceedings of the Southern Political Science Association*, Tenth Annual Meeting, 1937, pp. 13-16.

"Tenure and Turnover of the Indiana General Assembly," *American Political Science Review*, vol. 32 (February, April 1938), pp. 51-67, 311-31.

"Administrative Reorganization: An Adventure into Science and Theology," *Journal of Politics,* vol. 1 (February 1939), pp. 62-75.

"Tenure and Turnover of the Iowa Legislature" (in collaboration with Edmond F. Ricketts), *Iowa Law Review,* vol. 24 (May 1939), pp. 673-96.

"State Administrative Tribunals and 'Fair Play,'" *Iowa Law Review,* vol. 25 (March 1940), pp. 532-54.

"Who Makes Our Laws?" *Political Science Quarterly,* vol. 55 (December 1940), pp. 556-81.

"Grass Roots of Democracy," in Robert B. Heilman, ed., *Aspects of Democracy* (Baton Rouge: Louisiana State University Press, 1941), pp. 15-22.

"Executive-Administrative Power and Democracy," *Public Administration Review,* vol. 2 (Autumn 1942), pp. 332-38.

"The Army's Civil Affairs Training Program," *The American Political Science Review,* vol. 38 (April 1944), pp. 342-53.

"The Illinois Constitution and Democratic Government," *Illinois Law Review,* vol. 46 (September–October 1951), pp. 511-74.

"Federal Commissions—How Much Independence?" *Public Utilities Fortnightly,* vol. 49 (February 14, 28, 1952), pp. 211-22, 279-89.

"Methodology for Political Scientists: Perspectives for Study" (in collaboration with Jean M. Driscoll), *American Political Science Review,* vol. 49 (March 1955), pp. 192-217.

"Motivation, Incentives, and Achieving Agency Objectives," in Don L. Bowen and Robert H. Pearly, eds., *Administrative Leadership in Government* (Ann Arbor: University of Michigan Institute of Public Administration, 1959), pp. 15-23.

"Some Crucial Learning Experiences: A Personal View," in Robert H. Connery, ed., *Teaching Political Science* (Durham: Duke University Press, 1965), pp. 217-37.

# FOR FURTHER READING

There is a touch of censorship in every selective bibliography. Items that do not appear on the list are removed from attention; the items mentioned subject the reader to the bias of the man who compiled the list. It is with great reluctance therefore, that I recommend next steps in exploring a vast sweep of human concerns that have been under the scrutiny of scholars for generations. The few titles that are cited were selected with these considerations in mind. I omit the classic writings, even though I regard them as essential preparation for understanding contemporary problems and modern experience. I searched for general statements about the democratic way in government that stand on presumptions somewhat different from my own. On particular problems and aspects of the American experience, I intend to cite the most illuminating writings, and where many contend for a place I list a few that seem likely to be most accessible to most readers.

## The Democratic Idea and The Democratic Way

Brief statements of personal position and principal national experiences appear in most books designed to introduce college students to the study of political science. Thoughtful presentations will be found in J. A. Corry and Henry J. Abraham, *Elements of Democratic Government* (New York: Oxford University Press, 1958), 3d ed.; John C. Livingston and R. G. Thompson, *The Consent of the Governed* (New York: Macmillan, 1963); and J. Roland Pennock and D. G. Smith, *Political Science: An Introduction* (New York: Macmillan, 1964). A model of democratic government which has been highly influential among college teachers appears in the opening chapters of Austin Ranney and Willmoore Kendall, *Democracy and the American Party System* (New York: Harcourt, Brace & World, 1956).

Some small books that made an impact on my thinking when I started serious inquiry into the nature of democracy are: Carleton K. Allen, *Democracy and the Individual* (London: Oxford University Press, 1943); Carl L. Becker, *Modern Democracy* (New Haven: Yale University Press, 1941); C. Delisle Burns, *Democracy* (London: Butterworth, 1935); Alexander D. Lindsay, *I Believe in Democracy* (London: Oxford University Press, 1940); and Thomas V. Smith and Eduard C. Lindeman, *The Democratic Way of Life: An American Interpretation* (New York: New American Library, 1951). Books that provide more comprehensive treatment of basic ideas and enjoy high regard include: John H. Hallowell, *The Moral Foundation of Democracy* (Chicago: University of Chicago Press, 1954); Jay W. Hudson, *Why Democracy?* (New York: Appleton-Century-Crofts, 1936); Alexander D. Lindsay, *The Modern Democratic State* (New York: Oxford University Press, 1947); Henry B. Mayo, *An Introduction to Democratic Theory* (New York: Oxford University Press, 1960); J. Roland Pennock, *Liberal Democracy: Its Merits and Prospects* (New York: Holt, Rinehart & Winston, 1950); Giovanni Sartori, *Democratic Theory* (Detroit: Wayne State University Press, 1962); Alf Ross, *Why Democracy?* (Cambridge: Harvard University Press, 1952); Yves R. Simon, *Philosophy of Democratic Government* (Chicago: University of Chicago Press, 1951); and Herbert Tingsten, *The Problem of Democracy* (New York: Bedminster Press, 1965). Statements by several of the men listed above appear in two recent volumes that bring together definitions and personal testaments from a number of careful thinkers who have written about democracy: M. Rejai, *Democracy: The Contemporary Theories* (New York: Atherton Press, 1967); and Elias Berg, *Democracy and the Majority Principle: A Study in Twelve Contemporary Theories* (Göteborg: Scandinavian University Books, 1965). Finally, two books directed to special concerns: Thomas L. Thorson, *The Logic of Democracy* (New York: Holt, Rinehart & Winston, 1962) is an effort to justify or find in a comprehensive set of values reason for attachment to democratic regimes; and Neal Riemer, *The Revival of Democratic Theory* (New York: Appleton-Century-Crofts, 1962) urges more systematic study of democratic ideas and practice.

## The American Democratic Experience

I believe there is no comprehensive and incisive account of the growth of the idea, on the North American continent, that the people ought to control their government. The limited records of what was said in the Constitutional Convention of 1787 and the several state ratifying conventions are most readily accessible in two publications: Charles C. Tansill, ed., *Documents Illustrative of the Formation of the Union of the American States,* printed by the Government Printing Office in 1927 as House Document No. 398, 69th Congress, 1st Session; and Max Farrand, ed., *The Records of the Federal Convention of 1787* (3 vols.; New Haven: Yale University Press, 1911). The notes made on the Philadelphia debates are rearranged according to the main issues before the Convention in Saul K. Padover, *To Secure These Blessings* (New York: Washington Square Press, 1962). Debates in Congress during the first decades under the Constitution examined the popular basis of the new national government; they are partially reprinted in Charles S. Hyneman and George W. Carey, eds., *A Second Federalist; Congress Creates a Government* (New York: Appleton-Century-Crofts, 1967). The early state constitutional conventions also addressed themselves to provisions for popular control of government. The most pertinent of these debates are now assembled in Merrill D. Peterson, *Democracy, Liberty, and Property; The State Conventions of the 1820's* (Indianapolis: Bobbs-Merrill, 1966). Historians have provided us with several accounts of early experience in self-government. Of those I am acquainted with, these are among the best: Robert E. Brown, *Middle-Class Democracy and the Revolution in Massachusetts, 1691-1780* (Ithaca: Cornell University Press, 1955); Elisha P. Douglass, *Rebels and Democrats: The Struggle for Equal Political Rights and Majority Rule During the American Revolution* (Chicago: Quadrangle, 1965); Dixon Ryan Fox, *The Decline of Aristocracy in the Politics of New York, 1801-1840* (New York: Harper & Row, 1965); Roy F. Nichols, *The Invention of the American Political Parties* (New York: Macmillan, 1967); and Chilton Williamson, *American Suffrage: From Property to Democracy, 1760 to 1860* (Princeton: Princeton University Press, 1960). Most textbooks written for college courses in American government offer some explanation of how democratic goals are achieved in American political institutions and practices. Two that are especially attentive to the democratic character of our system are: Robert A. Dahl, *Pluralist Democracy in the United States* (Chicago: Rand McNally, 1967); and William H. Riker, *Democracy in the United States* (New York: Macmillan, 1953). Saul K. Padover attempts to do what his title suggests in *The Meaning of Democracy: An Appraisal of the American Experience* (New York: Praeger, 1963). Alexis de Tocqueville, the Frenchman who visited the United States in the early 1830's, gave us in his *Democracy in America* an interpretation and evaluation of our political system that stands to this day without a rival for shrewdness in perception, sureness in analysis, and imaginativeness in forcasting our further evolution. A very satisfactory edition is one by Phillips Bradley in the Vintage series of Alfred A. Knopf (2 vols.; New York: 1956). Another early observer who is too little read today is the novelist of the Leatherstocking Tales, James Fenimore Cooper. His *The American Democrat* is also in the Vintage series (New York: Knopf, 1956). Additional items dealing thoughtfully with the American effort to give the world a model of democratic practices are: Carl L. Becker, *Freedom and Responsibility in the American Way of Life* (New York: Knopf, 1945); Avery Craven, *Democracy in American Life; A Historical View* (Chicago: University of Chicago Press, 1941); Robert A. Dahl, *A Preface to Democratic Theory* (Chicago: University of Chicago Press, 1956); James Allen Smith, *The Spirit of American Government* (New York: Macmillan, 1912); and Martin Diamond, "Democracy and *The Federalist*; A Reconsideration of the Framers' Intent," *American Political Science Review*, vol. 53 (1959), p. 52. David Spitz, in his *Patterns of Antidemocratic Thought* (New York: The Free Press, 1965), traces dissent from our democratic commitment.

## Social Requisites of Democratic Government

The first of these bibliographic notes samples an extensive literature about the democratic way of life. These writings are definitional and descriptive, differentiating customs, institutions, and practices that meet the author's tests of democratic character from alternative ways that he considers to be non-democratic. Much of this writing expresses personal preferences; the author praises and condemns and urges his audience to hold steadfastly to the democratic values. Perhaps all such writers believe that some elements of a democratic social order constitute an indispensable environment for democratic government. If so, their beliefs are not always made explicit. Recently there has been more conscious effort to determine what previous experiences and what contemporary commitments and behaviors must exist in order for popular control of government to persist. In his recent book, *Democracy: The Contemporary Theories* (New York: Atherton Press, 1967), M. Rejai summarizes the debate and quotes extensively from more than twenty authors. His conception of "preconditions of democracy" includes extent and character of the land occupied by a population and political institutions and practices that I think of as on-going democratic government.

Of the writings directed more strictly to requisite social conditions and behavior, I find these most worthy of attention: "Cultural Prerequisites to a Successfully Functioning Democracy: A Symposium," *American Political Science Review*, vol. 50 (1956), p. 101; in the same journal, Seymour M. Lipset, "Some Social Requisites of Democracy: Economic Development and Political Legitimacy," vol. 53 (1959), p. 69; and William Kornhauser, *The Politics of Mass Society* (New York: The Free Press, 1959). Especially concerned with problems encountered and prospects for success in constructing democratic governments for non-industrialized populations are: Ivor Jennings, *The Approach to Self-Government* (Cambridge, England: Cambridge University Press, 1956); and John Plamenatz, *On Alien Rule and Self-Government* (London: Longmans, 1960).

## Populist, Pluralist, and Elitist Interpretations

In my effort to discover what induces American elected officials to act in accordance with popular expectations, I identified two demand-response systems, the populist and the pluralist. I described them as different systems, but I also said that they are closely interrelated and that both systems operate effectively at the same time. Perhaps most writers on American politics recognize the two systems, but they differ as to how those systems may be correctly described, as to their relative importance and effectiveness, and as to the desirability of making one or the other uppermost in national, state, and local governments. Controversy centers mainly on two big questions: (1) To what extent does the adult American act individually in political affairs, and to what extent do the groups to which he belongs mold his opinions and speak to public officials in his behalf? (2) Regardless of one's position on the first question, does government respond mainly to the de-

mands of limited sectors of the population (elites) or to the expectations and preferences of the great mass of adult population?

Helpful introductions to the debate are: Peter Bachrach, *The
Theory of Democratic Elitism: A Critique* (Boston: Little, Brown,
1967); and Harry K. Girvetz, *Democracy and Elitism* (New York:
Charles Scribner's Sons, 1967). Consciousness of the importance
of groups, in American literature, stems mainly from Arthur F.
Bentley, *The Process of Government* (first published 1908; re-
printed at Evanston, Illinois: Principia Press, 1949). Other land-
mark items are David B. Truman, *The Governmental Process*
(New York: Knopf, 1951); Pendleton Herring, *Group Repre-
sentation before Congress* (Baltimore: The Johns Hopkins Press,
1929), and *Public Administration and the Public Interest* (New
York: McGraw-Hill, 1936); Earl Latham, *The Group Basis of
Politics* (Ithaca: Cornell University Press, 1952); and Raymond
A. Bauer and others, *American Business and Public Policy: The
Politics of Foreign Trade* (New York: Atherton Press, 1963).
Charles E. Lindblom, *The Intelligence of Democracy: Decision
Making through Mutual Adjustment* (New York: The Free Press,
1965) seeks to explain how those who contend in the pluralist
arena state their claims, make compromises, and win victories or
suffer losses. Recent surveys of organized efforts to influence the
decisions and acts of elected and appointed officials include:
Donald C. Blaisdell, *American Democracy under Pressure* (New
York: Ronald Press, 1957); Abraham Holtzman, *Interest Groups
and Lobbying* (New York: Macmillan, 1966); Grant McConnell,
*Private Power and American Democracy* (New York: Knopf,
1966); Lester W. Milbrath, *The Washington Lobbyists* (Chicago:
Rand McNally, 1963); and Harmon Zeigler, *Interest Groups in
American Society* (Englewood Cliffs: Prentice-Hall, 1964).

Deprecation of the common man and exaltation of elite groups
as sources or repositories of political power are more highly
developed in European than in American literature. Writings by
Robert Michels, Gaetano Mosca, Vilfredo Pareto, and Oswald
Spengler are promontories in this literature. A good introduction
to this body of thought is provided in Carl J. Friedrich, *Man and
His Government* (New York: McGraw-Hill, 1963), chap. 18. It
seems probable that the debate in the United States is only beginning. Belief that decisions in high places respond to the few
is represented by C. Wright Mills, *The Power Elite* (New York:
Oxford University Press, 1959); Floyd Hunter, *Top Leadership,
U.S.A.* (Chapel Hill: University of North Carolina Press, 1959).
Less certain of the facts and less confident in their judgments

are such reputed scholars as Robert A. Dahl, V.O. Key, Jr., and Elmer E. Schattschneider. See Dahl, *A Preface to Democratic Theory* (Chicago: University of Chicago Press, 1956), and *Pluralist Democracy in the United States* (Chicago: Rand McNally, 1967); Key, *Politics, Parties, and Pressure Groups* (New York: Thomas Y. Crowell, 1958) 4th ed., or *Public Opinion and American Democracy* (New York: Knopf, 1964); Schattschneider, *The Semi-Sovereign People* (New York: Holt, Rinehart & Winston, 1960).

The search for origins and channels of influence has been pursued most rigorously in studies of local government. Diverse findings are reported. Studies that have won wide attention or promise to do so because of their quality include: Robert E. Agger, D. Goodrich, and B. E. Swanson, *The Rulers and the Ruled: Political Power and Impotence in American Communities* (New York: John Wiley and Sons, 1964); Robert A. Dahl, *Who Governs?* (New Haven: Yale University Press, 1961); Charles E. Gilbert, *Governing the Suburbs* (Bloomington: Indiana University Press, 1967); Floyd Hunter, *Community Power Structure* (Chapel Hill: University of North Carolina Press, 1953); and Wallace Sayre and Herbert Kaufman, *Governing New York City* (New York: Russell Sage Foundation, 1960). Other items are listed and characterized in Charles Press, *Main Street Politics: Policy Making at the Local Level* (East Lansing: Michigan State University Press, 1962). The findings of several studies and the methods pursued in reaching them are analyzed and evaluated in Nelson W. Polsby, *Community Power and Political Theory* (New Haven: Yale University Press, 1963); and Arnold M. Rose, *The Power Structure: Political Process in American Society* (New York: Oxford University Press, 1967).

## Democratic Government: Populist Model

My realization that democratic government is a system of competition for political power developed in conversations with Evron Kirkpatrick. I may have been encouraged in that interpretation by Alfred M. Bingham, *The Techniques of Democracy* (New York: Duell, Sloane, and Pearce, 1942). Later I read Joseph A. Schumpeter, *Capitalism, Socialism, and Democracy* (New York: Harper & Row, 1947), 2d ed.; I found that I was by no means out in front in my thought on this subject, nor have I found another book that rivals Schumpeter's as spokesman for this conception of what makes American government responsive to popular expectations. Willmoore Kendall was an aggressive champion of the idea that majority rule is the critical determinant of democratic character, that government is proven to be democratic when it acts in accordance with the wishes of a majority. I was never able to find out what population ought to be counted in order to determine whether a majority of the appropriate population was in favor of the governmental act. I think the best explanation and justification of majority tests is by Kendall and his co-author, Austin Ranney, in their *Democracy and the American Party System* (New York: Harcourt, Brace & World, 1956), chaps. 1 and 4. See also Kendall, *John Locke and the Doctrine of Majority Rule* (Urbana: University of Illinois Press, 1941), and the debate of Kendall and Herbert McClosky in *Journal of Politics*: McClosky, "The Fallacy of Absolute Majority Rule," vol. 11 (1949), p. 637, and Kendall, "Prolegomena to Any Further Work on Majority Rule," vol. 12 (1950), p. 694. The debate is carried further by Roland Pennock in "Responsiveness, Responsibility, and Majority Rule," *American Political Science Review*, vol. 46 (1952), p. 790, and Neal Riemer, "The Case for Bare Majority Rule," *Ethics*, vol. 62 (1951), p. 16. On equality as a condition to be approached, and for speculation as to whether measures of equality can be agreed upon, see Henry A. Myers, *Are Men Equal? An Inquiry into the Meaning of American Democracy* (Ithaca: Cornell University Press, 1955); Sanford Lakoff, *Equality in Political Philosophy* (Cambridge: Harvard University Press, 1964); and the essays in J. Roland Pennock and John W. Chapman, eds., *Equality* (New York: Atherton Press, 1967), vol. 9 in the *Nomos* series; Alan P. Grimes examines American aspirations and experience in *Equality in America: Religion, Race, and the Urban Majority* (New York: Oxford University Press, 1964).

## Preparation for Participation

I discuss personal observation and common talk, the school system, the press, and radio and television as main reliances for the ideas and knowledge essential to effective participation in control of government. Writing about the mass media is easily identified, but the uninitiated needs special help in his search for informative and critical discussion of the individual's ability to extract understanding from the people all around him. Further reading might well start with V. O. Key, Jr., *Public Opinion and American*

*Democracy* (New York: Knopf, 1961), chaps. 13-16. The principal
textbooks on the history of education in America supply reliable
accounts of our elaborate educational system and how it evolved
from its rude beginnings. Ellwood P. Cubberley, *Public Education
in the United States* (Boston: Houghton Mifflin, 1947), rev. ed.,
was long a leader. Other good ones are E. Freeman Butts and
L. A. Cremin, *A History of Education in the United States* (New
York: Holt, Rinehart & Winston, 1962), rev. ed.; and H. G. Good,
*A History of American Education* (New York: Macmillan, 1962),
2d. ed. More directly on the contribution of the schools to civic
education are: Gail Kennedy, ed., *Education for Democracy: The
Debate over the Report of the President's Commission on Higher
Education* (Boston: D. C. Heath, 1952); Franklin Patterson, *High
Schools for a Free Society* (New York: The Free Press, 1960);
and Donald H. Riddle and R. E. Cleary, *Political Science in the
Social Studies* (Washington: National Council for the Social
Studies, 1967). Reaching beyond the schools to other organized
efforts to excite political awareness and prepare young people
for political activity are two books by Charles E. Merriam, both
published by the University of Chicago Press: *The Making of
Citizens; A Comparative Study of Methods of Civic Training*
(1931), and *Civic Education in the United States* (1934). Writing
about the relation of mass media to civic education tends not to
make sharp differentiations between influence of newspapers,
magazines, radio, and television. Of the many books that deal
critically with the work of newspapermen, the best known is
Frank L. Mott, *A History of Newspapers in the United States
through 260 Years* (New York: Macmillan, 1959), rev. ed. Nearest
to a comparable treatment of radio and television are: Walter B.
Emery, *Broadcasting and Government* (East Lansing: Michigan
State University Press, 1961); and Charles A. Siepmann, *Radio,
Television, and Society* (New York: Oxford University Press, 1950).
On the initiating, shaping up, and dissemination of news about
government, see Douglas Cater, *The Fourth Branch of Government* (Boston: Houghton Mifflin, 1959); Dan D. Nimmo, *Newsgathering in Washington* (New York: Atherton Press, 1964); Leo
C. Rosten, *The Washington Correspondents* (New York: Harcourt, Brace & World, 1937); and Stanley Kelley, Jr., *Professional
Public Relations and Political Power* (Baltimore: Johns Hopkins
Press, 1956). Study of the impact of ideas and information on
individual minds is still in a pioneering stage. Speculation, theory,
and findings are reported in several volumes of readings, principal
collections being: Wilbur Schramm, ed., *The Process and Effects of*

*Mass Communication* (Urbana: University of Illinois Press, 1955);
and Charles S. Steinberg, *Mass Media and Communication* (New
York: Hastings House, 1966). The term political socialization embraces the many things that unite to transform the receptive mind
of the infant into the adult's cargo of curiosity, prejudices, convictions, knowledge, and predispositions to action in the realm
of public life. One may enter this literature by way of Herbert
H. Hyman, *Political Socialization* (New York: The Free Press,
1959); and Fred I. Greenstein, *Children and Politics* (New Haven:
Yale University Press, 1965). For advice on what to read beyond
my suggestions, consult two essays by Richard E. Dawson and
Bernard C. Hennessey in James A. Robinson, ed., *Political Science
Annual* (Indianapolis: Bobbs-Merrill, 1966), vol. 1.

## The Right to Vote

Generally the books on democracy cited in the first of these
bibliographic notes consider the question of who ought to be
admitted to suffrage by a people committed to democratic principles. See, for example, Henry B. Mayo, *Introduction to Democratic Theory* (New York: Oxford University Press, 1960), pp.
115 ff., where he discusses justification of adult suffrage. Present-
day requirements for voting are set forth and criticized in all
comprehensive textbooks on American political parties and elections. Perhaps the fullest treatment is in Howard R. Penniman,
*Sait's American Parties and Elections* (New York: Appleton-
Century-Crofts, 1948), 4th ed. There appears to be no up-to-date
compilation of the laws of the fifty states, but there is an informative tabulation of provisions in recent editions of *The Book
of the States* (Chicago: Council of State Governments). Of little
good for present practice but still authoritative on early development of the right to vote in Western countries is Charles Seymour
and D. P. Frary, *How the World Votes* (2 vols.; Springfield, Mass.:
C. A. Nichols Co., 1918). For a history of the development of the
suffrage in the United States see Kirk H. Porter, *A History of
Suffrage in the United States* (Chicago: University of Chicago
Press, 1918), and Chilton Williamson, *American Suffrage: From
Property to Democracy, 1760-1860* (Princeton: Princeton Uni-
versity Press, 1960). On the obstructions to voting by Negroes
and their use of the ballot to advance their interests, see: Paul
Lewinson, *Race, Class, and Party* (New York: Oxford University
Press, 1932); Samuel Lubell, *White and Black: Test of a Nation*

(New York: Harper & Row, 1966); Daniel L. Matthews and James W. Prothro, *Negroes and the New Southern Politics* (New York: Harcourt, Brace & World, 1966); Henry L. Moon, *Balance of Power: The Negro Vote* (Garden City, N.Y.: Doubleday, 1948); James Q. Wilson, *Negro Politics: The Search for Leadership* (New York: The Free Press, 1960); a selection of short essays by Harry A. Bailey, Jr., ed., *Negro Politics in America* (Columbus, Ohio: Charles E. Merrill Books, 1967); and two reports of the United States Civil Rights Commission: *Voting* (1961), and *Voting in Mississippi* (1965). Other than the college textbooks and a few reports on practice in a particular state, there have been no important studies of the administration of elections in recent years. Still useful, however, are Spencer D. Albright, *The American Ballot* (Washington: American Council on Public Affairs, 1942); and two books by Joseph P. Harris, both published by Brookings Institution of Washington, D.C.: *Registration of Voters in the United States* (1929), and *Election Administration in the United States* (1934). Also relevant is a *Report* of findings and recommendations by the President's Commission on Registration and Voting Participation (Washington: Government Printing Office, 1963).

## Political Organization and Activity

A great nation can control its government by popular selection and replacement of officials only if the electorate is associated in some sort of party organization. The necessity of political parties and the diverse forms which party organization may take are ably discussed in Maurice Duverger, *Political Parties: Their Organization and Activity in the Modern State* (New York: John Wiley and Sons, 1954). In addition to the comprehensive textbooks on parties and elections, a few books place special emphasis on interpretation and evaluation of the American party system. These include Pendleton Herring, *The Politics of Democracy* (New York: Holt, Rinehart & Winston, 1940); Elmer E. Schattschneider, *Party Government* (New York: Holt, Rinehart & Winston, 1942); Allan P. Sindler, *Political Parties in the United States* (New York: St. Martin's Press, 1966); and Frank J. Sorauf, *Political Parties in the American System* (Boston: Little, Brown, 1964). Seeing the American party system as grossly inadequate are: The Report of the Committee on Political Parties of the American Political Science Association, *Toward a More Responsible Two-Party System* (New York: Holt, Rinehart & Winston, 1950); and

James M. Burns, *Deadlock of Democracy* (Englewood Cliffs, N.J.:
Prentice-Hall, 1963). A remarkable amount of research has been
directed to the voter and the voting act since World War II. This
includes the voters' interests, alertness, competence, and preferences. The many research reports are sampled in more than a
dozen collections of essays intended for use in college class rooms.
The Survey Research Center of the University of Michigan is the
nation's principal center for such research; two of its most significant publications are authored by Angus Campbell, P. E.
Converse, W. E. Miller, and D. E. Stokes, and are published by
John Wiley and Sons of New York: *The American Voter* (1960),
and *Elections and the Political Order* (1966). We have not devoted nearly as much effort to study of how men rise to public
attention and win recognition as material for public office, the
strategies of balancing tickets, fashioning appeals to voters, and
waging campaigns for nomination and election. Two of the best
things on the nominating process are: Paul David, R. M. Goldman,
and R. C. Bain, *The Politics of National Party Conventions* (Washington: Brookings Institution, 1960); and Gerald Pomper, *Nominating the President* (New York: W. W. Norton, 1963). The most
thorough reports of a presidential campaign by a journalist are
by Theodore H. White, both published by Atheneum of New
York: *The Making of the President, 1960* (1961), and *The Making
of the President, 1964* (1965). For a scholarly study of the process
of choosing a president, drawing on a wide range of American
experience, see Nelson W. Polsby and Aaron B. Wildavsky, *Presidential Elections: Strategies of American Electoral Politics* (New
York: Charles Scribner's Sons, 1964). The studies of urban communities cited in the fourth of these bibliographic notes deal with
political organization and activity in local governments. See addi-
tionally: Edward C. Banfield and James Q. Wilson, *City Politics*
(New York: Random House, 1963); Edward C. Banfield, *Big City
Politics* (New York: Random House, 1965); and Charles E. Gilbert
and Christopher Clague, "Electoral Competition and Electoral
Systems in Large Cities," *Journal of Politics*, vol. 24 (1962), p. 323.

## The Decisional Apparatus

The three-level structure of offices and assignment of governmental
business which I call distributed self-government has not been
a popular subject for research and speculative inquiry among
political scientists in recent years. For nearly two decades after

World War II, Professor Morton Grodzins of the University of Chicago was the central figure in a small group that turned diligently and imaginatively to this field of study. Grodzin's own writing, uncompleted because of his early death, was brought between covers by one of his associates in Morton Grodzins, ed. by Daniel J. Elazar, *The American System: A New View of Government in the United States* (Chicago: Rand McNally, 1967). Also emanating from the Chicago group are: Daniel J. Elazar, *American Federalism: A View from the States* (New York: Thomas Y. Crowell, 1966), and Robert A. Goldwin, ed., *A Nation of States: Essays on the American Federal System* (Chicago: Rand McNally, 1961). Two other small books of recent date that are marked by imaginative analysis and conservative speculations are: Roscoe C. Martin, *The Cities and the Federal System* (New York: Atherton Press, 1965); and William H. Riker, *Federalism: Origin, Operation, Significance* (Boston: Little, Brown, 1964). Aaron Wildavsky, ed., *American Federalism in Perspective* (Boston: Little, Brown, 1967) is a selection of excellent short essays. See also the document commonly called the Kestenbaum Report, *A Report to the President* by the Commission on Intergovernmental Relations (Washington: U.S. Government Printing Office, 1955). Reading on the separation of powers and checks and balances among branches of government should begin with *The Federalist,* especially Nos. 47-51, 64-66, 73, 75-77. The thought of Hamilton and Madison in *The Federalist* was ably extended by members of the early Congresses under the Constitution; for some of their best statements see Charles S. Hyneman and George W. Carey, eds., *A Second Federalist: Congress Creates a Government* (New York: Appleton-Century-Crofts, 1967), chaps. 6-8. The history of doctrines of separation of powers and critical appraisal of thought on that subject are provided in two recent books: William G. Gwyn, *The Meaning of the Separation of Powers* (New Orleans: Tulane University Press, 1965); and Maurice C. J. Vile, *Constitutionalism and the Separation of Powers* (Oxford, England: Clarendon Press, 1967). Two articles that ought not be overlooked are: Malcolm P. Sharp, "The Classical American Doctrine of 'the Separation of Powers,'" *University of Chicago Law Review,* vol. 2 (1935) p. 385; and Benjamin F. Wright, "The Origins of the Separation of Powers in America," *Economica,* vol. 13 (1933), p. 169. Views about the actual division of authority and influence among the branches of the national government and judgments about their appropriate interrelationships abound in literature dating since World War II. I expressed my own position on these questions in *Bureaucracy in a Democracy* (New York: Harper & Row, 1950). Extended statements of position, all of them in significant respects different than mine, will be found in these books: Wilfred E. Binkley, *President and Congress* (New York: Random House, 1962), 3d ed.; James Burnham, *Congress and the American Tradition* (Chicago: Henry Regnery, 1959); James M. Burns, *Congress on Trial* (New York: Harper & Row, 1949), and *Presidential Government* (Boston: Houghton Mifflin, 1966); Alfred De Grazia, *Republic in Crisis: Congress Against the Executive Force* (New York: Federal Legal Publishers, 1965); Ernest S. Griffith, *Congress: Its Contemporary Role* (New York: New York University Press, 1961), 3d ed.; Louis M. Koenig, *The Chief Executive* (New York: Harcourt, Brace & World, 1964); Arthur M. Schlesinger, Jr., and Alfred De Grazia, *Congress and the Presidency: Their Role in Modern Times* (Washington: American Enterprise Institute for Policy Research, 1967); and Rexford G. Tugwell, *The Enlargement of the Presidency* (Garden City, N.Y.: Doubleday, 1960).

Most informative of recent writings about ideals and practice in respect to representation in legislative assemblies are: Alfred De Grazia, *Public and Republic* (New York: Knopf, 1951); John Wahlke, Heinz Eulau, William Buchanan, and L. C. Ferguson, *The Legislative System: Explorations in Legislative Behavior* (New York: John Wiley and Sons, 1962); Roland Young, *The American Congress* (New York: Harper & Row, 1958); and a book in press as I write and which I have not read: Hanna Pitkin, *The Concept of Representation* (Berkeley: University of California Press, 1967). A research study based on survey data and titled "Constituency Influence in Congress" constitutes the final chapter in *Elections and the Political Order* by Angus Campbell and others (New York: John Wiley and Sons, 1966). On control of administration by the elected branches of government see, in addition to my book cited above, Joseph P. Harris, *Congressional Control of Administration* (Washington: Brookings Institution, 1964); Richard E. Neustadt, *Presidential Power: The Politics of Leadership* (New York: John Wiley and Sons, 1960); and Aaron Wildavsky, *The Politics of the Budgetary Process* (Boston: Little, Brown, 1964). Some of the most discriminating thought about how administrative personnel can be held accountable for their conduct is in article-length essays. Critical analysis will be found in each of these: Charles E. Gilbert, "The Framework of Administrative Responsibility," *Journal of Politics,* vol. 21 (1959), p. 373; Carl J. Friedrich, "Responsible Government Service under the Constitution," *Problems of the American Public Service* (New

York: Commission of Inquiry on Public Service Personnel, 1935);
Herman Finer, "Administrative Responsibility in Democratic Government," *Public Administration Review,* vol. 1 (1941), p. 335;
and David M. Levitan, "The Responsibility of Administrative
Officials in a Democratic Society," *Political Science Quarterly,*
vol. 61 (1946), p. 562.

### Limitations on Government

I do not recall having seen a succinct statement of what legal
scholars believe to be the objectives and methods of Rule of Law
as it has been developed in the United States. The guides to legal
literature, such as *American Jurisprudence* and *Corpus Juris Secundum,* do not cite the term. Perhaps the most informative single
book discussing the American idea and experience is a collection of
addresses and ensuing discussion titled *Government Under Law,*
ed. by Arthur E. Sutherland (Cambridge: Harvard University
Press, 1956). Two other collections of lectures are also helpful:
Arthur L. Harding, ed., *The Rule of Law* (Dallas: Southern
Methodist University Press, 1961), and a symposium on "Post-war
Thinking about the Rule of Law" in *Michigan Law Review,* vol.
59 (February 1961), pp. 485-613. Excellent but probably difficult
to put a hand on is *The Rule of Law in the United States, A Statement* by the Committee to Cooperate with the International Commission of Jurists, The American Bar Association, Section on
International and Comparative Law (New York: American Fund
for Free Jurists, 1958). Of contemporary scholars, Friedrich A.
Hayek probably makes the strongest case for limited reliance
on government to solve social problems in his *The Constitution of
Liberty* (Chicago: University of Chicago Press, 1960). The ideals
and positive requirements associated with the term "equal protection of the laws" are elaborately set forth under that heading in
the two legal encyclopaedias, *American Jurisprudence* and *Corpus
Juris Secundum.* The constitutional requirement is most actively
invoked today, of course, in connection with racial discrimination.
On the Negroes' claim to equal protection, see my *The Supreme
Court on Trial* (New York: Atherton Press, 1963); and Robert J.
Harris, *The Quest for Equality* (Baton Rouge: Louisiana State
University Press, 1960). There are, of course, a great number of
articles on the subject in legal and political science journals. I
noted that the term "public interest" is widely used to embrace
the concerns which I discuss under the heading "general welfare."

Further reading on that subject might well start with the essays in Carl J. Friedrich, ed., *The Public Interest* (New York: Atherton Press, 1962), vol. 5 in the *Nomos* series. One who wishes to go beyond that should read Glendon Schubert, *Public Interest: A Critique of the Theory of a Political Concept* (New York: The Free Press, 1961); or Richard E. Flathman, *The Public Interest: An Essay Concerning the Normative Discourse of Politics* (New York: John Wiley and Sons, 1966).

The literature which expounds the constitutional limitations on American national, state, and local governments is staggering in volume. Most of it deals with the interpretations which the Supreme Court has given to the provisions of the national constitution. My study, *The Supreme Court on Trial* (cited above), attempts to state objectively how the Supreme Court has used its power to fix the meaning of vague and comprehensive provisions of the Constitution and to appraise the judicial process as a means of imposing restraints on the elected branches of government. Other books which have the same purposes, and most of which present judgments sharply differing from my own are: Alexander M. Bickel, *The Least Dangerous Branch: The Supreme Court at the Bar of Politics* (Indianapolis: Bobbs-Merrill, 1962); Charles L. Black, Jr., *The People and the Court* (New York: Macmillan, 1960); Louis B. Boudin, *Government by Judiciary* (2 vols.; New York: William Godwin, 1932); L. Brent Bozell, *The Warren Revolution* (New Rochelle, N.Y.: Arlington House, 1966); Edward S. Corwin, *Court over Constitution* (Princeton: Princeton University Press, 1938); and Martin Shapiro, *Law and Politics in the Supreme Court* (New York: The Free Press, 1964).

## Free Speech and Subversion

Deep concern about subversive activity and sharp differences in judgment about how to protect against it brought the free speech and press guarantee to the forefront of attention immediately after World War II. This cause for re-examination of our commitment to freedom of expression was augmented later by widespread determination to breach all barriers to speech, writing, and visual displays designated in law as obscene or pornographic. In keeping with these turns in public interest there has been a remarkable production of books and articles dealing with constitutional protection of expression that is impaired by efforts to safeguard other values. If one feels himself grossly uninformed on this subject he may be wise to start his reading with a look at beginnings. There is an excellent study of the antecedents of the American free speech policy, Leonard W. Levy, *Freedom of Speech and Press in Early American History* (New York: Harper & Row, 1963). The debates in Congress in connection with the adoption of the first ten amendments are reported, with no important omissions, in Charles S. Hyneman and George W. Carey, eds., *A Second Federalist: Congress Creates a Government* (New York: Appleton-Century-Crofts, 1967), chap. 11. Robert A. Rutland, in his *Birth of the Bill of Rights, 1776–1791* (Chapel Hill: University of North Carolina Press, 1955) sees more reason than Levy does to believe that the founders of our political system were devoted to present-day conceptions of free communication. Interesting parts of the Congressional debate on passage of the Sedition Act of 1798 are reported in chapter 12 of Hyneman and Carey, eds., *A Second Federalist* (cited above). In my judgment, the two most reliable accounts of experience under this legislation are: Frank M. Anderson, "The Enforcement of the Alien and Sedition Laws," in American Historical Association, *Annual Report for 1912,* p. 113 (Washington: Government Printing office, 1914); and James M. Smith, *Freedom's Fetters: The Alien and Sedition Laws and American Civil Liberties* (Ithaca: Cornell University Press, 1956). Our experience in combatting treason and subversion during and immediately after World War I is fully reported and severely criticized by Zechariah Chafee, *Free Speech in the United States* (Cambridge: Harvard University Press, 1941). One can only sample the writing since World War II that describes efforts to withstand subversion and inquires into the appropriate limits to speech and publication. I especially recommend two books by Sidney Hook, *Heresy, Yes—Conspiracy, No* (New York: John Day, 1953), and *The Paradoxes of Freedom* (Berkeley: University of California Press, 1962). A generous reading among the following items should correct against my bias: Alan Barth, *The Loyalty of Free Men* (Hamden, Conn.: Archon Books, 1965); Eleanor Bontecou, *The Federal Loyalty-Security Program* (Ithaca: Cornell University Press, 1953); William F. Buckley, Jr., and L. B. Bozell, *McCarthy and His Enemies* (Chicago: Henry Regnery, 1954); Thomas I. Cook, *Democratic Rights versus Communist Activity* (Garden City, N.Y.: Doubleday, 1954); Walter Gellhorn, *American Rights: The Constitution in Action* (New York: Macmillan, 1960); Milton R. Konvits, *Fundamental Liberties of a Free People* (Ithaca: Cornell University Press, 1957). Looking beyond contemporary problems and proposing a unique view of the Constitution's relation to purpose and content of messages is Alexander Meiklejohn, *Political Freedom* (New York: Harper & Row, 1960).

## The Negroes' Challenge

As one would expect, the Negro's demand for equality with the white man in the American society set off a flood of books and articles on the Negro's condition, his demands, his strategy and tactics, his prospects, and the white man's response to all of this. Starting with the Negro's status, whether directly or indirectly due to, or in no way the consequence of, the white man's discriminatory behavior, the following may be read with certain profit: Edward Franklin Frazier, *Black Bourgeoisie* (New York: The Free Press, 1957); Eli Ginzberg and A. S. Eichner, *The Troublesome Presence: American Democracy and the Negro* (New York: The Free Press, 1964); Charles S. Johnson, *Patterns of Negro Segregation* (New York: Harper & Row, 1943). The most comprehensive and best-known study of the Negro's former place in the society is Gunnar Myrdal: *An American Dilemma: The Negro Problem and Modern Democracy* (2 vols.; New York: Harper & Row, 1944). This research report is reduced to approximately 300 pages in Arnold M. Rose, *The Negro in America* (also Harper & Row, 1948). More limited in point of attention are Kenneth B. Clark, *Dark Ghetto; Dilemmas of Social Power* (New York: Harper & Row, 1965); Robert C. Weaver, *Negro Ghetto* (New York: Harcourt, Brace & World, 1948); and St. Clair Drake and H. R. Clayton, *Black Metropolis: A Study of Negro Life in a Northern City* (2 vols.; New York: Harper & Row, 1962). No doubt the best-known declaration of the Negro's right to a different status and his determination to win it is Martin Luther King, *Why We Can't Wait* (New York: Harper & Row, 1964). Surely fascinating reading for everyone, black or white, is Robert Penn Warren's *Who Speaks for the Negro?* (New York: Random House, 1965). This is a report of the conversations, most of them taken verbatim from a tape recorder, of more than thirty Negroes, both prominent and obscure from South and North. See also Leonard Broom and N. D. Glenn, *Transformation of the Negro American* (New York: Harper & Row, 1965). On Black Muslims and Negro nationalism, see Charles Eric Lincoln, *The Black Muslims in America* (Boston: Beacon Press, 1961) or E. U. Essien-Udom, *Black Nationalism* (Chicago: University of Chicago Press, 1962). Alan F. Westin manages to put something about nearly everything in an anthology of more than 800 pages titled *Freedom Now: The Civil Rights Struggle in America* (New York: Basic Books, 1964). Placing emphasis mainly on the Negro's condition, his campaign, and his prospects is this excellent collection of readings: Talcott Parsons and Kenneth B. Clark, eds., *The Negro American* (Boston: Houghton Mifflin, 1966).

Transcending present-day preoccupation with the strategy and tactics of the Negro, of course, is the fundamental question: What are the limits of the individual's obligation to obey the law currently in effect and to comply with the approved procedures in his efforts to get the law changed? This has been a recurring problem for Americans since the first of them worked up a temper about injustice suffered under his colonial or English rulers. In view of its importance, it is surprising to me that so little writing, sharply pertinent and mature in thought, has been addressed to this subject. The classic statements are more concerned with how to establish political obligation than with fixing limits upon it. Probably the best entry to this literature is David Spitz, "Democracy and the Problem of Civil Disobedience," *American Political Science Review*, vol. 48 (1954), p. 386. For analysis in the classic style see Thomas H. Green, *Lectures on the Principles of Political Obligation* (London: Longmans, Green, 1917), and John P. Plamenatz, *Consent, Freedom, and Political Obligation* (London: Oxford University Press, 1938). Recent writings in the classic tradition seem to me not to move the analysis forward. See Bertrand Russell, *Authority and the Individual* (Boston: Beacon Press, 1960); Joseph Tussman, *Obligation and the Body Politic* (New York: Oxford University Press, 1960); and Hanna Pitkin, "Obligation and Consent," *American Political Science Review*, vol. 59 (1965), p. 990 and vol. 60 (1966), p. 39. In his compilation, *Nonviolence in America: A Documentary History* (Indianapolis: Bobbs-Merrill, 1966), Staughton Lynd brings together personal manifestos and explanatory statements of Americans who have resisted political authority for one reason or another from colonial days to our own time. Thoreau's famous essay "On the Duty of Civil Disobedience" is included, as are two or three others that seem to me much more persuasive than Thoreau's. These references take one only a short distance into the vast area of concern that includes pacifism, religious withdrawal, the nonviolence teachings of Gandhi, and, beyond that, armed rebellion and revolution.

# INDEX

Adams, John, 223, 224–25, 227, 229
administration
   citizen and group participation in, 153–60
   control of, 161–71
Alien and Sedition Laws; see Sedition Act of 1798
Alien Registration Act of 1940, 233–35, 237–42
Allen, John, 254
Ames, Fisher, 147
Amish, 87, 90
Anderson, Frank Malloy, 228
Arkansas, opposes Supreme Court, 255
Arnold, Elliott, 74
autonomy, individual and group
   relation of, to two demand-response systems, 41–42, 51–52
   as requisite of democratic government, 28–30, 278–79, 280–83

Bill of Rights, see constitutional guarantees
Black, Hugo M., 202, 203, 204, 210
Black Muslims, 141
Breckinridge, John C., 256
British cabinet, 162–63
Brown v. Board of Education; see Segregation Cases
Bureau of the Budget, 167
Burns, James M., 46, 219
business, relation to government, 180–82

Calhoun, John C., 146–47
Campbell, Angus, 114
Capuya, Emile, 275
Carmichael, Peter A., 284
Carter v. Carter Coal Co., 204

Catholic schools, 87, 90
Chase, Samuel, 228
civil disobedience, 250–52
civil rights, 200–201
   see also constitutional guarantees; Negro
Civil Service Commission, 167
commonalty, 83, 102–103
   and racial antagonism, 273–74, 276
   relation of, to two demand-response systems, 41–42
   as requisite of democratic government, 31–32, 278–80, 285–86
   strengthening of, 286
communications services, 84–85
   press, 90–96
   radio and television, 96–101
Communist Control Act of 1954, 71, 233, 235
communists, 71, 227
Congress
   authority and power of, 146–47, 168, 183–84
   and control of administration, 161–66, 168–71
conspiracy, see subversion
Constitution, 6, 257
   enforcement of, 182, 194, 253–56
   see also constitutional guarantees
constitutional guarantees, 57, 198–201, 214–15
   Bill of Rights, 6–7, 19, 178, 200
   due process of law, 181
   equal protection of the laws, 182, 185–88, 193–94, 283–85
   see also religion; speech and press
Cooper v. Aaron, 256
Coulton, George G., 281
Cowley, Malcolm, 209

Curtis, Merle, 44

Declaration of Independence, 5–6
delegation of power, 183–85
democracy
    defined, 3–4, 8, 62–63
    tests of democratic character, 14–27
democratic government
    and relation to democratic way of life, 11–13, 24–26
    social requisites of, 27–33
    system of competition for power in, 64, 82, 102
*Dennis* v. *United States*, 204
Douglas, William O., 202, 203, 204, 210

education, 85–90
    *see also* voters, education of
elections, 104–105, 135
    administration of, 74–81
    electoral decisions in, 61–62, 133
    importance of, 56–61
electoral votes, 122–23
electorate, *see* voters
equal protection of the laws, *see* constitutional guarantees
equality, 11–12
    in control of government, 24–26, 55–56
    and relation to two demand-response systems, 40–41, 49
    as requisite of democratic government, 30–31, 278–79, 283–85
    of wealth, 22–24
equalization of influence thesis, *see* populist demand-response system

family, relation to government, 176–78
farm committees, 131, 159–60
Federal Communications Commission, 97–100
federal system, 128–33, 288–89
    *see also* state and local government
*Federalist, The*, 145, 147, 148, 149, 150, 194, 253
Federalist party, 225–26, 229, 230
first amendment, *see* constitutional guarantees
Frankfurter, Felix, 201–202, 209, 210, 212

Gallatin, Albert, 254

General Accounting Office, 167
government by law, *see* constitutional guarantees; limited government
group competition thesis, *see* pluralist demand-response system

Hamilton, Alexander, 147, 148, 149
*Hammer* v. *Dagenhart*, 204
Hand, Learned, 210
Holmes, Oliver Wendell, Jr., 208
Hook, Sidney, 251, 258
Hoover, Herbert, 148
Hoover Commission, 166
Humphrey, Hubert H., 207

Indiana, election board, 80
Internal Security Act of 1950, 233, 235
*International Brotherhood of Teamsters* v. *Vogt*, 204

Jefferson, Thomas, 224, 227, 230–31, 242
Johnson, Lyndon B., 115
Jusserand, Jean J., 281

Kendall, Willmoore, 135
Kennedy, John F., 114–15
Kentucky Resolutions, 229–30
Koenig, Louis W., 148
Konvits, Milton R., 208–209

lawlessness, 257–259
legislature, *see* Congress; representative assembly
liberty, 11–12
limited government, 5–7, 138, 197–200
    scope of authority, 176–82, 193
    *see also* constitutional guarantees
Livingston, Edward, 253–54
local government, *see* state and local government

McCarran Act, *see* Internal Security Act of 1950
McKean, Thomas, 224, 227
Madison, James, 7, 194, 253
majority rule, 55–56
Marshall, John, 204
mass media, *see* communications
medical licensing boards, 157
Meiklejohn, Alexander, 203
Mexico, suffrage, 72
Mill, John Stuart, 206
Miller, John C., 219, 228